Cold War Fantasies

Cold War Fantasies

Film, Fiction, and Foreign Policy

RONNIE D. LIPSCHUTZ

ROWMAN & LITTLEFIELD PUBLISHERS, INC.
Lanham • Boulder • New York • Oxford

ROWMAN & LITTLEFIELD PUBLISHERS, INC.

Published in the United States of America
by Rowman & Littlefield Publishers, Inc.
4720 Boston Way, Lanham, Maryland 20706
www.rowmanlittlefield.com

12 Hid's Copse Road, Cumnor Hill, Oxford OX2 9JJ, England

British Library Cataloguing in Publication Information Available

Library of Congress Cataloging-in-Publication Data

Lipschutz, Ronnie D.
    Cold War fantasies : film, fiction, and foreign policy / Ronnie D. Lipschutz.
       p. cm.
    Includes bibliographical references and index.
    ISBN 0-7425-1051-4 (cloth: alk. paper) — ISBN 0-7425-1052-2 (paper : alk. paper)
       1. War films—History and criticism. 2. War in literature. 3. Cold War in motion pictures. 4. Cold War in literature. 5. Motion pictures—Political aspects—United States.

PN1995.9 .W3 L57 2001
791.43'658 21
                                                                                2001040422

Printed in the United States of America

♾™ The paper used in this publication meets the minimum requirements of American National Standard for Information Sciences—Permanence of Paper for Printed Library Materials, ANSI/NISO Z39.48-1992.

≋

For those who survived the Cold War,
and those who did not,
and the children of both

Contents

Films and Novels Discussed
in This Book

Preface

What Did You Do in the Cold War, Daddy?

Watched TV, mostly. Back in the early 1960s, when I was youngster in Houston, Texas, and had not yet acquired a patina of sophisticated cynicism, I liked to stay up on Saturdays and watch "Weird," the local late-night horror film show. My favorite movies were those involving atomic mutants, such as *The Incredible Shrinking Man*. Such films were of a piece with everyday life, because the atom bomb was never very far from our minds. In school, we would practice for air raids, crouched under our desks, protected from flying glass and other shrapnel propelled through the air by the imagined nuclear blast. Then we would quickly run outside, because after such an attack, the buildings would be aflame.

In 1962, we found out there were missiles in Cuba. Houston was well within range. All I remember is my mother buying bottled water and canned food, and storing it in our cupboard as a precaution. For what reason? Against what threat? What would be left if the Soviet missiles hit us? All of these years I have pondered that question; my mother does not even remember buying the stuff.

One Saturday afternoon in 1964, when I was twelve, my father took me to see *Doctor Strangelove*. I was not yet initiated into the mysteries of nuclear deterrence but, living in Texas, I found Slim Pickens's final bronco ride to perdition enormously funny (but failed to recognize the phallic symbolism). I was also an avid reader of science fiction. In those days, postmodernism had not yet made it to the United States and the literature was still largely fixated on flying cars, aliens, and Communists. Not a few focused on how the world might appear after the bombs had fallen. World War III was never very far from my thoughts.

More than thirty-five years later, I often marvel that we are still here. Many people seem to take it for granted that the great ideological battles of the United States and the Soviet Union did not lead to a nuclear holocaust.

But the idea of the End of the World was so ingrained in me that one of my elementary school poems spoke of living and dying in a bomb shelter. It was difficult to imagine the world of forty years hence; now, it is difficult to recall the world of forty years ago. In this book, I try to evoke that world, and more recent ones, through both film and fiction.

I have written this as a volume neither of film nor literary theory nor criticism; indeed, I have consciously and deliberately chosen not to refer to that literature in any great detail because it is outside my field of knowledge and would not, I think, help the reader very much. Nor is this a book of cultural studies (such as Tom Englehardt's *The End of Victory Culture*, Basic, 1995). Rather, it represents an effort to illuminate U.S. Cold War history through reference to selected films and novels contemporaneous with the events they describe.

This cross-referencing between history and popular culture might help us to better comprehend both the reflective and the disciplining functions of these media. They are reflective in that they mirror the society they purport to describe (even in distorted form) while, at the same time, allowing us to view our society as both external observers and knowing participants. They are disciplining in that they also indicate where socially acceptable boundaries are and warn us what could happen if we transgress those lines. This exercise is particularly illuminating, I think, in light of the many "threats," both domestic and foreign, we are said to face today. (A shameless plug here: I have written several books on this last topic; they are listed in the bibliography.)

Although I am responsible for virtually everything that appears here, it would not have been possible without the help of Nicholas Towle, Sylvain Meyet, Andrew Park, and the students in the Politics 100 seminars and Politics 80T classes at UC-Santa Cruz during which I developed and wrote this book. Angela McCracken was extraordinarily helpful in finding books, searching for copyright holders to film stills, proofreading drafts of and making corrections in the book, and compiling the index. I am also indebted to Beverly Crawford, Rick Diamond, Jutta Weldes, Chel Lipschutz, and editors and staff at Rowman & Littlefield for their comments and encouragement. And, of course, the love and forbearance of Mary, Maia, and Eric were essential. Finally, comments, criticisms, cacophony, and notes on films and novels left out are always appreciated. Send them to: rlipsch@cats.ucsc.edu

∿∿ A Note to the Reader

In each chapter of this book, following the example of Brian Fawcett in *Cambodia: A Book for People Who Find Television Too Slow* (New York: Collier, 1986), I have provided two interpolated texts (although not in the top/ bottom split fashion of his book), separated by ∿. The first text, in *serif* font, is about the Cold War itself: history, events, people. The second text, in *sans serif* font, provides synopses of the movies and novels, and my commentaries on them. These discussions are hardly comprehensive, and the synopses are no substitute for viewing the films and reading the books (some of which are out of print, but are definitely worth locating).

Chapter 1

Film, Fiction, American Politics

Films are . . . not innocent entertainment but are thoroughly political arti-
facts bound up with political rhetoric, ideology, agendas, and policies.
Given their political importance and effects, it is . . . important to learn to
read films politically.

—James Conbo, *Movies, Politics*, pp. 69-70

"The world is a dangerous place," or so it is said. What could be more dangerous than a Russian nationalist with nuclear missile go-codes? Perhaps
an old American nuclear submariner with nuclear missile go-codes? The
latter could discipline the former, but who will keep an eye on the latter?
What if *he* launches the missiles?

This is the conundrum offered by *Crimson Tide*, a post-Cold War film
from 1995 that purports to draw on CNN Headline News for its subject of
nuclear terrorism and war. Although the film is ostensibly about nuclear
missiles, the real subject is closer to home: "war" within American society,
in this case, social warfare on a U.S. Navy sub.[1]

※
※※

"Gentlemen, We're Back in Business!"

Crimson Tide (Hollywood Pictures/Buena Vista, 1995, 112 min.)
Director: Tony Scott
Cast: Denzel Washington, Gene Hackman, Jason Robards

Vladimir Rochenko, a rabid nationalist at the head of an army of defecting
Russian soldiers, has launched a rebellion against Moscow in protest against
its acquiescence to NATO intervention in Chechnya. Rochenko has gained
control of a nuclear missile base close to the Chinese and North Korean borders. He warns that, if he or any of his men are harmed by the Russian
army, he will launch a nuclear strike against Japan and the United States.

1

This much we are told by Richard Valeriani, a CNN reporter aboard the French aircraft carrier *Foch* "somewhere in the Persian Gulf." (It is of some interest to note that the introductory news report was grafted onto what must have been an almost completed film, for the first Russian invasion of Chechnya took place in December 1994, only a few months before the film was released.)

To meet Rochenko's challenge, the U.S.S. *Alabama*, an American Trident SSBN (nuclear missile submarine), is called into action and sent into the Pacific. There, it is to take up station and wait until events in Russia clarify themselves or it becomes necessary to initiate a preemptive first strike to destroy the missile base.

The ship's commander, Captain Frank Ramsey (Hackman), is an old submariner, a protégé of Admiral Hyman Rickover and his original nuclear navy (Tyler, 1986). He is also, it would seem, an alumnus of the University of Alabama (hence, "Crimson Tide," Bama's football team). Ramsey operates under the "old rules." He and his crew go out to sea, cruise hither and thither, and keep in contact with the National Security Authority (NSA, aka, the president). If the sub should get the "go-code," he and his officers will let the missiles loose. Should the sub lose contact with the NSA, Ramsey can decide, at his own discretion, whether or not to attack Russia.

Much to Ramsey's sorrow, it would seem, those days are past. As he tells his officers at the pre-mission briefing, "Gentlemen, after a nice little vacation, it looks like we're back at it again. I hope you enjoyed the peace because, as of now, we're back in business. In the good old days of the Cold War, the Russians could always be depended on to do what was in their own self-interest. But this Rochenko's playing a whole new ball game, a whole new set of rules." Still, Ramsey clearly expects that, should it become necessary, the missiles will be loosed against this guy, too, even if he is not a "real" Commie.

Ramsey's regular executive officer (exo) is ill with appendicitis, and has been replaced by Lieutenant Commander Ron Hunter (Washington). Not only is Hunter a foil to Ramsey, he is also the captain's opposite. Hunter is of the new generation of submariners, a graduate of the Naval Academy at Annapolis. He has also spent a year at Harvard studying, we are led to believe, war, politics, and international relations. Hunter can quote Von Clausewitz ("War is a continuation of politics by other means"; see Von Clausewitz 1976) and he can also interpret Clausewitz in light of modern realities ("In this case, war is the enemy"). Hunter is cautious to a fault; he wants to ask questions first and shoot later, if necessary. Metaphorically, Ramsey is a gunslinging sheriff; Hunter is a lawyer. Oh, and, he is African American, too.

In other words, the Captain and Hunter are like oil and water. One represents the old, all-white society of Rickover's nuclear navy; the other, the new multicultural navy which, if it is to remain in business in this new, dangerous world, must cast the recruiting net more widely. Ramsey is threatened, all right, but not by the Russians.

When the NSA's order comes, unfortunately, the technology fails. Ramsey receives a command to launch the missiles and prepares to do so. Just as the sub initiates its dive to launch depth, another message begins to arrive. It, however, is cut off before completion. Hunter, thinking that the second message may countermand the first (and thereby stop a nuclear exchange), insists that Ramsey raise a communications buoy to confirm the first message. The winch controlling the buoy cable jams, the communications link to the surface is cut, and the confirmation is not received.[2]

To make a bad situation worse, at that very moment the crew discovers that one of Rochenko's hunter-killer subs is stalking the *Alabama*. The malfunctioning winch makes a noise, the enemy homes in on the Americans, and it fires two torpedoes. Fortunately, the sub's decoys work. The *Alabama* is able to destroy the hunter-killer, but not without suffering serious damage and the loss of several men in a flooded compartment.

Following this dramatic reminder of the world outside, the crew returns to its original task: preparation for launch. Ramsey, loyal to the old rules, insists that the first message is the operative one; Hunter, recognizing that a launch could precipitate a "nuclear holocaust," now wants to surface and confirm the order. Ramsey refuses, fearing that there may be other hunter-killer subs in the vicinity, and the two men begin to argue over what constitutes proper procedure.

The dispute gets rough, and what follows is nothing less than a football game. Hunter argues with Ramsey and orders him out of the control room. Hunter then takes over command and confines Ramsey to his cabin. Officers loyal to Ramsey free him, gain access to the gun locker, storm the bridge, arrest Hunter and his collaborators, and confine them to the officers' mess. Then, sailors loyal to Hunter free him, go to the gun locker, storm the bridge, and prepare to take over.

All during this time, preparations for launch continue; now the problem is to halt the countdown. But Ramsey, restored to his place on the bridge, has one launch key and the weapons officer has the other. Hunter must convince "Weapons," the officer in charge of the missiles, not to turn the key. He must also ensure that Ramsey does not get down to the launch console before he, Hunter, can get to the bridge and remove the launch key left there by Ramsey. Ultimately, of course, the launch sequence is halted. The *Alabama* surfaces and discovers that the second order does countermand the first one. Ramsey retires and, in a special hearing, Hunter is exonerated of charges of mutiny and recommended for immediate command of the next nuclear sub that becomes available.

First Down or Fourth?

What is *Crimson Tide* really about? Is it about Russian nuts with nukes? Is it about the nuclear navy, nuclear deterrence, and first strikes? Is it about following orders or resisting them? Actually, it is none of these. It is, rather, a football movie, from title to action.

Football appears in many American films, standing as a metaphor for competition and struggle among American men (Martin and Miller, 1999). Football is not about strategy or deterrence; it is about power and struggle, honor and victory. In *Crimson Tide*, the two protagonists struggle with each other, mobilize their followers, and rush for yardage. But the game is only a practice one. In contrast with a real football game, there is no enemy here. In an intrasquad scrimmage, one side wins, but both sides are part of the same team. What is important is besting your teammates, showing them up, without making them suffer losses any greater than a slight blow to their egos and a stern lecture from the coach (in the film, an uncredited cameo filled by Jason Robards, the admiral presiding over the panel hearing the charges of mutiny against Hunter).

Crimson Tide invokes other themes, of course. The fact that Hunter is black and Ramsey is white, and both are on (in?) the U.S.S. *Alabama*, cannot help but evoke memories of the civil rights movement and, one might add, affirmative action. These are part of the "game," too. What Ramsey does not seem to realize, however, is that Rochenko is not the only one playing with "a whole new set of rules"; so is everyone else (which is what makes the world so dangerous a place, especially for old white guys).

In this world, Ramsey is an anachronism. In the old days—during the Cold War—it was enough to go to sea and wait for the command to end the world. The old Polaris subs could not launch a first strike attack; their missiles were not accurate enough (Freedman, 1983). The nuclear missile subs were there to retaliate, to "make the rubble bounce," as one Air Force general put it. The new submarines, armed with Trident D-5 missiles, can initiate a pinpoint surprise attack and, therefore, need to be under much firmer control by the NSA. And, inasmuch as Russia is no longer the obvious enemy, extreme caution is in order.

The end of the Cold War has brought with it the end of the old game; Ramsey wants to play the crisis according to the rules he knows so well, but to do so would be foolhardy. Hunter knows the new rules and is not afraid to let Ramsey know; indeed, he is willing to imprison and even kill Ramsey should it become necessary. In the old days, a black man would never be allowed to do that on land, let alone sea (Rickover's nuclear navy was a white one). Hunter is, in other words, emblematic not only of the new nuclear Navy but also of the economic and social transformations working their way through U.S. society. Frank Ramsey: once he made us safe from the Communists. Now he's out of a job.

〰〰

Reflections in the Silver Screen

As is often the case, film is a mirror of the "real" world. The world is never, however, a single narrative; it consists of multiple and simultaneous stories, sometimes told by eyewitnesses to the same event.[3] Not all stories are torn from the headlines; just as often, they are based on fillers tucked away on the back pages of newspapers. Those narratives tell us something about society's concerns, interests, fears, and obsessions. In this respect, *Crimson Tide* is not at all atypical of American film and fiction, even if it is more exaggerated than most. After all, what do we get when we go to see a movie or read a novel? Obviously, we get a story. Sometimes it is linear narrative, at other times it is circular and confusing. But there is more to such works than "just" the story.

Inasmuch as films and novels are products of particular places and times, we can also regard them as reflections of those places and times. In the telling, they also tell us something of those places and times and the contexts in which they were created. More than this, films and novels that address themes and ideas drawn from the times in which they appeared can give us a sense of what people living in those times feared and hoped, alone and together. In this sense, they can also be windows into the past (see, e.g., Rollins, 1983).

Of course, what one gets in such fictional works is never "pure," just as no one is born a fully conscious and socialized adult. Films and novels reflect not only their own times but also those that came before; often, they "quote" earlier films or novels or events in order to convey to the audience or reader not only the recollection of those earlier works, but sets of beliefs and associations, as well (Ryan and Kellner, 1988; Nichols, 1981). In doing this, a linkage is set up between the time in which the film is seen or the book is read, and that earlier time. Culture is dynamic but also a product of accretion, and the "knowing" viewer or reader, through her awareness of this culture, becomes a part of an appreciative historical/cultural community "in the know." There is nothing to require, however, that this be "high" culture; it can also involve, as in Crimson Tide, widely held popular views of both society and national security.

Rambo: First Blood, Part II, a film discussed later in this book, is another example of such mirroring. In 1985, when it was first released, Sylvester Stallone's Rambo was regarded by many—myself included—as more of a cartoon than a political icon. Consequently, I did not see the film until many years after its release, when I was teaching about the Cold War. Once I viewed it, however, I realized that the film tapped deeply into the American political psyche, reflecting politics as they were in 1985 and influencing the political landscape as it was in 1985.

Whether or not one believed that POWs and MIAs had been abandoned in Vietnam was beside the point; Rambo's sheer determination to defy his superiors was something with which everyone could identify, and did. His bloody unilateralism was deplorable, but who, in those days (or these) fully trusts the government? Not only did the film receive wide distribution around the world—where many saw it as indicative of U.S. foreign policy under President Reagan—the term "Rambo" entered the English language to become, itself, a trope whose meaning and associations everyone understood, then and now.

Not all films and novels have quite this impact on society and politics, but their authors and directors all draw on similar cultural reservoirs. In turn, they all try to leave their mark on the culture (and make money, too). Leaving those marks is what makes a hit film or best seller. Works with an explicitly political focus—although not too ideological—can be especially influential, because they resonate with broadly held feelings and provide a framework for explaining what is "going on." Viewing and reading these works with the benefit of hindsight can be, for us, both informative and educational. Because, to paraphrase Santayana, many of us are too young to have experienced the past, perhaps we can use such films and novels to avoid being condemned to repeat it.

Plan of the Book

The films and novels I discuss in this book are only a few of the hundreds, if not thousands, with international and foreign policy themes, that appeared between 1947 and 1998 (more are listed in the "Resources" section following chapter 10). Most have to do with the Cold War between the United States and the Soviet Union, although some also draw on its aftermath. Virtually all—except those that offer some vision of the future—are roughly contemporaneous with the events they purport to describe or the issues they address. And, the ones I have included are not always the best known. Nonetheless, I have selected them for the reflections of the times that they provide, as well as insights into particular political notions that they help to illustrate.

The chapters are organized in a roughly chronological and topical fashion. Each chapter takes a particular issue or period, situates it historically, and illustrates how specific films and novels addressed the issue and reflected the times. In chapter 2, I begin with a look at the transition "From Hot War to Cold War," the ten or fifteen years of growing domestic fear and international tension following the end of World War II (1945-60). The times were, for many, gray and ruinous, the atomic bomb promising a dismal future of war and destruction. Versions of the world as it was, and as it might become, filtered out into popular consciousness through newsreels, films, and novels. Among these were *The Big Lift* (1950), a film about the Berlin Airlift and a primer for distinguishing good Germans from bad ones; *The Third Man* (1949), a film noir based on a novel by Graham Greene; and George Orwell's *1984* (1949), a "novel of the future," as reported on the cover of the book's paperback version.

The Big Lift stars Montgomery Clift as Danny McCullough, a U.S. Army Air Force officer who takes up with a German war widow during his brief breaks between flights into and out of Berlin during the airlift mounted in response to the Soviet blockade of the city. McCullough is after romance, but his inamorata is after a visa. Lessons are learned by actors and viewers alike. *The Third Man* is set in a dreary postwar Vienna, reduced to rubble, stricken by poverty, and occupied by the Four Powers (at that time, the United States, Soviet Union, France, and Britain). Orson Welles plays Harry Lime, a black marketeer selling tainted penicillin, which has killed or injured a number of people. Lime is the epitome of amoral self-interest. He is a realist who seeks only to help himself. George Orwell's book is set in a not dissimilar landscape; its protagonist, Winston Smith, is also highly self-interested, although the reader cheers him on as he seeks to break free of control by "Big Brother." *1984* has been read in many ways; one of the best is as a mirror of the United States of 1947 and one man's vision of that present projected into ours. It remains very pertinent, however, in its depiction of the totalitarian uses of technology, and should make us think twice about the promises of the "information revolution" and the potential for continuous surveillance of citizens by both state and capital (Lyon, 1994).

Chapter 3 asks whether there are "Reds among Us?" The expansion of communist rule in Europe and Asia, the Soviet acquisition of the atomic bomb in 1949, the sudden outbreak of the Korean War in June 1950: all of these events led to a national hunt for brainwashed spies in the form of ex-GIs and traitors, with many convinced that the country was being subverted from within. The country did not know whom to trust; even President Eisenhower was thought by some to be a stooge of the Kremlin. As a child, I worried, along with my schoolmates, about being "brainwashed" (although in typical childhood fashion, I imagined it to involve soap and water). Richard Condon's *The Manchurian Candidate*, published in the late 1950s, provided an extreme, and often sardonic, account of what Americans foolishly feared. As we shall see, Condon's convoluted plot invokes not only Lenin, Stalin, and Mao, but also Freud, Lewis Carroll, Joseph McCarthy, and Heinz ketchup.

Invasion of the Bodysnatchers—the black-and-white version of 1956, based on a novel by Jack Finney (1955)—raised the possibility of being taken over unawares—by whom or what is never made very clear—without knowing it. This is another theme that has contemporary resonance in current culture war debates over sex and violence in film and on television and the Internet. In the original version, the film painted a hopeless picture; everyone was doomed. Subsequently, a new conclusion was grafted on, in which the country was saved by the FBI.

Such assurances hardly made a difference. Numerous other films and books warned, as well, how easy it was to be turned into a Red, what tell-tale signs might indicate that family or friends had "gone over," and how to protect the nation through good citizenship and national duty. (A classic along these lines is the Defense Department's half-hour situation comedy

Red Nightmare from 1953. The film, narrated by *Dragnet's* Jack Webb, imagines a family man awakening to find his town conquered and occupied by Communist forces and bureaucrats.)

Chapter 4 searches for "Spies." There were, it was claimed, secrets essential to the national security that, if discovered, would surely lead to the country's destruction and the death of all (much as the uproar over alleged Chinese theft of nuclear secrets, and the arrest and release of Los Alamos scientist Wen Ho Lee, have been claimed to pose a mortal threat to U.S. national security; see the *Cox Report*, 1999). Hence, each side wanted what the other knew, and wanted to find out what the other side knew and did not know. Spies could do what diplomacy could not—what James Der Derian (1992) has called "anti-diplomacy."

Indeed, the CIA's subversion of legitimate governments in Iran and Guatemala in 1953 and 1954—regimes tagged "leftist" or "radical" by Washington—seemed to demonstrate that covert action could do what diplomacy and military force could not. (As Henry Kissinger put it twenty years later, just because the people of a country are irresponsible enough to go communist does not mean we should let them do so; quoted in McCormick, 1989: 186.) But the life of a spy was hardly as glamorous as suggested by Ian Fleming's James Bond novels and the films based on them.

Kiss Me Deadly (1955), a late film noir based on Mickey Spillane's detective Mike Hammer, glamorizes the private eye's life but also suggests that it can be "nasty, brutish and short." It is a story of a detective's search for a "whatsit," as Velda, his beautiful lover/colleague/Girl Friday, puts it. Whatever the whatsit is, it is atomic and, in a chase through sordid buildings and back alleys, the whatsit destroys everyone who tries to get it. John le Carré's *The Spy Who Came in from the Cold* (1963), although British in origin and temperament, remains one of the best novels of the espionage genre. It serves as an illustration of how grim and gray the entire business of spying really is. Le Carré also suggested that, where the business was concerned, morality was, as the central figure in the book might have put it, "rubbish"; instead, spies were all that kept the two sides from blowing each other up in atomic war.

The threat of nuclear war cast a shadow over almost all walks of life, as we see in chapter 5, "Nukes." The 1950s and 1960s saw a flood of books and films about the end of the world; there was not much about which to be optimistic, although in a few novels, such as Pat Frank's *Alas Babylon* (1959), authors thought that atomic war would cleanse the Earth, allowing only the fittest and purest of heart to survive (guess whom they would be?). There were, however, a few works that were more hopeful.

Red Planet Mars (1952), a little-remembered film, stars Peter Graves of television's *Mission Impossible* fame. The film expressed hope for a deus ex machina that would convert the Russians and rescue the world from nuclear holocaust. It underlined the abiding religious faith in God of many Americans as the means of global salvation (*The Next Voice You Hear*, another film from the early 1950s, actually depicted God speaking to the world, by radio, on this topic).

Fail-Safe (1962), written by Eugene Burdick and Harvey Wheeler and published in the same year as the Cuban Missile Crisis, was much more pragmatic. In their novel, a holocaust is avoided by the simultaneous nuclear destruction of both New York and Moscow. The president expresses hope that these terrible events might lead to a new era of nuclear disarmament and peace, while his chief nuclear strategist mentally calculates how, in the future, he will make a living. *Dr. Strangelove, or How I Learned to Stop Worrying and Love the Bomb* (1964), turned Burdick and Wheeler on their heads, although quite unintentionally. In this black comedy, one of Stanley Kubrick's finest films, a "Doomsday Machine" puts an end to everyone (a threat first issued in 1951 by Klaatu in *The Day the Earth Stood Still*).

Chapter 6 explores "The Final Frontier." The tired conclusion of the Eisenhower presidency and arrival of the Kennedys in Washington raised contradictory hopes among the American public. It also, for the first time, provided a prominent place for academics—a number coming from Harvard—to play a central role in the making of foreign policy. The results were not pretty. Many believed that the Democrats would take a more energetic stance against communism, through a combination of carrots and sticks: economic liberalism, on the one hand, as evidenced in the Alliance for Progress, and confrontation where necessary, on the other. But Kennedy inherited a going concern from the Republicans—including an ill-planned invasion of Cuba—that demonstrated it was none too easy to change direction. The ill-fated Bay of Pigs led, via a convoluted path, to the Cuban Missile Crisis and, according to some, a point just short of World War III.

In *The Ugly American* (1958), William Lederer and Eugene Burdick provided what appeared to be a foolproof formula for defeating the Communists in Asia, where Vietnam was a growing but not yet widely known obsession of Washington. The book also warned that Americans made poor diplomats, tended to be obnoxious, and lived too high on the hog. Instead, the author argued, a folksy, culturally sensitive but manipulative approach to Asians would yield much better results. In any event, that formula was never applied. Costa Gavras's *State of Siege* (1972) showed how Americans really operated in the developing world, beefing up police and military forces to keep uppity students and radicals down.

Chapter 7 considers "Vietnam, Over and Over." The Vietnam War is generally considered a watershed in U.S. foreign policy as well as in political culture. BV (Before Vietnam), foreign policy had been "bipartisan" and the president spoke for America beyond the ocean's edge; AV, a cacophony of voices were raised, a president was deposed, the counterculture so despised by the neo-conservatives was born, and some 57,000 Americans, along with millions of Asians, were killed. For many who served in Vietnam, the experience was a traumatic one. An endless and always introspective stream of works has come out of the period, beginning with *The Green Berets* (novel and film, the latter starring John Wayne) and ending, most recently, with *Heaven and Earth*, directed by Oliver Stone, based on a riveting memoir by Le Ly Hayslip (1990).

Francis Ford Coppola's *Apocalypse Now* (1979) still stands as one of the most visually stunning and horrifying films on Vietnam. Based in part on Joseph Conrad's *Heart of Darkness*, it depicts a journey upriver into both the physical and mental realms of madness. It illustrates the fine line between the rationality of flexible response, a theory of graduated attack against a nuclear-armed enemy, and the insanity required for its implementation on the ground against a conventionally armed, guerilla-based military force.

The logic of the entire Vietnam endeavor was never very clear. Novels such as Daniel Ford's *Incident at Muc Wa* (1967), later filmed as *Go Tell the Spartans* (with Burt Lancaster and several other later well-known actors), tells the story of an unsuccessful American effort to establish a military outpost on the site of a former French fort that had also been a tactical failure. Ford suggested early on that the war had become a bureaucratic and meaningless affair; even today, however, there are those who still seek to instill the war with spiritual and philosophical meaning.

The 1980s began with a celebration of America's "renewal" and "return," marked both by calls for struggle with the Soviets and warnings about the threat and consequences of world war. It was too late to win in Vietnam, so war was replayed in a number of films, one of the best known of which was *Rambo: First Blood, Part II* (1985). In that film, Sylvester Stallone plays a disaffected vet who singlehandedly defeats the "Evil Empire." Ronald Reagan was said to have joked, "After seeing Rambo last night, I know what to do next time this happens" (quoted in Christensen, 1987: 203). Evidently, he didn't; at the same time that the film was such a hit, Oliver North and his colleagues were bringing cakes and Bibles to Teheran, in a failed effort to free American hostages in Lebanon (Draper, 1991).

Chapter 8, "Renewing the Cold War," illustrates the fundamental contradiction between the rhetoric and reality of efforts to contain communism. Renewal, such as it was, began around 1976, but it did not bloom until 1980. The Reagan administration and its supporters hoped to use the threat of nuclear war to cow the Soviets. Their efforts were immortalized in Robert Scheer's book *With Enough Shovels* (1982), whose title came from the remark of T. K. Jones, a Boeing employee working for the Defense Department. He advocated digging trench shelters, putting wooden doors over them, and covering the entire affair with dirt as a means of surviving nuclear war; "With enough shovels," he said, "everyone is going to make it."

But what would World War III look like? *Red Dawn* (1983), directed by John Milius (author of the original screenplay for *Apocalypse Now*) thought it could come as a "bolt from the blue," with planeloads of Central American guerillas arriving in the guise of tourists. The film, starring a young Patrick Swayze, invokes frontier, football, and freedom fighters and accuses Americans of being gutless and unprepared for the challenge to come. By the end of the film, there is not a dry eye in the house, although much of what comes before begs belief.

Tom Clancy's "Red" novels set the tone for a more technically meticulous challenge to the USSR. *The Hunt for Red October* (1984) proposed that Soviet technology might soon outrun America's, while *Red Storm Rising* (1986) was a detailed and seemingly endless account of the coming East-West war. Clancy provided a highly detailed exposition of why and how World War III could begin—oil shortages in the Soviet Union brought about by domestic Islamic terrorism—and how it could be fought and won without nuclear weapons (a point disputed by films such as *The Day After* (1983) and *Testament* (1983), released at the same time). By the time the two sides get around to talking, Clancy's World War III turns out to have been a "misunderstanding." In the end, the world survives, although the reader might not. It takes courage and dedication to make it to the end of the book. But the Second Cold War did not become a hot one—even Ronald Reagan said that a nuclear war could not be won—and it astonished everyone by ending in a completely unexpected and peaceful manner. Still, more surprises were in store. With the loss of the old enemy, a new one had to be found.

Chapter 9, "New Competitors, Old Enemies" takes up this theme, one that became the mantra of Bill Clinton's 1992 presidential campaign. By the end of the 1980s, Americans were being warned that the country was "in decline" and needed to become more "competitive" in order to remain prosperous and secure. Paul Kennedy, a heretofore unknown British naval historian transplanted to Yale, hit the best-seller list with *The Rise and Fall of the Great Powers* (1987). Kennedy's thesis, borrowed from the "hegemonic cycle" theories of obscure international political economists (Gilpin, 1980), suggested that the United States had been overreaching itself and was, historically, doomed to decline. Kennedy saved his predictions for later books, but the grist was in the mill. Who would be the next threat?

Along with many others, Michael Crichton thought Japan. In *Rising Sun* (1992), a xenophobic and misogynistic potboiler, he depicted what could happen if we allowed Japan to purchase our economic patrimony: Americans would be "snatched" and sapped of their strength (cf. *Invasion of the Bodysnatchers* and the ravings of General Jack D. Ripper in *Dr. Strangelove*).

Falling Down (1992) illustrated what Japan might do to the average

American. It tells how Bill Foster (Michael Douglas), a very tense, recently downsized, white male defense technician living in Los Angeles, becomes a "stranger in a strange land." Foster, like the United States, begins in familiar territory—the freeway—which isn't functioning as it should. He goes "over the hill" only to find himself in a place he no longer understands. As Foster proceeds westward, toward Venice and the Pacific Ocean, he becomes more and more deranged and, eventually, turns into Rambo. But Rambo wins to kill another day, in *Rambo III* (1988). Foster doesn't and dies for our sins.

What happens after "after the Cold War" or as chapter 10 puts it, "Now What?" As the "post-Cold War period" comes to an end, to be replaced by what some have called the "coming anarchy," and others the "post-post Cold War," U.S. foreign policymakers remain in a state of confusion (Lipschutz, 2000). What will the future look like? What should we do? Who will save us? Two "modern classics" from the 1980s offer interesting answers. Ridley Scott's film *Blade Runner* (1982) and William Gibson's novel *Neuromancer* (1984) offer illuminating pictures of a future as seen from the mid-1980s: polyglot, highly stratified, and class-ridden societies in which states hardly exist, in which corporate struggles for commerce and data dominate, in which the environment has been all but destroyed, and in which most people are, as the police sergeant in *Blade Runner* puts it, "little people."

The main character in *Blade Runner*, Rick Deckard (Harrison Ford) is a "blade runner." His profession is the execution of androids, human clones who have illegally migrated to Earth from the colonies. The only thing that distinguishes humans from androids is the latters' four-year life span, which is artificially imposed. What, then, is the difference between the two? Who, exactly, is human, and what makes them so? *Neuromancer* has to do with surfing through cyberspace—"jacking into the matrix" is the expression—and stealing corporate secrets. Hacking, in other words. Information is the ultimate currency—power in its purest form—but you can't eat it. Gotta make a living.

Onward, Through the Fog

The history of the Cold War presented in the chapters that follow is one "veteran's" account. As such, it should not be regarded as either authoritative or complete. I was never in the U.S. military and I did not attain political awareness much before age ten, during the Cuban Missile Crisis in 1962. Not long afterward, I went "AWOL," and refused to play my assigned role in the Cold War any longer (although I cannot say I rebelled actively).

There are many other histories of the time written by enthusiastic participants and articulate opponents, some of which are listed in the Resources section following chapter 10. The reader is encouraged to consult them for contrasting views of Cold War film, fiction, fantasy, and foreign policy from 1945 to 1995.

♒

Chapter 2

From Hot War to Cold War

We've Got the Gold, We Make the Rules

In August 1945, World War II came to an end. Americans were euphoric; they danced in the streets. The expectation was that peace would reign, unimpeded, around the world. That the United States was the most powerful country in the world, and the sole possessor of the atomic bomb, only reinforced this belief. After all, American intentions were of the best, and no one could doubt them . . . could they?

For the most part, the United States had been untouched by the fighting. There were a considerable number of American casualties, of course, but nothing like the 20 million dead in the Soviet Union or the 30 or 40 million dead in Europe and Asia. There had been rationing of certain goods and shortages of various kinds of foods, but nothing like the complete collapse of a functioning economy in parts of Central Europe. And there had been fears of German and Japanese invasion—accompanied by incarcerations and false alarms that bombers or subs had been sighted—but nothing like the devastation that laid waste to cities in the middle of the battle zones or the death camps discovered by Allied armies throughout the areas of German conquest.

All of this left Americans sanguine about the future, more so, perhaps, than was the case in some quarters. In Washington, D.C., especially, there were rumors and concerns that future relations among the victorious Allies might not be so smooth. American and British leaders saw signs, they thought, that the Soviet Union might prove less than willing to go along with Western plans for the postwar world. And what were these plans? Nothing less than to make over the world in the image of the United States, in which happy citizens would be able to spend their dollars in flourishing markets.

15

The immediate postwar environment looked nothing like this, however. Two films—*The Big Lift* and *The Third Man*—and one novel—*1984*—offer us a look into the grim, gray world of the late 1940s, before prosperity returned to the West. These are works that warn of corruption by the outside world even as they play on notions of the inherent beneficence of the "American Way." In the films, naked self-interest taints people; in *1984*, uncontrolled power taints the state. Both power and self-interest were central to the emerging Cold War.

Soon after their entry into World War II, the United States and Great Britain began to plan the reconstruction of the global economy in a way that would benefit both countries as well as, they hoped, foster international peace and cooperation. The institutional manifestation of these hopes came to be called the Bretton Woods institutions—the World Bank, the International Monetary Fund, the dollar as an international currency, and what would later become the General Agreement on Tariffs and Trade (Block, 1977). The agreements setting up these institutions were signed in 1944 but, already by 1946, it was clear that they were hardly up to the task. The critical question became how to rebuild Europe? The fear in Washington was that a poor and hungry continent awash in rubble and refugees would be fertile ground for demagogues and radicals, and that the United States could not prosper if European markets were not open to American goods.

As a result of the Allied victory in Europe, Germany and Berlin, as well as Austria and Vienna, were divided into four zones of occupation: American, British, French, and Soviet. Different schemes for dealing with Germany were bruited about. FDR's treasury secretary, Henry Morgenthau, wanted to strip the former Third Reich of all remaining industrial capacity and return it to peasant agriculture. Others wanted to squeeze reparations out of Germany and leave the people to fend for themselves. In the end, however, the Western Allies concluded that a revival of the European economy as well as peace within Europe depended on the reconstruction of Germany's industrial zones and its economic integration into Europe.

The Soviets were not unalterably opposed to this plan, although they were more interested in extracting resources from Germany in order to rebuild *their* industries. For good reason, the Soviet leader, Joseph Stalin, was much more concerned about a future German military "threat" than the economic prosperity of the recent enemy; hence, the Soviets preferred to keep Germany weak, poor, and disarmed. But they were to be disappointed in this hope. Not long after the end of the war, the Western allies began to coordinate the economies of their respective three zones—what they called "Trizonia"—and to deny reparations from Trizonia to the Soviet Union.

In 1948, as the next step in stabilizing the economy of Trizonia, the three Western allies initiated a currency reform, replacing the old, almost-worthless Reichsmark with a new "Deutschmark." Stalin believed—correctly, but not inevitably, as it turned out—that this represented an attempt to pull Trizonia into Western Europe. In order to prevent the old Reichsmarks from flowing into the Soviet zone, where they were still legal tender, Stalin ordered his military forces to block all movement between Trizonia and the Eastern part of Germany. This included the Western sectors of Berlin, a city located far inside the Soviet zone. The result was the first Berlin crisis. Rather than cancel the economic reform, however, the United States, France, and the United Kingdom launched the Berlin Airlift. Over the following year, the effort included more than 278,000 flights that supplied the western parts of the city with 2.3 million tons of food, coal, and other goods (Davison, 1958). Eventually, it was the Soviets who ended the blockade, in 1949, but not before Germany was split along an East-West axis, which helped to create the confrontation zone in Central Europe that would remain until 1989.[1]

The defeat of Germany and Japan in the war, and the beginnings of the Cold War, posed an epistemological problem for the United States. The enemy, which had been demonized through news reports, propaganda, film, experience, and the Nuremberg Trials, was now an ally. The Soviet Union, which had been lionized through the same methods, was now becoming an enemy. While it was not difficult for Washington to rationalize this change, it was less easy for the public to accept. Not until the Berlin crisis were the lines between East and West clearly drawn. As a result, there came to be "good" Germans and "bad" ones. The former were in the West (and some had been Nazis during the war), while the latter were in the East (and some had been anti-Nazi during the war). But, inasmuch as there was not yet a wall to keep the two kinds apart—the Berlin Wall was not built until 1961—one could never be sure from appearances who was good and who was bad.

※

Heavy Lifting

The Big Lift (20th Century Fox, 1950, 119 min.)
Director: George Seaton
Cast: Montgomery Clift, Paul Douglas, Cornell Borchers, O. E. Hasse, Bruni Lobel

The Big Lift was shot in Berlin when much of the city was still in ruins, and most of the cast are Berliners. The film takes the Berlin Airlift as its central theme, focusing on Air Force Sergeant Danny McCullough (Clift). Hank Kowalski (Douglas) is McCullough's friend, an ex-POW who hates all Germans. When the Berlin crisis erupts, McCullough is assigned to fly on supply planes into Tempelhof airfield, a dicey proposition given both bad weather and the approach path, which requires flying between the apartment buildings ringing the airport.

Normally, flight crews are not permitted to leave the airfield because of fears for their safety but, when McCullough arrives on the plane carrying the one millionth ton of supplies, a celebration is held in which he somewhat unwillingly must participate. There, he meets an attractive German *fraülein*, Frederika Burkhardt (Borchers), who tells him that she is a war widow. She gives him her address and asks him to look her up when he has a chance. When, at a later date, he is permitted to go into the city, McCullough heads out in search of Burkhardt.

Walking through the rubble of Berlin, Danny arrives at her address, only to discover that it is in ruins. Frederika is nearby, however, digging up bricks that will be used to rebuild the city. She and Danny begin a relationship and, whenever he gets leave time between flights, he goes into Berlin to see her. Hank, permanently based in Berlin, also strikes up an affair with a German woman, Gerda (Lobel). He, however, treats her abusively and thinks her stupid because she continually asks him questions about politics and economics. McCullough's girlfriend is, apparently, much more sophisticated and not very interested in such topics.

When Danny receives word that he is to be sent home, he decides to marry Frederika, who is only too happy to agree. But on their wedding day, he discovers her plan to travel with him to the United States, get a divorce, and reunite with her lover in St. Louis. Heartbroken and disgusted, McCullough confronts her and she confesses all. Gerda, meanwhile, demands that Hank treat her properly, as a good democrat should. She refuses to marry him in order to stay in Berlin to help rebuild the free part of the city.

The theme of "good" versus "bad" German emerges most clearly in the person of Frederika's neighbor (Hasse), who lives in the apartment across the hall. He, it turns out, is spying for *both* Americans and Russians; indeed, as he describes the situation in Berlin, it seems as if almost everyone is working for one side or the other in order to survive. How, then, is one to tell who is good and who is bad? Clearly, Frederika is a "bad" German, interested only in herself. Gerda, however, learns the meaning of democracy and capitalism, and Hank comes to realize that she is much smarter than he has believed her to be. She is a "good" German.

The key feature of a "good" German, in other words, is the recognition of the virtues of the American way of life. Even those Germans who had been committed Nazis could become "good," while even those Germans who had opposed Hitler from the very beginning were "bad" if they became Communists. *The Big Lift,* in other words, offers moviegoers a lesson in the relationship between morality and geopolitics.

~~~
~~~

Good Cop, Bad Cop

By 1949, Soviet-backed governments had gained power in all of the countries of Central and Eastern Europe except Austria. U.S. policymakers feared that Communist-dominated or controlled governments might take over throughout Western Europe, too. The Communist parties of several countries—in particular, France and Italy—had played prominent roles in the wartime resistance against Nazi Germany, which gave them a certain degree of moral authority and political potential. They could not be denied a role in the newly constituted coalition governments of these countries. Moreover, a fair number of industrial unions were either Communist or dominated by them. Alone, these factors would not have been of very great concern but, in Washington, some people believed that the dismal economic conditions found throughout Europe might provide the opportunity for Communists to win parliamentary majorities and form governments. Or, with support from the unions, the Communists might be able to grab power and put in place pro-Soviet governments. Were that to happen, many reasoned, the United States would be cut off from European markets and the Depression would surely return. Thus was the rationale for covert aid provided by the newly established CIA to European unions, political parties, newspapers and magazines, academics and intellectuals, and other individuals and organizations (Agee and Wolf, 1981). Indeed, it was often said that the CIA won the elections in France and Italy for the conservative anti-Communist parties.

For Washington, however, the manipulation of public opinion and elections was not enough to prevent Communist takeovers. Friendly governments, by themselves, could not rebuild Europe. Economic growth and prosperity were seen as the key to keeping Western Europe out of Soviet hands. Some means were needed to generate investment in Europe and bind the region to American capital. This economic effort began in earnest, in 1947, with a rather fortuitous event, brought on by the impending bankruptcy of the United Kingdom (Jones, 1955).

One Friday afternoon in March, the British ambassador to the United States delivered a diplomatic note to the State Department. The note stated that, after 1947, Britain would no longer be able to maintain its commitment to the financial and military support of the Greek government. The note caused consternation in Washington and initiated several days of furious consultations and planning. The Greek civil war, between a conservative monarchy and an opposition force led by the Greek Communist Party, had waxed and waned since 1944. In 1947, it was once again increasing in intensity. Many thought the war was being directed by Yugoslavia, whose leader, Marshall Tito, was providing aid to the Greek opposition against the express orders of Stalin. If the Greek monarchy were to fall, the entire Balkan Peninsula would come under Communist rule and they would be in a position to threaten Mediterranean shipping routes. Whether Greece was as strategically crucial as would soon be claimed is arguable; the problem, as framed in Washington, was one of *credibility*.

President Truman, presenting to Congress what came to be known as the Truman Doctrine, went further than the Balkans. He promised that the United States would put its power and reputation on the line to defend free peoples *everywhere*, and not just in Greece. Turkey was added to the list, too, even though there was no civil war there. Truman implied, too, that the Middle East (and its oil) would be imperiled by a failure to act. The $400 million he requested for these two countries was just the first installment on an invoice to keep the Free World free that would, by 1989, run into trillions of dollars. For good measure, China would soon be added to the list, too. There, a corrupt and inept Nationalist government was losing control of the country to the Chinese Communists (again, despite Stalin's support for the Nationalists), a debacle that would culminate in the flight of President Chiang and his minions to Taiwan.

To mobilize support for the Truman Doctrine, and the Marshall Plan that followed, the administration invoked the specter of communism on the march, intending to "scare the hell" out of the public at the advice of Senator Arthur Vandenburg (a strategy that subsequently backfired, when the Truman administration was judged by Senator Joseph McCarthy and others to be insufficiently anti-Communist). Thus, Dean Acheson, Truman's secretary of state, warned members of Congress, "Like apples in a barrel infected by one rotten one, the corruption of Greece would infect Iran and all to the east. It would also carry infection to Africa . . . , and to Europe through Italy and France . . . ." And Senator Vandenburg, in 1947 a new convert to activist internationalism, told anyone who would listen that "[The] fall of Greece, followed by the fall of Turkey would establish a chain reaction around the world which could very easily leave us isolated in a Communist-dominated earth" (quoted in LaFeber, 1993). Truman got the money he asked for, but it was not enough for the job. More had to be found, and fast!

Call the Marshall (Plan, That Is)

The problem was a fairly simple one: the currencies in circulation in Europe were "soft," that is, they could not, in general, be used by the citizens of one country to buy goods from the citizens of another. Dollars were "hard"— the reader is left to interpret the significance of the two terms—and were legal tender the world over. More than that, if there was nothing in the markets to buy, money was not much good. After the war, a good deal of the economic exchange going on in Europe was based on barter and the use of ersatz currencies, such as cigarettes. Barter was not a basis on which to develop economies. The Bretton Woods institutions were meant to solve the money problem, but they didn't. Why not?

Economic conditions existing in Europe after the end of the war were much more serious than anyone had anticipated. Moreover, within a period of three years, the system had been converted from one whose goal was economic stability to one aimed at fighting the Cold War (although some historians have argued that the Cold War was launched precisely in order to stabilize the economic system; see Pollard, 1985). Ultimately, the entire Bretton Woods system did not begin to operate until the late 1950s, and it functioned in its entirety only until 1972.

Interestingly, the USSR was among the signatories of the original Bretton Woods agreements. There was nothing that prohibited a country with a centrally planned economy from participating. The catch was that full involvement would require the Soviets to reveal a great deal of information about the operation of their economy. It would also permit a significant degree of external intervention in the operation of their economy. Stalin thought this might create serious domestic political troubles and decided to stay out. A few years later, refusal to participate was seen as a hostile act.

The first stumble in the project was not, however, the fault of the Soviet Union. Rather, it came about as the result of Britain's economic distress and the demands of its creditors. During World War II, Britain's economy had operated within what was known as the "Sterling Zone." All international monetary transactions within this zone were conducted in soft (non-convertible) pounds sterling. The British government would borrow funds from other countries (usually ex-colonies), promising to repay after the war in hard sterling, that is, money that could be used internationally. It then bought and sold goods with what were basically sterling-based promissory notes. In doing this, Britain was, in effect, kiting checks. There was nothing in the Royal Treasury—in the way of gold or dollars, for instance—to back up these notes, and no real prospect of redeeming them after the war. The operating assumption was that Britain would produce goods that these other countries would want, which they could purchase with the promissory notes, but this turned out not to be the case.

In order to help restore Britain's financial position, and to make the pound sterling convertible, in late 1945 the United States provided a large stabilization loan, on the order of $3.8 billion dollars (quite a sizable sum at the time, equal to at least $50 billion in today's dollars). But Britain's creditors did not believe that the pound would maintain its value, and demand for conversion of sterling into hard dollars was unexpectedly great. So many countries wanted to redeem their notes that the loan was used up rapidly, and convertibility of the pound was suspended. The effect of this was to greatly limit the amount of liquidity (i.e., cash in hand) available in the international system because it meant that sterling could not be used freely in international trade. This liquidity shortage acted, in turn, as a constraint on economic growth. If the pound could not be freely exchanged for dollars, countries holding pounds (and not having any dollars) could not use them to buy goods from the United States (which had no use for soft pounds, since Britain had little to sell). Finally, this limited the export markets that were being relied on to support the American economy and to forestall a return to Great Depression conditions (Gardner, 1980).

Under ordinary conditions, a situation like this should have been handled by the International Monetary Fund, which would have provided a short-term stabilization loan to support the pound. But the IMF lacked sufficient funds to provide for Britain's needs and, anyway, it was never really intended to support currency convertibility. Congress refused to consider providing any more funds to Britain, and no other sources of finance were available. The only alternative was for the United States to start pumping large quantities of money into the international economy. This would "prime the pump," so to speak, by providing dollars that could be used to purchase capital goods from the United States. Such equipment could then be used to rebuild industrial infrastructure which, in turn, would allow countries to export manufactures back to the United States, thereby earning dollars, and so on. This, then, was one of the contexts for the Marshall Plan.

The demand for dollars coincided, more or less, with the British decision to halt its support of government forces in the Greek civil war and the subsequent enunciation of the Truman Doctrine. But Truman Doctrine funds were hardly enough, and they were not targeted at Western Europe; more had to be supplied. Secretary of State Marshall's announcement of the European Recovery Program (ERP, aka, the Marshall Plan) at the Harvard commencement of 1947 was thus part and parcel of a larger effort. Two things about the ERP should be noted. First, as with Bretton Woods, it was not closed to the emerging Eastern Bloc. Indeed, a Czech delegation attended the initial ERP meetings, but left early as the result of Soviet pressure.

Second, although the ERP ultimately provided about $13 billion in assistance to participating countries, this only represented a relatively small fraction of the total sum invested in European reconstruction. Most of the capital came from the Europeans themselves. The ERP did accomplish three critical things. First, it provided dollars to Europe—many more than could have been provided by the World Bank. Second, it offered a sort of guarantee to European investors that their funds would not vanish or be nationalized. Third, it ensured that European capital would be linked into an integrated, Europe-wide economy, rather than limited to national ones, thereby providing larger markets and greater profit potentials. The forerunner of the European Community, the European Coal and Steel Community, was established in the late 1940s for precisely this last purpose.

As with Bretton Woods, the Soviet Bloc decision not to participate in the Marshall Plan was based largely on Stalin's belief that to do so would open the East up to Western economic and cultural penetration and lead to a loss of political autonomy (in other words, the same conditions found in Russia today). But in the context of the times—Greece, Turkey, Berlin, and so on—this refusal was cast as a hostile response rather than a cautious step. Very quickly, the ERP became the second half of the Cold War walnut, matched to the Truman Doctrine: a program intended to protect Western Europe from penetration by Soviet communism (Pollard, 1985; LaFeber, 1993).

The Marshall Plan was meant to continue through the end of 1951. By that time, it was assumed, the Western European economies would be able to operate on their own. Again, however, the planners did not get it quite right. By the time 1949 rolled around, economic recession once again reared its ugly head. The industrial reconstruction of Europe was proceeding, but not nearly as fast as had been anticipated. The dollar shortage continued. Postwar demand for goods slackened. What it took for the transatlantic economy to really succeed was, curiously enough, the Korean War and the quadrupling of the American defense budget. Rearmament pumped dollars into the international system—at the same time, reinvigorating domestic demand in the United States—to cause an international economic boom. The Japanese economic miracle was also the result of the influx of funds and the American demand for goods resulting from Korea and rearmament. But that is getting ahead of our story.

ᨫᨫ

Down at the Bottom of the Barrel

The Third Man (British Lion, 1949, 104 min.)
Director: Carol Reed
Cast: Orson Welles, Joseph Cotton, Alida Valli, Trevor Howard

Carol Reed's film is about Acheson's "rotten apples." Based on a short story and a screenplay by Graham Greene, it is set in the Europe of 1948, a time and place that has not yet escaped World War II, and which is just beginning to come under the Cold War shadow. The Vienna depicted in the film is still occupied by the Four Powers (it would remain so until 1955, when the occupiers agreed to Austrian neutrality). It is a city half in ruins, full of people without enough to eat, where cigarettes are far more valuable than schillings. (By the time the film was released, however, prosperity was beginning to return). But business is business, as the film's protagonist, Holly Martins, (Cotton), reminds us in an introductory voiceover. In Vienna's black market, anything can be had for the right price and the right currency.

Martins is a writer of Westerns and other potboilers. He has come to occupied Vienna at the invitation of his old friend, Harry Lime (Welles), who has offered Martins a job doing publicity for his "charitable foundation." Since employment is in short supply in Europe—and why Martins is in Europe is never made clear—he has decided to take up Lime's offer. Unfortunately, Martins arrives at Lime's apartment building just in time to see Lime's coffin being carried off to the cemetery. His friend has been run over and killed by a truck.

Martins is at a loss about what to do. He has no return ticket, no prospects, and no money. The British major in charge of the case, Calloway (Howard), offers to get him out on a flight the next morning. Martins is ready to leave when he discovers inconsistencies in the details of Lime's death, including the presence of a mysterious "third man" at the scene of the accident. So, he decides to stay. As the film proceeds, Martins begins to suspect that, quite possibly, Lime is not dead at all. Martins also becomes involved with Lime's girlfriend, Anna Schmidt (Valli). Anna has forged Austrian identity papers, is in Vienna illegally, and is in danger of being repatriated to her native Czechoslovakia by the Soviets.

Bringing his suspicions about his friend to the British authorities, Martins is told that Lime was a wanted man. A black marketeer and a murderer, he was guilty of diluting and selling contaminated penicillin on the black market, leading to the injury and death of a number of children and adults. Hence, if Lime remains alive, the police want him. When the police dig up Lime's coffin, it is not his corpse that they find, but that of one of his associates who has gone missing. Martins continues his search.

Lime, of course, is still alive. In a classic scene on Vienna's famed (and still-operating today) giant Ferris wheel, Martins finally comes face-to-face with his friend. Lime is sanguine about his sins; after all, a man has to make a living. Looking out of the open door of the Ferris wheel cab at the people on the ground far below, he says to Martins,

> Look down there. Would you really feel any pity if one of those dots stopped moving forever? If I offered you 20,000 pounds for every dot that stopped would you really, old man, tell me to keep my money? Or would you calculate how many dots you could afford to spend? Free of income tax, old man, free of income [sic]. That's the only way you can save money nowadays.

Martins is unimpressed, but very frightened, realizing that Harry could kill him, too. For a moment, Harry looks as though he might push Martins out the door of the cab; instead, Lime offers to cut Martins in on the business. Martins refuses, and decides that, this time, he really will leave Vienna. But just before returning to the Russian zone, where he has been hiding, Lime offers one final bit of insight.

> Don't look so gloomy, after all, it's not that awful. What was it the fellow said? In Italy for 30 years under the Borgias they had warfare, terror, murder, bloodshed but they produced Michelangelo, Leonardo da Vinci, and the Renaissance. In Switzerland they had brotherly love. They had 500 years of democracy and peace, and what did that produce? The cuckoo clock.

Martins is still not fully convinced that his friend is rotten. But Major Calloway shows Martins the evidence against Lime and takes him to view some of the victims of Lime's black market scheme. Horrified by what he sees, Martins agrees to entrap Lime and, in a final chase scene through Vienna's sewers, Lime is hunted down and killed. He is buried, once again. Martins, planning again to leave, decides to remain in Vienna, perhaps to patch things up with Anna, perhaps not. Certainly, she shows no signs of wanting to have anything to do with Martins.

Back in the Saddle, Again

The vision of Europe—the Wild, Wild East—conveyed to American viewers by films such as *The Big Lift* and *The Third Man* could not have been very attractive. *The Big Lift* was filmed in Berlin, among the ruins, with Berliners playing the extras. By the time the film was released, the "good" Germans were on our side, while the "bad" Germans were in the East. But this was long before the East was sealed off from the West, and there was still a flow of Germans across the dividing line between the two zones. *The Big Lift* showed that beliefs, not actions, distinguished the good from the bad. One might be fooled by appearances, but devout followers of democracy and capitalism could be told from opportunists not by what they did, but by what they professed. The same is true in *The Third Man*.

Ostensibly, *The Third Man* is a detective film—one not all that dissimilar from some of Holly Martins's novels. It also falls into the category of *film noir,* a genre in which there are no real heroes, and even the villains may be of a sympathetic sort (O'Brien, 1991; Martin, 1997). But Vienna's darkness and gloom also reflect the moral and political ambiguity with which Americans saw postwar Europe. The victory over the Nazis was a glorious one, to be sure, but the follow-up proves a dismal affair. On the one hand, the Allies are supposed to impose law and order on the Viennese who, like Baron Kurtz (Ernst Deutsch), one of the minor characters in the film, cringe at the kinds of corrupt activities in which they must engage. On the other hand, it is clear that all kinds of truck and barter must go on for people to survive. Those who have connections or protection or are well placed will do well; others will simply become "dots" and die. As Lime puts it to Martins, "Nobody thinks in terms of human beings. Governments don't. Why should we? They talk about the people and the proletariat, I talk about the suckers and the mugs. It's the same thing. They have their five-year plans, so have I."

After the film was released, Graham Greene claimed that he never intended The Third Man to convey either a political or moral message; as he wrote in the introduction to the short story that was the basis for the screenplay of the film, "We had no desire to move people's political emotions. . . . Reality in fact was to be only the background to a fairy tale . . ." (Greene, 1976:8). Nonetheless, Harry Lime embodies both political and moral qualities of a questionable nature. He is a classic American confidence man and an avatar of the "Wild West" American capitalism that soon would arrive and thrive throughout Europe, Vienna included. Not only is Lime out to make a pound however he can, he has no compunctions about how he does it (as Baron Kurtz says to Martins, "You do better to think of yourself."). Indeed, in pursuit of "life, liberty and happiness," Lime finds it prudent and profitable to stage his own death, seek the protection of the Russians, and even turn Anna over to them.

In 1948, Greene could hardly have imagined how the Cold War might turn out, with not only the Russians losing but naked self-interest a triumphant and almost universally respected value. (Greene was surprised, however, to return to Vienna three months after his initial visit and find it already on its way to future prosperity.) The Vienna he describes is one in which order is paramount—as in, "I was just following orders"—even when such order is carried to an extreme. Each power has its own sector, each its own rights, each its own rules. The Russians go so far as to seek to recapture those who have "gone astray" from their newly founded empire in Eastern Europe. This includes Anna, whose native Czechoslovakia has just seen a democratic government deposed by a Communist coup. There is no justice as such in Vienna, although even among the International police one might buy it for the right price. As the British soldier says to Anna when she is being taken from her apartment to the International Police Station, "It's just protocol, miss." (Anna says, "I don't know what that means." He replies, "Neither do I, miss.") This is not a terribly attractive sort of order, but it is a message moviegoers could hardly have missed.

Graham Greene was well known not only for his novels but also for his Catholicism, which was central to many of his works. While The Third Man is hardly a Catholic film—Martins is asked to give a propaganda lecture on the modern novel and "the crisis of faith," even though he hasn't the faintest idea what that means—some of Greene's beliefs do seep in. When Major Calloway shows Martins convincing evidence of his friend's heinous misdeeds, the latter, temporarily believing that Lime was, indeed, murdered, responds, "Whoever killed him, there was some sort of justice." But, inasmuch as Lime is not dead, justice has not been done and things must be set in order. This task falls to Martins, the somewhat naïve writer of Western novelettes (e.g., The Oklahoma Kid) in which the hero always triumphs. Lime is hunted down and shot, underground in the sewers, but dies reaching for the unattainable sky. Even in chaotic postwar Vienna, there is some sort of justice.

Is it too much to read an allegory of the emerging Cold War into this underground mise en scène? Harry Lime is the avatar of amorality in the face of opportunity, and a bit Anglified, to boot. He is a realist—in the international relations sense—and sees his interests best served by the Soviets. Martins, the idealistic American, contemplates Harry's offer of business and rejects it out of hand—even at the risk of death. His sense of morality triumphs, in this instance, over naked self-interest. Only the United States, one might conclude, could get the Europeans out of their hole. Moreover, to keep them from dealing with Stalin, we would have to make them a better deal, one they could not refuse. Ultimately, however, money was not enough; power was needed, too. Atomic power.

≋

"First We Got the Bomb, but That Was Good"[2]

This was the world in which the Hot War became a Cold one. The United States was doing quite well, thank you, although there was an ever-present fear that a new Depression might be just around the corner. Peacetime military Keynesianism had not yet been applied—Truman was too intent on balancing the budget and minimizing defense spending—and American prosperity seemed reliant on foreign markets. But Europe remained poor and short of hard currency. Britain lurched from one balance-of-payments crisis to another. The winter of 1948 was one of the coldest in recent memory, and there were renewed threats of food shortages and starvation.[3] The future appeared none too promising.

By late 1949, with the ongoing troubles in Europe—Berlin, Czechoslovakia, Communist regimes in Eastern Europe, powerful Communist parties in France and Italy, the Soviet atomic bomb, and a Communist victory in China—U.S. policymakers were beginning to worry that their level of commitment to the Free World project was insufficient. Not only was the strategy of economic reconstruction apparently working poorly, but communism seemed to be on a march. In Malaya, a Communist insurgency threatened British control. In the Philippines, the Huk rebellion was approaching its peak. In Indochina, the French attempt to suppress nationalist opposition was beginning to heat up. And, at home, the Red Scare was beginning. All of the gold in Fort Knox was not enough, it seemed, to keep communism at bay. And the threat of economic recession was an ever-present one. The United States did, however, hold one trump card.

On August 6, 1945, nuclear weapons—that is, atomic bombs—became a reality of international political life and a force to be reckoned with. American policymakers were well aware that the blast over Hiroshima signified a major change in foreign affairs. Stalin recognized it, too. At a summit of foreign ministers, Truman's first secretary of state, James Byrnes, joked with his Soviet counterpart, Vyacheslav Molotov, about the new "gun" on his hip (Molotov did not find this amusing but, then, he was rarely amused about anything). Harry Truman exulted that, with the bomb, the Soviets could no longer bully him (had they been bullying him?). And, there grew a conviction among U.S. leaders that the bomb more than made up for the size of the Red Army in Europe, and this emboldened the Americans to flaunt it (LaFeber, 1993). Subsequent proposals to internationalize atomic energy—offered by the United States in the Baruch and Acheson-Lillienthal Plans—were couched in such terms as to maintain the American monopoly and they gave little or nothing to the Soviets. As a result, and quite deliberately, these efforts came to naught. What has been called "atomic diplomacy" (Alperovitz, 1994) and was later renamed "containment" (Gaddis, 1982) became an important element of the American response to Soviet actions in Europe and Asia.

For example, when the Soviets triggered the Berlin Crisis in 1948, President Truman sent atomic-*capable* B-29 bombers to air bases in England. He intended this to signal to Stalin that the United States would use the bomb, if necessary. Whether the message had any effect on the USSR is not clear, although it is unlikely that the planes could have delivered any atomic bombs on short notice. It normally took several days and a great deal of specialized equipment to load the bombs and prepare the planes, and none was available in England (George Orwell called England "Airstrip One" in *1984*; see below). At any rate, the nearest atomic bombs (of which there were no more than fifteen at the time) remained safely at home in the United States. Such atomic diplomacy was, in any event, a tactic whose utility proved to be time-limited (although, as we shall see, threats to use nuclear weapons were made again and again during the following decades; see Blechman and Kaplan, 1978).

The American atomic monopoly, predicted by some to last at least until 1960, came to an early end in August 1949. The first Soviet atomic test came as no great surprise to most of the atomic scientists, and it was not of great strategic importance. To politicians and the public, however, the Soviet test appeared a catastrophe. Rather than admit that they had ignored the assessments of those who knew better, the authorities began to seek atomic spies (see, e.g., U.S. Congress, 1951; Dallin, 1955; Pilat, 1952). The search did uncover several in the United States and Britain, some of whom had supplied useful information to the Soviets, but it also claimed as one of its victims Robert Oppenheimer, the "father" of the atomic bomb. Along the way, Julius and Ethel Rosenberg became the only individuals ever executed by the U.S. government for atomic espionage.[4]

Strictly speaking, there were no atomic secrets; if anything, the key bit of information was that the bomb worked. Once that was clear, it was only a matter of putting the pieces together correctly. In any event, the Soviets had been furiously pursuing an atomic bomb almost from the moment they learned that the United States was working on one. The Soviets wasted no time, either, in developing the atom bomb's successor, the thermonuclear fusion explosive that is now the standard for all nuclear weapons. At the time, this was called at the time the "super," and later became known popularly as the hydrogen or "H" bomb. (The USSR actually tested an H-bomb before the United States, in 1953, although it was physically as big as a building. The race for the first bomber "deliverable" H-bomb was won by the Americans not long afterward.)

The power (and terror) of the bomb lay in its terrible destructiveness. From almost the moment the first one was detonated at Alamagordo, New Mexico, it was reckoned that such weapons could hardly be employed in war. Ten dropped on an enemy's cities, as was noted some years later, would be a catastrophe beyond imagining, and there was no way to conceive of such weapons being useful on the battlefield. Upon hearing of the successful test, the wartime British prime minister, Winston Churchill, told Henry Stimson, Truman's secretary of war, "Stimson, what was gunpowder? Trivial. What was electricity? Meaningless. This Atomic Bomb is the Second Coming in Wrath!" (quoted in Freedman, 1981: 16). Bernard Brodie, one of the first academics to theorize about the bomb's utility in international relations, noted in 1946, "Thus far the chief purpose of a military establishment has been to win wars. From now on its chief purpose must be to avert them. It can have no other useful purpose" (quoted in Freedman, 1981:44). That this was the informed opinion of a fair number of scholars in the new field of nuclear strategy did not deter the bomb's aficionados from trying to devise ways to use them on the battlefield—as we shall see in chapter 5.

By 1950, it was generally recognized that the reasons for developing the super had more to do with national prestige than military strategy and, as Oppenheimer put it, the "technical sweetness" of making the thing work.[5] The debate over the super that went on during 1950 between Edward Teller and his supporters, on one side, and Oppenheimer and his, on the other, had little to do with whether thermonuclear weapons could ever be employed, much less questions about the morality of their existence. Oppenheimer was not opposed to atomic weapons; he simply believed that the super was much too destructive to be of any use, and that what later came to be called "collateral damage" would be hazardous, if not fatal, to one's own troops. He thought it would make much more sense to develop low-yield bombs, scaling their destructiveness down to a usable level—on the order of 5-10 kilotons or less (the Hiroshima bomb was 15-20 kilotons). Then, howitzers could lob nuclear shells onto the enemy's formations and, after a suitable period of time, properly protected troops could move in to take control of the rubble.[6]

While Oppenheimer lost the fight over the super—and, eventually, his security clearance for not being sufficiently enthusiastic to quell either Teller's or the government's suspicions about his loyalty—his views did triumph to some degree. Along with the decision to build the H-bomb came a second to focus on the development of battlefield and theater atomic weapons. During the 1950s, therefore, not only were bigger air-launched thermonuclear weapons designed, developed, and deployed, so were nuclear land mines and artillery, as well as "dial-a-yield" warheads for short-range missiles, which literally allowed the launch officer to decide how powerful the blast would be (Cochran, Arkin and Hoenig, 1984; Schwartz, 1998).

But these innovations were not part of the world's introduction to the Atomic Age, and they had little to do with the way in which the Hot War initially turned Cold. Many feared that a new Hot War was imminent, although few thought much about what might follow. George Orwell did.

∿∿∿
∿∿∿

Say Hello to Big Brother. He's Watching, You Know

1984: A Novel, George Orwell (New York: Harcourt Brace; 1st American Edition, 1949)

Winston Smith, the thirty-nine-year-old protagonist of *1984*, is a member of the Outer Party and a mid-level employee at the Ministry of Truth (Minitrue in Newspeak, the language of Oceania) located in London, Airstrip One. His job is to "rectify" errors in the historical record, in line with the Party's dictum "Who controls the past, controls the future; who controls the present controls the past." Smith revises and rewrites published materials such as newspaper articles so that they will reflect either actual events—as opposed to what had been predicted—or what the Party wants people to think happened. This will cast a favorable light on the Party and its far-sighted leadership, personified in the cult of Big Brother (who may or may not be a real individual).

But Smith is a heretic. While he enjoys his job, he believes in nothing, except Truth. He longs to find those who oppose the Party, an ultra-secret group rumored to be called "The Brotherhood," led by one Emmanuel Goldstein. Goldstein, modeled on Leon Trotsky, was purged in the 1960s. Although his whereabouts are unknown—indeed, he is probably dead—the Party finds it convenient to keep his memory and threat alive so that he can be blamed for whatever goes wrong: sabotage, food shortages, setbacks in war.

Winston does not know how to contact the Brotherhood, but he believes that he has found a soul mate in O'Brien, his superior in the Ministry of Truth and a member of the Inner Party. Seven years earlier, O'Brien gave Winston a sympathetic, knowing look while the two passed in a hallway. But more contact than this is not possible. The Thought Police, aided by spies, listening devices, and two-way telescreens, are constantly on the alert for traitors, and only too ready to vaporize them and turn them into "nonpersons," removed from the pages of history.

Somewhat unintentionally, Winston becomes involved in a love affair with Julia, a young women who also works in the Ministry of Truth. Julia maintains a strictly orthodox outward appearance, but revels in violating Party norms, especially those concerning celibacy. Eventually, Winston and Julia are able to arrange a face-to-face meeting with O'Brien whom, they hope, will induct them into the Brotherhood. O'Brien warns the two that, in joining the Brotherhood, they will be exposed to great danger, will be alone, and will be expected to sacrifice their lives to a future they will never live to see. He then gives Winston and Julia a copy of the Brotherhood's "book"—*The Theory and Practice of Oligarchical Collectivism*, by Emmanuel Goldstein—which, he tells them, will explain everything.

Unfortunately for Winston and Julia, O'Brien is not a member of the Brotherhood. In fact, he works with the Thought Police and has been keeping an eye on Smith ever since the day of that look, seven years earlier. Winston and Julia are set up and captured by the Thought Police and taken off to the Ministry of Love (Minilove). There, they are tortured, shown the error of their ways, forced to confess their crimes, and tricked into betraying each other. Eventually, they will emerge from imprisonment and express their love for and devotion to Big Brother. Then, they will be executed.

And so it comes to pass.

It Can't Happen Here . . . Can It?

To the first-time reader, what is striking about Orwell's novel is its unrelenting grimness. The world of Winston Smith is gray, shabby, dusty, hungry, poor, brutish, ignorant, stagnant, and without hope. It is in a constant state of war—although with whom is hardly important. War serves, on the one hand, to sop up excess production that might otherwise be used to improve general living standards while, on the other hand, it allows the Inner Party to maintain its hegemony over the Outer Party through an ideological and unquestioning frenzy. The apparent paradox is that this world continues to exist, even though several hundred atomic bombs had been dropped on cities in the 1950s. As Goldstein (Orwell) presciently points out, "Thereafter, although no formal agreement was ever made or hinted at, no more bombs were dropped. All three powers merely continue to produce atomic bombs and store them up against the decisive opportunity which they all believe will come sooner or later" (Orwell, 1983: 160). Thus, war is normal but change is not, since that would upset the established order of things and might even lead to nuclear holocaust. The echo here of the Cold War nuclear stalemate, in which "war" was a constant and the East-West confrontation frozen and unchangeable, is striking.

After publication, Orwell's book was often regarded as a prediction of life in the future were the Soviet Union to succeed in conquering the world. Indeed, in 1984, numerous commentators trumpeted the failure of *1984* to materialize as

Orwell seemed to predict (Howe, 1983), and there has been no end of interpretations of the book (as illustrated by perusal of any bibliographic database using the keywords "George Orwell"). But there are still some truths to be found in the novel. For example, there is evidence that Orwell actually used the United States as his model for Oceania. In a fascinating, unattributed paper that appeared on the World Wide Web (but has since been disappeared),[7] the author linked Orwell's dystopic novel to the growing influence of American culture and industrialism on Britain. As the writer of the essay put it, Orwell meant to romanticize England and he "needed the moronic inferno of American brutality and insanity, complete with the fire and brimstone of atomic weapons, to complete his romantic construction of English life and values."

To one who has read *1984* several times, Orwell's Hobbesian vision remains striking for its warnings about history, language, truth, and order as means of gaining and maintaining power within the state. By controlling history and language, the Party is able to manipulate "reality" so as to buttress its authority and order. Infallibility means that the Party cannot be challenged by contrary "truths," and the limits on technology mean that no one can acquire the tools needed to undermine the Party or its hegemony.

It is a version of Orwell's two-way telescreen—what in the 1990s was called, for a time, the "information superhighway"—that today threatens to fulfill the most disturbing part of his vision. The telescreen, which can never be shut off, pours forth an unending stream of "facts," statistics whose evident claims are not only unclear, they are not even necessarily "true." Thus, for example, even as he is adjusting a report on boot production issued by the Ministry of Plenty, Smith reflects,

> In any case, sixty-two millions [pairs of boots] was no nearer the truth than fifty-seven millions, or than a hundred and forty-five millions. Very likely no boots had been produced at all. Likelier still, nobody knew how many had been produced, much less cared. All one knew was that every quarter astronomical numbers of boots were produced on paper, while perhaps half the population of Oceania went barefoot (Orwell, 1983: 37).

What *does* information mean when one is drowned in it and has no way of distinguishing among "facts"? For that matter, of what significance is it that more than one trillion dollars of currency trading takes place every day, while a billion people or more are without clean water? (As Ronald Reagan once said, "facts are stupid things.")

Orwell's depiction of totalitarianism seems to come up short or, at least, to be only of historical or literary interest, and the rubble of *The Third Man* and *The Big Lift* are only memories, visible, now, on the telescreen. But there is a very real sense in which our world is a descendent of the two fictional ones of Orwell and Greene. In Orwell's world, the Party is the ultimate determinant of "reality"; in our world, we are faced with a somewhat contrary problematic that looks quite different: the tyranny of the "free" market. But how different is it? The market is the most "efficient" means of arriving at political outcomes; the market is the place where consumers "vote" for the truth, where societies live and die, where those who have money also have ultimate power. Rather than the totalitarianism of oligarchy, we face a totalitarianism of the market, which we are not allowed to question. Harry Lime may be dead, but his spirit is alive and well on Wall Street and the world's bourses. After all, aren't the best consumers the "mugs and suckers," those who don't question or challenge the ruling ideology of the day?

~~~
~~~

Is War Peace? Is Freedom Slavery? Is Ignorance Strength?

What kept the Cold War from breaking out into a Hot One during the late 1940s and throughout the 1950s? As we shall see in later chapters, it was as much fear as anything else—a fear that nuclear strategists named *nuclear deterrence*, in order to make it respectable. Orwell's Emmanuel Goldstein, sworn enemy of Big Brother, put it better when he suggested that "The effect [of using atomic bombs] was to convince the ruling groups of all countries that a few more atomic bombs would mean the end of organized society, and hence of their own power" (Orwell, 1983: 160). Slowly, American policymakers—and, much more slowly, the military—came to realize that the utility of nuclear weapons lay not in their usefulness in battle—as demonstrated by President Eisenhower's decisions not to use the bomb in either Korea or Vietnam, despite pressure from his military advisers—but, rather, in their *deterrent* quality, their ability to induce fear.

That is to say, it was the *threat* of use, rather than use itself, that was seen as most useful. So long as the adversary was unwilling to risk the great destructiveness associated with atomic attack, she would not try to start anything. The problem, as it later developed, was that the adversary had to be *convinced*—absolutely and unalterably—that nuclear weapons *would* be used *if* she tried anything. Since any use of nuclear weapons by one side would probably result in retaliation by the other, resulting in similar levels of destruction, it became increasingly difficult to project a conviction that one would actually initiate the end of the world in the face of a *conventional* attack to prevent one. The outcome was the same: no nuclear war. As in the world of *1984*, there were plenty of peripheral wars, almost all of them in colonial or newly independent countries. The "superstates"—Europe, the United States, the Soviet Union—enjoyed peace.

But was it truly peace? In *1984*, Orwell issued a warning about order and power that, in some ways, depicts the same sort of bureaucratic order seen in the Vienna (and Berlin) of 1948. While Orwell was clearly concerned about totalitarianism—his experiences in the Spanish Civil War had not endeared the Communists to him, or him to them, and many thought his book a direct criticism of Stalinism—it is telling that his Oceanian superstate encompasses the former terrain of Anglo-American democracy. That "Ingsoc" ("English Socialism") could become the ruling ideology of even the United States says much about Orwell's fears for the future. Moreover, there is some reason to think that, perhaps, he merely got some of the details wrong; there is much in his world that, if we look, we can find in ours.

Always Check under the Bed

There were no Thought Police in the United States of the 1950s, but some ideas were treated with great suspicion. It used to be said that, in the USSR, "everything that was not explicitly permitted was forbidden" while, in the United States, "everything that was not explicitly forbidden was permitted." There were, however, things that were not explicitly forbidden that a "good" American would never even contemplate. One of these was membership in any kind of leftist organization. Another was associating with members of any kind of leftist organization. Another was having been married to a former member of any kind of leftist organization . . . and on and on and on.

Chapter 3

Reds among Us?

The antipathy of slavery to freedom explains the iron curtain, the isolation, the autarchy of the society whose end is absolute power. The existence and persistence of the idea of freedom is a permanent and continuous threat to the foundation of the slave society; and it therefore regards as intolerable the long continued existence of freedom in the world.

—NSC-68, April 7, 1950

World War III!

On June 25, 1950, word came to Washington that Communist North Korea had invaded South Korea. Almost immediately, plans were made by the United States to respond to this provocation with force. What was not clear at first, however, was the import of the invasion. Was it an isolated event, or the first shot in World War III? The invasion came close on the heels of the declaration of the People's Republic of China in Peking (Beijing) by the victorious Chinese Communists in late 1949, and an extended visit by Party Chairman Mao Zedong to Moscow. Many in the West thought general war would soon break out, and war fear, fever, and fervor began to stalk the land (see, e.g., *Life Magazine*, Dec. 18, 1950).

What was most troubling to Washington, however, was how such Communist victories had been possible. Where had the United States failed? Who was responsible? How could the further expansion of communism be prevented? The onset of the Korean War increased already existing suspicions that not only was the U.S. policy of preventing Soviet expansion badly flawed, but also that there were traitors actively working from within the West to undermine America's security. The search for Reds began in earnest, and no stone was left unturned in seeking them out (Fariello, 1995; Foster, 2000).

35

The 1950s were the heyday of U.S. Cold War economic power and domination. The dollar was king. U.S. products were in worldwide demand (indeed, in those days, the labels "Made in Japan" and "Made in Hong Kong" indicated shoddy product quality). And what American corporations wanted, they got (Gilpin, 1975). Indeed, the U.S. government even intervened on their behalf in places such as Iran and Guatemala (see chapter 4). But the exercise of external influence also led to major social changes in the domestic arena, and these were unsettling to American society. During World War II, for example, large numbers of African Americans had migrated from the South to northern and western cities, where jobs in the defense industry were readily available. Greater involvement in international affairs also meant more exposure to foreign cultures, especially among the soldiers fighting in Europe and Asia. The cosmopolitanism of the country's elites became increasingly visible through the new medium of television, and both were fascinating as well as alien at the same time (Englehardt, 1995). Science created the atomic bomb, which could not only destroy cities in a flash but also, it seemed, cause unpredictable mutations in living things. Change was in the air, and not only was it disturbing, it was also politically charged.

Most fundamentally, such changes raised questions about identity and belonging (many of these questions are still being asked today). Who was American, who was not? What kinds of beliefs should "good citizens" hold, and what should be done about those who did not hew to them? What effect might such "heretics" have on the body politic, especially if they occupied high positions in the country's political and cultural hierarchy (as a rule, such subversives were not to be found among the economic elites, who were, for the most part, firmly Republican and wedded to capitalism). Finally, could "good" Americans fall prey to these heretics, even as unwilling victims?

Such concerns were expressed, in part, through two themes: *corruption* and *possession*. Both have long been present in American politics and society, dating back to early days of European settlement in North America. The notion of corruption is evident in those works that link crime with communism. And, although we now think of corruption as having to do with illegal or "under-the-table" activities, especially economic ones, the word derives from the Latin term meaning "to break to pieces." As used in more recent history, it also invokes perversion, contamination, spoilage, rot, and bodily decay, in this instance, of the body politic.

Possession is also an idea with a long history. Things happen, people change, customary ways of living are upset, and there are no obvious explanations—except, perhaps, the devil and his minions or some other inimical force. What was familiar and stable is no longer so, and the roles one thought were fixed are now seen as fluid and changeable. Followers take charge and leaders become the hunted. How to explain the world turned upside down, especially by those who know better (Groh, 1987)?

During the 1950s, these themes emerged in three forms, the first focused on crime, the second on atomic radiation, the third on possession by Communist ideas. The first became popular in *films noir*—such as *I was a Communist for the FBI, My Son John, Pickup on South Street*—in which fathers, sons, and husbands, among others, have been changed, some becoming homosexuals, some traitors, a few, both. These films also provided viewers with instructions in the detection of corruption. Atomic radiation, with its power to do damage invisibly, was central to a flood of monster films portraying giant ants (*Them!*, 1954) and grasshoppers (*The Beginning of the End*, 1957), sea monsters (*It Came from Beneath the Sea*, 1955), invincible aliens (*The Thing*, 1951), and bizarre mutants (*The Incredible Shrinking Man*, 1957), among others. Finally, possession was best illustrated by a 1956 film, *Invasion of the Body Snatchers*, set in the fictional California town of Santa Mira, which went so far as to suggest that one could become a Commie simply by adopting subversive ideas (see also *Invaders from Mars*, 1953). *The Manchurian Candidate* (1959), a novel by Richard Condon, satirized the Korean War fear of remote control through "brainwashing." Several of the novel's premises became all too real only four years later, however, when President John F. Kennedy was apparently shot by Lee Harvey Oswald, an ex-marine whose political proclivities and mental stability were none too clear.

In many ways, it was this period, during the early 1950s, that set the political tone for the next several decades. The magnitude of the apparent Communist threat and its seemingly relentless march across the world could not be attributed, people thought, to any rational or logical reasoning inherent in the ideology and its practice. Clearly, capitalism and democracy were much more attractive in what they had to offer the "underdeveloped areas," as Harry Truman called them in his 1949 inaugural address. If these areas did not accept such evident logic, why then they must be falling victim to lies and deceit emanating from Moscow!

The effort to halt the spread of communism was called *containment*. As we shall see, while the outline for this strategy was largely the brainchild of a single individual, George Kennan, who never meant it to be foolproof or leakproof, it was eagerly adopted and taken to extremes by U.S. policymakers (Gaddis, 1982). Containing Communists abroad was necessary but not sufficient; they must also be contained at home. This was one source of the domestic Red Scare. The problem was how could you tell who was a Communist? Were there telltale signs? Did Communists behave in peculiar ways? Might one be turned into a Red unawares?

 ∿∿∿
 ∿∿∿

Look Out! Save Yourselves! They're Coming! They're Here!

Invasion of the Body Snatchers (Allied Artists, 1956, 80 min.)
Director: Don Siegel
Cast: Kevin McCarthy, Dana Wynter, Carolyn Jones, Sam Peckinpah
(The film was remade in flashy but inferior versions in 1978 and 1994.)

Dr. Miles Bennell (McCarthy) returns from a medical conference to his home in Santa Mira (in Spanish, *mira* means "to be on the lookout; to watch for") to find a mysterious hysteria spreading throughout the town. People think their friends and family are not who they are supposed to be, although there are no evident changes short of emotional deficits (brought on, according to the town's psychiatrist, by fear). Bennell and his love interest, Becky Driscoll (Wynter), soon discover that people are being taken over and reborn as duplicate bodies that emerge from alien pods. The pods have come "out of the sky" and taken root on the farms around the town. The replacements are superior in every way to the "real" people they take over, in that they all belong to a soulless collective and have no feelings, emotions, or worries. Those who have undergone the change swear it is the best thing that has ever happened to them; those who have not—such as Bennell—try to escape in order to protect their "humanity."

Eventually, Bennell, with the entire population of Santa Mira in pursuit, including Becky, manages to reach the main highway. From there, he hopes to escape to Los Angeles(!), although no one will pick him up. In the final scene, at an LA hospital, Bennell tells his story to two incredulous doctors who are prepared to have him committed to a lunatic asylum. At the last minute, however, a policeman arrives at the hospital with an injured truck driver who, the cop tells the doctors, was driving a rig carrying the strangest things: large pods. The FBI is called in on the case, presumably to eradicate this evil plague on the land. The movie ends with a closeup of Bennell who, although vindicated, has been driven to the brink of madness by his close call. (In the film's original version, Bennell is last seen screaming into the camera "You're next! You're next!").

I Only Trust Myself and You . . . and I'm Not too Sure about You

Not many films combined the themes of corruption and possession as did *Invasion of the Body Snatchers*. And what was not entirely clear, either, was whether the film depicted possession by Communists or McCarthyites (by 1956, Senator Joseph McCarthy was no longer a political power in the

United States). The film's director, Don Siegel, claimed that the film was anti-Communist, but it can also be read as a diatribe against conformity—a topic addressed elsewhere in print (William Whyte, *The Organization Man*, 1956) and film (*The Man in the Gray Flannel Suit*, 1956).

At first watch, *Invasion* appears to be a fairly straightforward science fiction film: aliens invade and take over. One man escapes and warns the world. Still, as with the occupied citizens of Santa Mira, the story is not quite so simple. There are a number of peculiar subthemes that run throughout, involving liquor, sex, and madness.

From a contemporary perspective, the frequency of social drinking in the course of everyday life in Santa Mira seems astonishing. Dr. Bennell and his associates imbibe copious quantities of liquor, during both social occasions and in times of stress. While never visibly intoxicated, Bennell is frequently accused, by those who have been taken over by the pods, of being drunk, suffering from hallucinations, and not seeing straight. Certainly, he does not see the world from the same point of view as the rest of the town but, whereas we think him sober, most Santa Mirans claim he is not.

Bennell and Becky Driscoll, his old flame, are also newly drunk—and, perhaps, a bit insane—over each other. High-school sweethearts, they went their separate ways, married, divorced, left town, and returned. A single reunion and they fall head over heels in love again. The film is laced with what, for the times, seem fairly strong sexual innuendos. Each time Bennell makes a suggestive remark to Driscoll, she responds coyly that madness would be sure to follow such violations of the social norm ("What's wrong with madness?" Miles asks Becky. "Madness," she replies). In the "new" Santa Mira, taken over by aliens, any emotion whatsoever is against the social norm, and love is impossible. One cannot belong to the collective if one loves (although hate seems permissible). Finally, when Bennell reaches the main highway and tries to stop traffic, warning people of the "madness" at large in Santa Mira, he is regarded as mad or drunk. Even a truck driver, carrying a load of pods to Los Angeles, yells at him to get out of the way. Once he makes it to the city, he is stonewalled by psychiatrists at the hospital to which the police, presuming him to be mad, have brought him.

The paradox here is that much of what is described as "madness" is actually fairly ordinary or expectable behavior, albeit a manifestation of emotion that must be contained, as it is contained by those who have been occupied. In Santa Mira, conventional standards have become extraordinary, and Bennell must be contained so as not to reveal to outsiders what has happened in the town. He escapes from the "plague zone" to warn others that this illness must be contained, lest terrible things happen to the rest of the country. What is never made exactly clear, however, is the nature of the plague that has arrived from "out there." Perhaps the pods are not alien at all; perhaps they are the result of mutation by atomic radiation. Perhaps society has become so twisted by its fears of "things from the sky" that it will do anything to suppress wayward emotions. Perhaps the pods represent the virus of communism or the bacterium of McCarthyism. The answer is left to the viewer's imagination.

Invasion of the Body Snatchers is, ultimately, a film that warns us that we may not be who we think we are even if, for all intents and purposes, we have not visibly changed (or been changed). After all, how can what we believe or feel have an effect on who we are? One might as well ask how the people of a country can go, almost overnight, from being peace-loving to becoming a Party of War? To stop having to worry about the "issues of the day" (e.g., atomic destruction) would, in the 1950s, have been as much as anyone might have asked for. But the political solutions that were offered were not solutions at all. At the end of the day, they would have turned the country into something quite different, something no longer identifiable as the United States. In other words, change (aka, "instability") was the problem. Best to freeze everything and keep it familiar. This was, by and large, the goal of containment.

≈

Containing Commies: Kennan and the Long Telegram

How did containment become the guiding light of U.S. Cold War strategy? Almost by accident. In 1946, George Frost Kennan was chief of mission at the U.S. embassy in Moscow. He had had long experience with and in Russia, but had not risen much above the middle staff level in the Foreign Service. His analyses of Soviet affairs were valued, but had never been singled out as exceptional. He was not an American "mover" or "shaker"— at least, not yet. But he was soon to acquire a notoriety that he never escaped, largely the result of a single, long analysis that he sent to the State Department in Washington that year.

Between late 1945 and the middle of 1946, U.S. foreign policy was somewhat aimless, inasmuch as there was a good deal of cleaning up to do. Viewing the world through the geopolitical lens made popular during the war, policymakers tended more and more to see the world in zero-sum terms: what one Great Power was able to gain came as a loss to others (Dalby, 1990). And, as noted in chapter 2, relations with Moscow were beginning to deteriorate. Nevertheless, no one was able to offer a clear and compelling assessment of Soviet strategy that would satisfy U.S. policymakers as to Stalin's intentions in Europe and elsewhere. Was the USSR an insecure state seeking to avoid a repeat of invasions by Napoleon, the World War I allies, and the Third Reich? Could it become a trusted partner in the management of world affairs, through the UN Security Council and other international organizations? Or, was it like Hitler's Germany, bent on expansion all the way to the English Channel (and beyond)? Events, especially as they transpired in Central and Eastern Europe and elsewhere during the years after the end of World War II, seemed to indicate malign intent, even though there were always several possible explanations for what was happening.

For example, the Soviets appeared reluctant to end their wartime occupation of Northern Iran and, before leaving in 1946, tried to encourage secessionist efforts in Azerbaijani areas in the northern part of the country. In Germany, the Soviets systematically stripped their occupation zone of its industrial capacity, extending even to railroad tracks. Through their Yugoslav allies, Moscow appeared to be aiding and abetting the leftists in the Greek civil war (which turned out not to be the case). Stalin made unprecedented—and many thought hostile—demands on Turkey, asking for revisions in the conventions governing passage through the straits between the Black and Mediterranean seas. The Soviets proved intransigent in negotiations undertaken over various issues, including the atomic bomb (although with respect to the bomb, they were offered deals by the United States that they could and did refuse). The Kremlin failed to live up to its commitments to hold free elections in Eastern Europe and Stalin seemed to be encouraging the Communist parties in Western Europe to seize power, through the ballot box, if possible, and through destabilization, if necessary. And so on (Kuniholm, 1980; LaFeber, 1993; McCormick, 1995).

Taken as a piece, such actions puzzled and troubled the Americans, and stoked paranoia. Such activities might be those either of an aggressive, expansionist power or a conservative, insecure one. Both views, and various combinations, were proposed by various people in various positions of power and authority. Kennan was one of those polled on this question. In response, he wrote and sent to the State Department what came to be called the "Long Telegram," an extended analysis of Soviet thinking and intentions. It was here that the term *containment* first appeared.

In the intervening decades, containment came to acquire an almost mystical significance. After all, that was what kept the Russians out and, eventually, led the West to win the Cold War—or so goes the popular interpretation. But what, exactly, did Kennan *argue*? It was not nearly as ambitious as the policy to which he was eventually linked. Rather, he laid out what he saw as the irreducible interests of the United States: national security and freedom from external interference, and national welfare to be promoted in a peaceful, congenial international environment. These objectives were to be pursued through what Kennan called a "particularized" approach to foreign policy, rooted in his recognition of the thirst for power as the basic driving force of international life. This philosophy he contrasted to a "universalistic" approach that tried to convert the entire world to American principles. In the language of the 1930s, in other words,

Kennan was a "realist" and not an "idealist," one who saw the world as it was, rather than as it should be (Gaddis, 1982; Carr, 1939).

From this framework, Kennan derived four corollaries. First, it was essential that no more than one of the five great industrial power centers of the time—North America, the United Kingdom, Germany, Japan, and the Soviet Union—be under the control of a country hostile to the United States. Second, the internal organization and politics of a country were of no concern to the United States, so long as said country was not demonstrably under direct Soviet control or a clear and present danger to the United States. Third, there was no conflict between the demands of security and those of principle, so long as the first was understood to come before the second. Maintenance of the balance of power was the best way to ensure that this hierarchy of goals remained intact. Fourth, and last, Kennan insisted on using interests as the way of evaluating threats, rather than using threats to determine interests. He argued that following the latter course would be too costly and probably impossible. Nonetheless, it was that practice that became strategy in a very short time and which led to a vast increase in defense expenditures during the 1950s (Gaddis, 1982).

It was not, however, Kennan's principles of foreign affairs that proved so compelling to Washington but, rather, his explanation of Soviet behavior. The Soviets, he argued, were driven by an historical insecurity that had roots in both Czarist and more recent times. Given Russia's experiences with invasions by Napoleon, the West during the Bolshevik Revolution, and Germany during World War II, the Soviets had little reason not to think that the world was unremittingly hostile, explained Kennan. This, combined with the ideological rationalizations of Marxism-Leninism, made it clear that Soviet expansion could, in theory, have no limits. The implication was that the United States might well have a problem on its hands. But Kennan himself did not believe that Stalin would risk war with the West, even though, by 1946, the Soviet military far outnumbered anything the West would have been able to mobilize on short notice (and, hence, the reliance on atomic weapons).

Instead, Kennan was more concerned about the *psychological* manipulation of Western Europe—what would later be called "Finlandization"—as the result of demoralization and the destruction brought about by the war. If this happened, Europe might well be lost to the United States, an outcome that the United States was duty-bound to resist. If a totalitarian Europe had been unacceptable in 1941, how could it be acceptable in 1946? Fortunately, while war was out of the question, the influence of affluence was not. The threat of intimidation could be countered through financial and military assistance, and the United States was much, much richer than the Soviet Union.

In 1947, Kennan's analysis was published in *Foreign Affairs*, the semi-official journal of the U.S. foreign policy establishment, under the title "The Sources of Soviet Conduct" and the pseudonym "Mr. X." It proved extremely popular. By 1950, almost all of America's foreign policy was, somehow, rationalized through the strategy of containment. But Kennan's proposals counseled patience, and they were not sufficiently proactive for U.S. policymakers. In 1950, he resigned from the State Department, feeling that his ideas were being twisted and misused (Gaddis, 1982).

War Is Peace!

In early 1950, in response to the apparent expansion of Communist influence, especially in Asia, Washington began to think about a mobilization strategy for what appeared to be an almost inevitable World War III. Not only would mobilization prepare the country for war, it could also have salutary economic impacts, an important consideration given that there had already been several postwar recessions. Some American policymakers reasoned, on the one hand, that only World War II had rescued the United States from the Depression and, on the other, that America's international credibility required greater military and economic commitments to its allies. The Policy Planning Staff of the State Department, directed by Paul Nitze, began a response to the presidential order: "That the President direct the Secretary of State and the Secretary of Defense to undertake a reexamination of our objectives in peace and war and of the effect of these objectives on our strategic plans, in the light of probable fission capability and possible thermonuclear bomb capability of the Soviet Union" (NSC-68, 1980: 236).

The result was NSC-68, a strategy document that went far beyond the mere assessment of military objectives requested by the president.[1] It also explored the ontologies of both the United States and the USSR, proposing an essentially Manichaean analysis of the world situation. Thus, according to the report,

> [T]he Soviet Union, unlike previous aspirants to hegemony, is animated by a new fanatic faith, antithetical to our own, and seeks to impose its absolute authority over the rest of the world. . . . [This] design . . . calls for the complete subversion or forcible destruction of the machinery of government and structure of society in the countries of the non-Soviet world and their replacement by an apparatus and structure subservient to and controlled from the Kremlin (NSC-68, 1980: 237-38).

Describing the underlying and contrasting ideology of the United States, NSC-68 asserted that "[T]he free society does not fear, it welcomes, diversity. It derives its strength from its hospitality even to antipathetic ideas. It is a market for free trade in ideas, secure in its faith that free men will take the best wares, and grow to a fuller and better realization of their powers in exercising their choice" (NSC-68, 1980: 239). In that marketplace of ideas, could any choice be more clear?

The report warned that the United States would need to remain vigilant and on guard against both Soviet attack and Soviet subversion. In some ways, the first problem would be easier for, as the report later admonished,

> It is quite clear from Soviet theory and practice that the Kremlin seeks to bring the free world under its dominion by the methods of the cold war. The preferred technique is to subvert by infiltration and intimidation. Every institution of our society is an instrument which it is sought [sic] to stultify and turn against our purposes. Those that touch most closely our material and moral strength are obviously the prime targets, labor unions, civic enterprises, schools, churches, and all media for influencing opinion (NSC-68, 1980: 263).

Reading NSC-68 in its entirety a half-century later is a mind-numbing experience. It is a fascinating historical document, unless one makes the mistake of reading beyond the first page or two. Then, the reader is quickly overwhelmed by turgid prose and imponderable statistics (how many pairs of boots?). Even had it not been a highly classified report, NSC-68 would never have been a bestseller. Nonetheless, it did become important as a policy plan, although only by accident.

What the authors of NSC-68 proposed was relatively straightforward: increased military spending (aka, Keynesian fiscal stimulus) as a means of, first, responding to the Communist threat; second, pulling the West out of the economic doldrums that had hit in 1949; and third, reinforcing the credibility of American commitments to allies by making it clear that the U.S. *would* go to war to save Europe. To accomplish this, four central proposals were put forward:

- Move from what was called *strongpoint containment* to *perimeter defense*, which meant threatening the use of military force in response to any provocative Soviet action;
- Recognize the disutility of nuclear weapons in countering Soviet advances—an argument for greater reliance on and a buildup in conventional armaments—while nonetheless building the H-bomb;
- Increase the military budget from $13 billion to about $50 billion to pay for the shift to conventional weaponry, especially in Europe; and

* Focus on frustrating the Kremlin's "design" through political and psychological efforts aimed against the Soviet Union (Gaddis, 1982).

Presented with a draft document in early 1950, Truman was not terribly impressed. In particular, he believed that there was no way, given the economic situation, budgetary constraints, *and* a Republican Congress, that defense spending could be quadrupled (it is important to remember that, at the time, Keynesian pump priming was not yet the accepted economic wisdom, as it would become ten years later). Balanced budgets were not merely rhetoric, as they came to be during the 1980s, they were religion. So Truman provisionally approved the document and returned it to the National Security Council for further consideration, where it might have languished, except for a quite unexpected event.

On June 25, 1950, a sort of deus ex machina—the Korean War—breathed new life into NSC-68. Subsequently, it became the blueprint for the militarization of the Cold War and the emergence of the military-industrial complex as two of the dominant facets of subsequent American foreign policy. From then on, there were few foreign problems that, it was believed, could not be substantially solved without an injection of military power, and fewer domestic problems that could not be addressed through Congressional appropriation of funds for national security. Oddly, while the U.S. defense budget did quadruple by the end of 1950, most of the funds were directed not to *Korea* but to the military buildup in *Europe*. That was where the main battles of the Cold War and World War III would be fought, and that was where the risks of nuclear war—and the incentives to avoid it—were greatest. But military rearmament was only part of the strategy; containment at home was also essential (Gaddis, 1982).

Reds on a Roll?

The Korean War was not a success, and Harry Truman suffered for it. South Korea was almost "lost" during the first few weeks of the war, and Democrats lost control of the White House two years later. Under the auspices of the United Nations, General Douglas MacArthur led an invasion at Inchon, in South Korea, which succeeded in establishing a defensive perimeter behind North Korean lines. This became the basis for a military campaign that pushed the North Korean forces all the way to the Yalu River, the peninsula's northern border with China. There was some concern in Washington that "Red" China, as Americans then called it, might enter the war, but MacArthur pooh-poohed this fear and dismissed as hearsay reports of Chinese Communist regulars fighting on the North Korean side.

Fear soon proved fact, however, as massive numbers of Chinese soldiers crossed the Yalu and pushed MacArthur's men back toward the South (Whiting, 1960). That failure became one of the central factors in MacArthur's eventual dismissal by Truman, which Republicans turned into another black mark against the Democrats. Not until 1953 was an armistice established, with the dividing line drawn just about where it had been prior to 1950.

By then, however, another election had come and gone. Truman, thrust into the presidency without much warning in 1945, and elected to a full term in 1948 in the face of intraparty challenges from both Left and Right,[2] decided not to run again. His designated successor, Adlai Stevenson, lost badly in the general election of 1952 to the Republican candidate, Dwight D. Eisenhower. "Ike" was a genuine war hero. His political proclivities had not been very clear prior to 1950, and he was wooed by both parties. He came late to the Republican Party, pushing Senator Robert Taft, an isolationist, out of the race. But Eisenhower was also not above suspicion of having Communistic leanings, due to his "internationalist" credentials and support for the United Nations.

Eisenhower's secretary of state, John Foster Dulles, however, was as anti-Communist as they came, promising to roll back the Reds throughout Europe and Asia, and to reply with "massive retaliation"—nuclear weapons—whenever and wherever the Soviets made a sally against the West. Rhetoric was not the same as action, of course, although it terrified Western publics who nervously watched the sky. In 1954, Eisenhower refused to use nuclear weapons to relieve the siege of the French army at Dien Bien Phu in North Vietnam (chapter 7), even though he regarded nukes as not much more than very powerful conventional bombs. But he also did nothing to liberate the "captive nations" of Eastern Europe, failing to offer assistance to the Hungarians when they rose up against the country's Soviet-bloc government in 1956. An avid believer in economy and efficiency, Eisenhower also refused to spend as much money on defense and containment as some Cold Warriors thought necessary (his treasury secretary, George Humphrey, was said to fear a budget deficit almost as much as he feared Communists; Gaddis, 1982: 135). Rollback was empty talk and massive retaliation was never put to the test.

Nonetheless, in a larger sense, containment was a success: few countries went Communist after 1952. But the United States's apparent inability to roll back Reds abroad frustrated many at home. Suspicions were aired about the loyalty of those who had been and were in government and had failed to prevent Communist expansion. Traitors there must be, and they must have been at work long before the 1950s. Surely the deals worked out among the Allies during World War II at Yalta,

Potsdam, and other such places had given too much to the Soviet Union, and now Eastern and Central Europe were captive nations, trapped on the other side of the Iron Curtain. Stalin had not been such a great bargainer that he could have gotten these deals without secret help on the American side. Treason was clearly indicated, with the result that containment must be applied not only abroad but at home, too. And so it came to pass.

~~~

Reds on Parade

How can you tell who is a Red? During the early 1950s, this particular skill was of considerable concern in many quarters (see below). A number of films were released during this period that offered pointers, and there was no dearth of magazine articles that tried to do the same. Several films along these lines are of particular interest. *I Was a Communist for the F.B.I.* illustrates what is necessary to counter the threat. *My Son John* tells what happens when a mother discovers what the Communist Party can to do a family. *Pickup on South Street* is a story of crime, espionage, and unwitting involvement in a Soviet spy ring. Finally, *Red Nightmare*, a Defense Department short, utilizes a television situation comedy format to warn against domestic subversion.

I Was a Communist for the FBI (Warner Brothers, 1951, 83 min.)
Director: Gordon Douglas
Cast: Frank Lovejoy, Dorothy Hart, Phil Carey

Based on a true story! A Pittsburgh steelworker, Matt Cvetic, goes under-cover for the FBI and joins the Party in order to trap Communists in the labor unions. He succeeds in this endeavor but loses everything else in the process.

My Son John (Paramount, 1952, 122 min.)
Director: Leo McCarey
Cast: Helen Hayes, Robert Walker, Dean Jagger, Van Heflin

In this film, a patriotic American Catholic family discovers that the eldest son is a Communist, even as the younger one goes off to war. The former is ostracized and comes to a bad end.

Pickup on South Street (20th Century Fox, 1953, 80 min.)
Director: Samuel Fuller
Cast: Richard Widmark, Jean Peters, Thelma Ritter, Richard Kiley.

While riding on the New York City subway one morning, Jean Peters is pick-pocketed by Richard Widmark. She is unaware that she has been recruited by her Communist boyfriend to carry secret microfilm for delivery to the head of a spy ring. Unknowingly, Widmark has lifted the secret microfilm. Various complications follow. When, however, the crooks in the film (Widmark, Ritter) discover what's up, they turn state's evidence. It's one thing to steal, it's another to spy! Even thiefs are patriotic Americans and not Commie scum!

Red Nightmare (U.S. Department of Defense, 1953, 30 min.)
Director: George Waggoner
Cast: Jack Webb, Jack Kelly, Jeanne Cooper, Peter Brown

Propaganda film made by the U.S. Department of Defense which deals with a typical American citizen who finds himself in a Communist village and is rudely awakened to his civic responsibilities.

How to Spot a Communist

Films such as these were common in the early 1950s, a period during which the search for traitors was at its peak. The war in Korea was underway, and there was widespread fear and paranoia not only that captured soldiers were being turned into Communists, but also that solid U.S. citizens might be, too. The social changes and instability that followed World War II threatened the hegemony of the country's economic and political elite, through a kind of liberal populism fostered by upward mobility, expanded access to education (especially through the GI bill), and liberal culture (propagated by those who had flirted with communism during the 1930s, were now resolutely opposed to it, and, in many cases, would transmogrify into neo-conservatives in the 1970s).

The hunt for Reds, which began not long after the end of World War II, picked up steam in the late 1940s and blossomed under the direction of Senator Joseph McCarthy (R-Wisc.) during the first half of the 1950s (Rovere, 1959). In the furor that followed, declarations of loyalty to the United States (satirized in Joseph Heller's 1961 novel *Catch-22*) became one litmus test for detecting subversives, while FBI investigations became another. In the case of the former, however, bona fide Communist Party members would probably take the oath, while those who were not sometimes refused. The former would keep their jobs, the latter would be fired.

Were there Communists throughout the government and society, as so many claimed? If so, were they a threat to the country and its survival? Today, these questions hardly seem to matter, yet they are still being debated, for several reasons. First, during the past decade or so, both Soviet archives and FBI files have been opened, allowing investigators to examine raw materials, so to speak. Second, there remains a kind of post hoc desire to justify the Red Hunt and its excesses. After all, if there was no mortal danger from domestic subversives, why were suspects pursued so fervently? The evidence is mixed and far from conclusive. Those who believe there was danger continue to find evidence of it; those who do not, roundly reject the possibility (Haynes, 1996).

∿∿

I Have in My Hand a List

The first big investigations into Communists in government were set in train by the Truman administration in the 1940s. Ironically, by 1950, Truman and his associates were being pilloried by the Republicans for their "Communist sympathies." In the next few years, the assault would only grow more intense. Among the stars of these early hearings and loyalty searches was Whittaker Chambers, who led Richard Nixon to search for microfilm in a pumpkin field. Chambers had once been a member of the U.S. Communist Party (CPUSA) but later became an ardent Red Hunter. He testified to passing secrets to Alger Hiss, a high-level State Department employee whose guilt or innocence is still debated today (Breindel, 1996; Lowenthal, 2000).

Nixon was another beneficiary of the Red Scare. He made his name as a congressman by pursuing Hiss until the latter was convicted of perjury in 1950. Nixon advanced to the Senate by accusing his opponent, Helen G. Douglas, of being "pink." In 1952, he parlayed his rising star into the Republican vice presidential nomination (Mitchell, 1998). And, of course, Senator McCarthy told the world that he had a list of 57—or was it 205? or 81?—Communists in the State Department. He also accused Truman's secretary of state, George C. Marshall (of eponymous Marshall Plan fame) of involvement in a "conspiracy so immense and an infamy so black as to dwarf any previous such venture in the history of man" (cited in LaFeber, 1993: 111). The search led to the firing of numerous government employees, although solid evidence of treason was never found.

The hunt for Reds did not stop in the government. The U.S. House of Representatives Committee on Un-American Activities (HUAC), which had begun its search for traitors in the late 1930s, began to look into the role of Communists in Hollywood and the entertainment business. With the help of supporters and the fearful in the media, a "blacklist"—whose existence was never openly admitted—of writers, producers, singers, and actors suspected of being "fellow travelers" was produced. Those so listed were unable to work openly for years to come (Rouverol, 2000).[3] Academics were expected to take loyalty oaths and were fired if they refused. The 1950 McCarran Act required Communist organizations and their members to register with the government, but obeying that law would open them to criminal charges under the Smith Act of 1940. Wives were warned to watch

their husbands for behavior that might indicate membership in a subversive group (symptoms that resembled, as well, indications of homo-
sexuality). Even the publishers of comic books were required to appear
before HUAC, where they were charged with what amounted to the
subversion of America's youth (Englehardt, 1995: 137-39).

The fear of internal subversion continued throughout the 1950s and
into the following decade, although never again reaching quite the level of
stridency achieved during that first, full decade of the Cold War. But why
was there so much dread and concern, especially when solid evidence of
subversion was so sparse? One possibility suggests itself. The Cold War
was very different from the Hot War that preceded it. World War II was
characterized by armies, navies, and air forces engaged in clearly
demarcated battles (none of which took place, of course, on the soil of the
continental United States). Enemies' appearance or language clearly
marked them as being from the "other side" (which led to excesses at
home, such as imprisonment of Japanese Americans). And virtually everyone supported the war effort, believing it to be a righteous cause (see, e.g.,
Terkel, 1984). The Cold War had none of these features; rather, it was about
influence, psychology, and secret maneuver. Countries and people could be
taken over, occupied, without a shot being fired or anyone being the wiser.
That, at least, was the message communicated by those who claimed to
know.

Consequently, anyone who might harbor or express radical tendencies
during this time risked being charged with having been "brainwashed."
The notion of brainwashing grew out of the relatively new field of
psychology and the apparent manipulation of U.S. prisoners of war in
North Korea, some of whom publicly condemned the UN defense of South
Korea (Hunter, 1953; Schein, 1961). It was believed that repeated conditioning, especially in harsh surroundings, could make people hate what they
once loved, and oppose that which they once supported. This dovetailed
rather nicely, too, with the growing field of advertising, which relied
heavily on ideas about such conditioning. No evidence ever demonstrated
clearly the possibility of brainwashing, but the fear became an integral part
of the political culture. Richard Condon satirized this fear in one of his
greatest novels.

$$\approx$$

In the Realm of the Queen of Diamonds

The Manchurian Candidate, Richard Condon (New York: New American Library, 1959)

Raymond Shaw is an American hero, a Medal of Honor winner in the Korean War. He is also such an unpleasant person that no one can stand to be near him. Shaw is the stepson of Senator Johnny Iselin (modeled on Joe Mc-Carthy) and the son of Eleanor Iselin. She is determined to climb to the pinnacle of power by ensuring that her husband, a fairly mindless drunk, will become president of the United States.

But how has Shaw become a hero? While in Korea on a nighttime reconnaissance mission, he and his patrol are kidnapped by a joint Russian-Chinese platoon, and transported to Manchuria. There they are all brainwashed. Shaw, as the stepson of a prominent American politician, receives special programming inasmuch as he, at some time in the future, will see service as an agent of the Kremlin. His programmers instruct him that, whenever he is given the order, "Raymond, why don't you pass the time by playing a little solitaire?" he will do so until the Queen of Diamonds appears. He will then sit quietly, awaiting further instructions from his American operator.

As a test of his conditioning, Shaw is politely ordered to kill two members of the patrol. This he does, to the satisfaction of the watching audience of Chinese and Russian observers (the patrol members have been conditioned to think they have been marooned in a garden club meeting during a heavy rainstorm). The two dead patrol members will later be reported as "killed in action."

The patrol is then returned to UN lines, where the members tell of a battle in which Shaw heroically rescued his colleagues. In recognition of his action, Shaw is recommended for the Medal of Honor by his commanding officer, Ben Marco. Shaw returns home to a hero's welcome (which fills him with disgust but provides his stepfather and mother with endless publicity). He also goes to work for a New York newspaper until such time as the Communists need him.

Shaw's operator turns out to be his own mother, whose connections to the Communists go way back but who, in order to gain power, has turned husband Johnny into the epitome of a McCarthyite anti-Communist, complete with a list of traitors in government (when he presses Ellie about how many there are on his list, she sees a bottle of Heinz ketchup and answers "fifty-seven").

Ellie intends to have Johnny nominated as the vice presidential candidate of his party in 1960. Raymond, under her orders, will shoot the presidential nominee as he is giving his acceptance speech to the convention. In the chaotic aftermath, Johnny will succeed to the presidential nomination by acclamation. But Ellie does not want only national power, she also wants global power. Infuriated with what the Soviets have done to her son—she was not told that he would be their assassin—Ellie swears vengeance. Once Johnny is president, she means to annihilate Moscow with a nuclear attack.

Ellie's plan does not proceed unnoticed, however. Shaw's cover is gradually being eroded, because Ben Marco and another patrol member are having strange nightmares. In his dreams, Marco sees the patrol seated in an auditorium, not with the garden club members but before an audience of Russian and Chinese observers. For Marco, the vision of the garden club is crossed with flashes of Communist faces and the memory that Shaw has killed two of his colleagues. Marco gradually realizes that Shaw has been programmed to commit some kind of action in the United States, but he is not sure what. Fortunately, Marco gets to Shaw before it is too late, and reprograms him to shoot not the presidential nominee, but the Iselins. Shaw does so and then kills himself with a gun Marco gives to him. As Marco says afterward, "No electric chair for a Medal of Honor man."

Marx Meets Freud

The Manchurian Candidate was made into a film in 1962. Directed by John Frankenheimer, starring Frank Sinatra (Marco), Laurence Harvey (Shaw), Janet Leigh (Marco's love interest), and Angela Lansbury (Ellie Iselin), it is much less powerful or entertaining than the book. Sinatra owned the film rights and withdrew it from circulation after the assassination of JFK (apparently due to a conflict over film rights, although rumor had the film's disappearance linked to Kennedy's death). It was not seen again in public until some twenty-five years later.

Where *Invasion of the Body Snatchers* is about the transformation of collective identities by forces alien or unknown—or familiar and well known— *The Manchurian Candidate* plays havoc with Id, Ego, and Super-Ego.[4] Once again, the FBI is involved in hunting down a mortal threat to the body politic, but this time the threat comes in the guise of American wife and mother. Condon's book should probably best be regarded as pure satire, playing on American fears of both Freud and Marx, of both soul and body. Indeed, there is even the suggestion that we should fear Freud *more* than Marx, that it is the former that ought to be contained in the interests of the nation's security and sanity.

Condon's apparent intent in writing *The Manchurian Candidate* was not only to satirize McCarthyism and raise questions about just *whose* interests were being served by the Red Scare but also to delve into the psychological and political aspects of these phenomena. Throughout the 1950s, as noted earlier, it was widely believed that U.S. soldiers taken prisoner of war in North Korea had undergone some kind of special mental torture that turned them from loyal Americans into Communists, ready to denounce and even betray their country. While there was no evidence that anyone was ever actually "brainwashed"—or that such a process is possible—even U.S. school children routinely threw such accusations back and forth (without really knowing what they meant). In retrospect, the very concept of brainwashing was probably another response to the social changes following World War II. There were more subtle (and capitalist) ways of accomplishing the same thing, as suggested by one short-lived hysteria about subliminal advertising on television and in films and later controversies over the fluoridation of water (immortalized by General Jack D. Ripper in the 1963 film *Doctor Strangelove*; see chapter 5).[5]

Moreover, if one could be stripped of love for one's country, what was to prevent other things in the mind from being changed, as well? Not only are instructions implanted in Shaw's super-ego, his id is modified, too. As a favor, Lo Chen, Shaw's Chinese brainwasher, removes his sexual inhibitions. The result is not only a flowering of sexual experience after his return to the United States but, eventually, incest with Ellie, his operator, mother, and the emotional manipulator of the American body politic (this did not appear explicitly in the film; in the film, Ellie kisses Raymond passionately). Shaw's mother had incestuous relations with her father but had never consummated her marriage to Johnny Iselin. Instead, she does so with her son, the "Medal of Honor" man. Whom *can* you trust?

In the end, the threat is contained. But what, exactly, has been contained? Who was in control of whom? The Soviets think they control Ellie and Johnny Iselin through Raymond. Ellie Iselin thinks she controls Johnny and Raymond, and intends to gain control of the United States. Ben Marco almost loses control of himself, only to find it and gain control of the whole monstrous conspiracy. Condon seems to suggests that, perhaps, the origins of the threat are not "out there" but "up here." Marx can't hold a candle to Freud.

〰〰

Eye Spy!

One of the primary elements of Eisenhower's approach to containment—called the "New Look"—was increased reliance on espionage. As we shall see, spies were thought to be a relatively inexpensive means of countering the Soviet threat. Moreover, the Soviet Union did not hesitate to employ all kinds of secret intelligence methods against the United States, as demonstrated by repeated experience. But too much was, perhaps, expected of secret operatives. They were, after all, only human beings.

∿∿
∿∿

Chapter 4

Spies!

The Midas Touch

Goldfinger was one of the big film hits of 1964, and set off a craze for the further adventures of James Bond, that, even today, has not died out. This and the other Bond films were based upon a character and a series of novels created in the mid-1950s by Ian Fleming. A somewhat embittered Englishman, Fleming could not forgive the United States for having shouldered aside the British after World War II. Bond was Fleming's revenge, forever saving the Americans from both their clumsiness and the Russians.

Goldfinger was typical in this way. In the novel, published in 1959, the Soviet Union contracts with the fabulously wealthy German Auric Goldfinger to create an international economic crisis by greatly diminishing the world's supply of gold. This will undermine the West (the eternal nightmare of Nazi revenge!) and, in the process, make Goldfinger a very rich man, inasmuch as he collects gold as well as things golden. The crisis is to be triggered by exploding an atomic bomb over Fort Knox, wherein is stored America's gold supply (in recognition of changing international verities, in the film it is the Red Chinese who want to nuke Knox). The gold provides backing for the U.S. dollar and, in theory, any foreign country can redeem its dollar holdings for gold. Once irradiated, however, the gold will be useless as will the dollar. Its value will plummet and the United States will lose its dominant position in the world economy. Europe will have to give up on the United States, and the Commies will be triumphant. Bond, of course, manages to defeat Goldfinger and the enemy and saves both the day and the global economy.

Neither the film nor the novel got the problem exactly right, however. Goldfinger calculates that, by irradiating Fort Knox, a major portion of the world's gold supply will be removed from circulation. The laws of supply and demand will drive up the price of nonradioactive gold, and Goldfinger, having most of that, will become even wealthier. But Fort Knox gold was not available for public use and, by law, U.S. citizens were forbidden from holding gold coins or bullion for monetary purposes. Only governments could redeem U.S. dollars for gold, and they would store the metal in their bank vaults in order to support their own currencies. So, although the value of the dollar would drop, irradiating Knox would not reduce the world's circulating gold supply (although demand might, of course, rise precipitously).

It is of some interest to note, therefore, that by the 1960s, the United States *was* running into a gold crisis that had nothing to do with either the Russians or Chinese but was directly the fault of Cold War economic relations with U.S. allies. The dollar was the international reserve currency, and was backed by gold. Foreign governments could convert their dollar holdings into gold if they did not want dollars and wished to do so. In *Goldfinger*, the crisis would arise because, without the gold backing, no one would want to accept dollars, the United States would not be able to use them to buy goods, and the global economy would collapse.

In real life, the U.S. government had been so profligate in providing military and economic assistance to allies and others that, by the late 1950s, there were too many dollars in circulation to be fully backed by the gold in Fort Knox. Hence, if everyone holding dollars were to demand gold instead, as did the French government in the late 1960s, an economic crisis would ensue, without the need for help from the Bomb. Rather than risk such an eventuality, in 1971 President Nixon suspended the convertibility of the dollar into gold (Gowa, 1983). Spies, however, rarely bothered themselves with economics, and neither readers nor filmgoers were concerned about what was called the "Triffin Dilemma."

In any event, those engaged in the intelligence business had better things to worry about. Bond was a suave and debonair character and his mission was always to save the world. Between the fancy toys supplied to him by MI-5, and his innate intelligence and fabulous skills, he was virtually unbeatable by the Soviets and at the box office. Indeed, Bond's invulnerability created both a host of clones (*Our Man Flint; The Man from U.N.C.L.E.*) as well as parodies (*Get Smart!; What's Up, Tiger Lily?*).

The actuality of espionage was far removed from both adventure and comedy. Real spies were not ladies' men and they tended to die like flies. In the language of the intelligence business, they were "expendable." Alec Leamas, the protagonist of John le Carré's 1964 novel *The Spy Who Came in from the Cold*, is intelligent and determined like Bond, but resembles the latter in almost nothing else. Leamas can rely only on himself and his network of agents in East Germany, who, by the time the novel begins, are all dead. More than this, as the novel progresses, good does not always triumph, plans often go awry, and the spy does not always "get" the girl

[sic]. The world of espionage is a gray and dreary place, where time passes slowly and meaningful discoveries are few and far between. Fleming and the Bond films glorified the spy business and, if always far from the truth, made it seem attractive and necessary to the public (aka, the "great moronic mass," as Leamas puts it; le Carré, 1975: 210). Le Carré's novels were always much closer to the dismal reality.

This difference might not have mattered, except that the Cold War helped to transform espionage from a somewhat marginal element in U.S. foreign policy to the full-blown $30-plus billion industry it is today, a decade or more after the fall of the Berlin Wall. The key to this enormous growth was (and is) the idea that there are secrets, and that they make a difference. But do they? Why do we need spies? Whom do they serve? What do they do?

For the United States, the 1950s were the Golden Age of Espionage. The Central Intelligence Agency saw its greatest successes abroad even as the Federal Bureau of Investigation ferreted out traitors at home. And, not only did spies appear to be effective, they were also economical. Indeed, Dwight Eisenhower's "New Look," a security strategy aimed at reducing the budgetary costs of containing the Soviet Union, was very explicit in its reliance on psychological warfare and covert operations (Gaddis, 1982).

By the beginning of the 1960s, with James Bond's appearance on the screen, and his endorsement by President John F. Kennedy, spies had become glamorous. Yet even then, disillusionment was already setting in, as a result of the debacle at the Bay of Pigs. Le Carré's novels, and films such as Robert Aldrich's *Kiss Me Deadly* (1955), illuminate not only the role of espionage in the Cold War but also its seamy and immoral aspects. Moreover, they force us to question the purpose, practices, *and* usefulness of intelligence agencies, personnel, and operations, questions that are still germane even today (Nelson, 1999).

Other People's Letters

Rhodri Jeffreys-Jones, an historian of the CIA, has argued that "Democracy depends upon secret intelligence for its survival . . ." (1989). Yet, it was not so many decades ago that, on being urged to revive America's intelligence capabilities, which had largely lapsed after World War I, then-secretary of state Henry Stimson responded that "Gentlemen don't read other people's letters." Let us begin, then, by asking what might be the rationale for a country to have an intelligence capability?

There are at least three possible reasons. First, a country's citizens presumably want their leaders to make informed decisions—even though this does not always appear to happen. There is the need, therefore, to collect openly available data that tells what is going on in other societies so that decision making that will affect relations with those countries can be made on a clear-headed basis. This type of information can be acquired in a variety of ways: from newspapers, books, journals, casual conversations, and so on. Agents can be locals, tourists, academics, or businessmen.

Second, there may be secret information needed in order to ascertain motives or plans of other countries. The rationale for this type of activity is not very different from what goes on between competing businesses. Proprietary information is closely held so as to maintain a competitive advantage, and competitors often try to find out what other companies are up to. Similarly, it can be argued, a decisionmaker needs to be able to anticipate the acts of another country's leaders by knowing both the other's capabilities and their plans. This type of intelligence can be acquired from individuals in official positions ("moles" or double agents), who have somehow been convinced that it is in their monetary or other interest to supply secret information (*humint*, in the jargon). Secret intelligence may also be collected via various technological means, such as satellites, listening posts, wire-tapping, message interception, and so on (*sigint*).

Finally, one country might try to manipulate another through various covert or unpublicized activities (as opposed to open activities, such as trade fairs and libraries). It is this last part of the whole business that, ironically, seems to garner the most publicity (even though it must be the most secret). The goal of covert activity is to somehow influence target governments in a way favorable to one's own interests. Such influence can be acquired in three ways.

First, one can try to generate favorable publicity about one's country through various means, such as secret financial assistance to newspapers, civic organizations, and unions, or unfavorable publicity about opponents or critics through disinformation sent via the same channels. Second, one might try to acquire influence with those in power, either through bribery or the proffering of aid or information to them, or by threatening them in some fashion. And, third, one could simply set up activities outside of official channels with the intent of influencing or undermining governments or putting obstacles in the way of oppositional activities. As we shall see, all of these means and ends have been used by U.S. intelligence agencies, and especially the CIA.

But why? There are several standard arguments for American reliance on intelligence operations and operatives. The most prominent one is that, as a global power with global interests of both a security and economic nature, the United States must know what is going on around the world that might threaten these interests. Furthermore, where we can take action to ward off existing or future threats to our interests, we should be able and willing to do so (moral considerations notwithstanding).

A second line of reasoning rests on the political nature of the United States and its adversaries. We are open and democratic, goes the argument, and our opponents are closed and totalitarian (notwithstanding the fact that Israel, Japan, Taiwan, and France spy on us, as we do on them). If we are to anticipate what our opponents might do, it is not enough—indeed, it is entirely inadequate—to depend on open sources of information. We must, therefore, have the means to penetrate the innermost recesses of these countries and acquire such information as is needed to protect our interests and guarantee our survival. As we shall see, this was the rationale behind the establishment of the CIA: a very specific reaction to the nature and actions of the Soviet Union. That such actions have been and are now taken by our supposed allies, such as Israel (even as we do the same to them), does not lessen the force of the argument, at least not in the open debates in Congress and the media.

Finally, it is often said, we need to fight fire with fire. Our adversaries do not shirk from undertaking nefarious activities that threaten us both abroad *and* at home. We must be able and willing, therefore, to respond accordingly, and even to match those activities where necessary. If they disrupt, we disrupt. If they misinform, we misinform. If they assassinate, we assassinate. And so on.

Now, for some these may be very convincing arguments, but they also pose some troubling moral questions. And they are based on two dubious assumptions: that, a fortiori, the particular ends desirable for American democracy and security cannot be achieved by open means; and that there is secret information that is threatening to us and not available by any other means. The archetypal example of what happens if such information is not obtained is the Japanese attack on Pearl Harbor (and fear of future "Pearl Harbors" is rife throughout the corridors of Washington, D.C.; see Lipschutz, 1999).

Yet, Pearl Harbor might not even stand as a good example of the importance of intelligence, inasmuch as the United States did have some indications that an attack might be in the offing (Stinnett, 2000; Kahn, 2000). The problem in that instance was that the incoming data were incorrectly interpreted and that they were, in any case, downplayed. Moreover, the attack on Pearl Harbor was, in some respects, the direct result of a number of very overt and hostile actions taken earlier by the United States against Japan (Feis, 1950; Iriye, 1967). The surprise was as much in the temerity of the attack as in its perfidy and audacity.

During the Cold War, large-scale resort to covert activity by the United States was rationalized largely as a response to what was seen as the emerging Soviet threat (recall the discussion of NSC-68 in chapter 3), in particular, covert activities engineered by the NKVD, the predecessor of the better-known Soviet intelligence service, the KGB. In the United States there was, at first, a fair amount of opposition to establishing something like a Central Intelligence Agency. To some, it seemed better to keep intelligence activities fragmented, lest such a centralized organization become a government unto itself, like Hitler's Gestapo. Of greater importance, some thought, was what was seen as a fundamental "defect" in the American system: there were times when particular actions *of a secretive nature* would be necessary, and not even Congress could be allowed to know too much so as to prevent tipping America's hand to the enemy.

Certainly, there is ample evidence to suggest that Congress "leaks" secrets but, when it suits the president, so does the White House. The fundamental defect in the American system—if, indeed, it is a defect—has not so much to do with the keeping of secrets as it does with public constraints on presidential freedom to act in the "national interest." The Constitution specifies that the president is to carry out foreign policy, but the Congress has the power to appropriate whatever funds are required to carry these policies out. Therefore, it would seem, the Congress has a need to know for what it and the American public are paying. To reveal what is being bought, however, is not only to tell secrets to Congress but also to introduce delays into preparations. By the time the purchase order has arrived, the war might well be over. There is also the problem of legality, so to speak. If Congress is allowed to decide whether to fund particular projects, it may also choose to pass on their legality, with the consequence that they might not happen at all (not that this need be an undesirable outcome).

Consequently, U.S. presidents since Truman have tended to view Congress as an *obstacle* to foreign policy, as something to be avoided, deceived, or stonewalled. Presidents have routinely approved, in a plausibly deniable way (see below), covert activities meant to accomplish foreign policy goals while not getting caught in domestic politics. Congress has been relatively acquiescent in this process, passing budget appropriations in "black form," as a lump sum, leaving any necessary deliberations to be carried out in closed session by special committees. Even this very weak constraint has proved to be too much for some presidents (such as Ronald Reagan, who had Oliver North mount an operation completely external to the CIA; see Draper, 1991).

And, so long as such capabilities exist, they will be used. The likelihood of their being used in the pursuit of narrowly defined interests is high, as well. And, such projects—touted, when they become public, as having been in the "national interest"—have a high probability of going awry, if only because the situations that covert operators confront are often so fluid and variable that failure is almost axiomatic (Mailer, 1991, although fictional, nicely illustrates this point). Moreover, defining these activities as being in the national interest almost certainly guarantees that they will *not* be undertaken in broad national interests, but only those of economic and political elites who, after all, imprint *their* subjective notions of interest on the public. This, then, is the tradeoff of secret intelligence in a democratic system: objectives are easier to achieve—in theory, at least—but possibly at the cost of perverting the common good. If we must meddle everywhere so as to protect ourselves, there is probably something amiss with that which we wish to protect.

◊◊◊

I Spy!

The Spy Who Came in from the Cold, John le Carré (London: Gollancz, 1963)

Le Carré's novel is, in the opinion of many critics and readers, the best spy novel ever written, if only because it deliberately does not glorify the business or the "good guys." Indeed, the novel shows just how desolate and debilitating an activity espionage can be. At the beginning of the story, we are introduced to Alec Leamas, a British agent who has been running an espionage network in East Berlin. Apparently there is a leak somewhere in the operation, for all of his agents but one have been killed. Leamas is waiting for the last one, Karl, to come over at Checkpoint Charlie, the crossing point between East and West Berlin (which were divided by the Wall in 1961). As he watches his agent wobble across the line on his bicycle, a shot rings out and Karl is killed.

After this last failure, Leamas returns to London, ready to retire—he is past the normal age for operators, in any event. Before leaving, however, he is put up to one last caper by Control, the director of the "Circus" (MI-5, the British foreign intelligence service). Control observes that the source of Alec's failure is, quite evidently, Deiter Mundt, the head of the Abteilung, East Germany's counterintelligence agency. Control proposes an operation to eliminate Mundt. Leamas eagerly accepts the plan, which is to fake Alec's defection to the East and entrap Mundt.

To do this, Leamas must let himself go to seed—in concert with rumors that he has been denied a full pension by MI-5—and get himself thrown into jail. After he is released some months later, it is hoped that he will be approached by Soviet Bloc intelligence services, who will try to get him to defect (which he will appear to do). Once Leamas does go over to the other side, he will be debriefed by his new masters. During this interrogation, he is to suggest, through the information he provides to his interrogators, that Mundt is a double agent working for the British. This should lead to Mundt's arrest and execution.

Leamas follows the plan but problems develop. Somewhat unexpectedly—or so we are led to think—prior to being jailed, he falls into a love affair with Liz Gold, a member of the British Communist Party. The day before the contrived attack on a grocer that will land him in jail, Leamas breaks up with Liz, presumably for good.

After his release, some time later, the plan is put into motion. Alec is recruited by the "Bloc" and brought to East Germany. There he meets Leslie Fiedler, Mundt's second-in-command, who suspects that his boss really is a British mole and who has been accumulating evidence to support his accusation of treason against Mundt. Leamas feeds Fiedler's suspicions, with the result that Mundt is brought before a tribunal of the East German Communist Party, where he is to be judged.

The hearing seems to be going against Mundt when a surprise witness is brought in to the hearing room: Liz. She has been invited on an all-expenses-paid trip to the German Democratic Republic (the East), supposedly to see how the Party operates at the community level. Responding to questions from the tribunal, she inadvertently mentions that, the night before he got into the fight, Leamas seemed to expect to go "away." She also reveals that Alec's associates in the Circus have helped her to purchase the lease on her flat. Leamas knows nothing of this, although it is now becoming clear to him that he and Liz have been set up by MI-5. The evidence now suggests that Leamas and Fiedler are engaged in a plot to have Mundt eliminated. Mundt is, therefore, exonerated of all charges against him. Fiedler is arrested for treason, and Alec and Liz are thrown into prison, there to await their fate.

In the middle of the night, Mundt comes to see Liz and Alec. He frees them, gives them a car, and instructs them to drive to East Berlin. There they will pick up a guide who will show them where and how they are to climb the Berlin Wall and cross over to the West. But things turn out badly.

Mundt really is a British double agent. The entire operation has been set up to protect him, with Alec as the patsy and Liz as the bait. The two arrive at the Wall and they begin to climb. But contrary to the promise made by Mundt, only Leamas will be allowed to cross. Liz knows too much and, as a member of the British Communist Party, cannot be allowed to return to England where she might reveal the truth. She is shot and killed. As the searchlights beam down on him, Alec, in a moment of literally blinding clarity, faces the moral consequences of his behavior and his life. He climbs down to join Liz and dies, too. (In 1965, a film based on the book was released, starring Richard Burton, Claire Bloom, and Oskar Werner. It is, however, extremely telegraphic and difficult to understand if you have not read the book.)

The Spy's Ethos?

Le Carré makes no bones about the moral position of the spy. And as with the spy's moral position, the world of Alec Leamas is unrelievedly gray. This absence of moral clarity seems to lead, in that final blinding moment, to his demise. In contrast to James Bond, Alec Leamas is not an agent of the good; indeed, in the world of espionage, the notion of *good* hardly has a meaning. As Control says to Leamas, early in the novel,

> The ethic of our work, as I understand it, is based on a single assumption. That is, we are never going to be aggressors. . . . Thus we do disagreeable things, but we are *defensive*. . . . We do disagreeable things so that ordinary people here and elsewhere can sleep safely in their beds at night . . . (le Carré, 1975: 15).

But Control does not leave it there. "He grinned like a schoolboy."

> Of course, we occasionally do very wicked things. . . . And in weighing up the moralities, we rather go in for dishonest comparisons; after all, you can't compare the ideals of one side with the methods of the other, can you now. . . . I mean you can't be less ruthless than the opposition simply because your government's *policy* is benevolent, can you now? That would *never* do (id.).

Leamas cannot make out what Control is talking about. He has never really given the point much thought, it would seem. As with Fiedler, later in the novel, Alec is concerned only with doing his job and ensuring the success of his operations. By this metric, Leamas is a complete failure, inasmuch as he has lost all of his agents.

But Control's offer to him is irresistible. In it Leamas sees the opportunity to become a moral agent (for good, moreover) and recoup his losses. By helping to eliminate Mundt, whom he regards as the personification of evil, Leamas will avenge his dead agents and prove himself worthy as a spy. Unfortunately for him, Leamas not only stays out "in the cold" a little longer, he is also left "out in the cold" by Control. Circus is only too willing to sacrifice additional agents, if necessary, in order to protect the bigger fish on the other side.

Nevertheless, in the end, and even though aware of the betrayal, Leamas still professes allegiance to the universal principles of espionage. As they are heading, unknowingly, toward their deaths, he says to Liz:

> There's only one law in this game. . . . Mundt is their man; he gives them what they need. That's easy enough to understand, isn't it? Leninism—the expediency of temporary alliances. What do you think spies are: priests, saints and martyrs? They're a squalid procession of vain fools, traitors, too. . . . I'd have killed Mundt if I could, I hate his guts; *but not now*. It so happens that they need him. They need him so that the great moronic mass you admire can sleep soundly in their beds at night. They need him for the safety of ordinary, crummy people like you and me (le Carré, 1975: 211; emphasis added).

"I've Got a Secret!"

And what of America's intelligence apparatus? Its current, highly decentralized form was not inevitable, but today there are ten or more distinct U.S. intelligence agencies, if one includes those belonging to the military services (the agencies include: the Central Intelligence Agency, the National Security Agency, the Defense Intelligence Agency, the National Technical Surveillance Agency, and a host of others).

Prior to 1947, there was much discussion, in public as well as behind closed doors, of the merits and demerits of a "Central Intelligence" organization. That there would be intelligence agencies was not questioned; that there should be a *central* one in charge of all the others was not, however, self-evident. The arguments against such an arrangement had to do with bureaucratic resistance and concern about creating an American "Gestapo," as noted earlier. The arguments for a centralized system simply suggested that "everyone else does it," so we should, too. But we should also coordinate what we do, to eliminate waste and duplication.

Before World War II, the U.S. system of intelligence gathering had been fragmented and not very comprehensive. The war created a need for such capabilities, leading to the establishment of the OSS (Office of Strategic Services) in 1942 (Smith, 1983). This was not the first U.S. wartime intelligence agency, but it was the one that led, more or less directly, to the CIA. The OSS had the twin wartime jobs of collecting and analyzing strategic information for the Joint Chiefs of Staff, and planning, directing, and executing what were called "special services," or covert interventions, in enemy territories.

The OSS was not, however, allowed to engage in domestic work; during the war, this was left to the FBI, whose area of operation also extended into Latin and South America (we see here that the sphere of American homeland defense encompassed the entire Western Hemisphere, a mindset which continues even today). Via its various activities in occupied Europe and Asia, the OSS managed to organize and support resistance groups as well as make contacts with the enemy that would, in later years, be revived in pursuit of the Cold War.

The OSS was disbanded in 1945. It was not apparent then, as it would become by 1947, that there might be a future need for such an organization. Some individuals, such as "Wild Bill" Donovan, head of the OSS during the war, made the rounds of Washington in 1946 and 1947, arguing in favor of a new central agency. He was interested not so much in the elimination of "waste" and "duplication"—which is the argument he made—but in the maintenance of the operations begun during the war. Still, there was resistance throughout the U.S. government. On the right, a CIA was seen as a continuation of the "big government" policies of the New Deal; on the left, there was fear of a police state (similar arguments are made, with some justification, even today). It was not until a conception of the "national security state" crystallized in 1947 that the CIA finally got to see the light of day.

The idea of the "national security state" is not one that can be found in American planning documents or laws. Indeed, it seems as though the 1947 National Security Act, which authorized the establishment of the CIA, did not even really focus on threats from the clandestine services of the Soviet Union. Among other things, the act created the Defense Department, bringing the Departments of War, Army, and Navy under one cabinet office. The act also authorized creation of the National Security Council and the now long-forgotten National Security Resources Board. The formulators of the National Security Act saw the CIA not so much as a place where all intelligence operations would originate as one that would keep track of the many other agencies engaged in such operations (already in 1947 there were as many as a half-dozen). Thus, the DCI—the director of central intelligence—was supposed to oversee all intelligence operations, even though he was the immediate director of only the CIA (Hogan, 1998).

From its very inception, the CIA was an agency with a confused and confusing mission, because of its two somewhat contradictory functions. One part of the Agency was in the business of collecting and analyzing information in order to provide a realistic assessment of the international political environment within which American policymakers had to operate. The other part was in the business of "fixing" those things that might complicate operating within that international environment.

So far as the first responsibility was concerned, there were limits to what could be discovered, even through humint. In 1947, there was not much in the way of a U.S. intelligence-collecting capability within the Soviet Union, and efforts to place operatives behind the Iron Curtain were almost all failures. This contributed to tendencies toward "worst-case analysis" where the USSR was concerned. Even so, the early estimates of Soviet capabilities and intentions made by the agency were reasonably accurate. The Soviets, argued CIA analysts, were unlikely to launch any overt military attacks against the West, although they might engage in covert activities. Furthermore, instability in places such as the Philippines, Burma, and Malaya could not be laid at the Kremlin's door. There were major failures of prediction, too, such as the first Soviet A-bomb test in 1949 or the North Korean invasion of the South in 1950.

"And I Aim to Do Something about It!"

Analysis alone was not enough to justify the CIA and its siblings. While covert operations required careful analysis beforehand in order to ensure their success—indeed, in order to judge whether an operation was even necessary—such a reasoned approach to espionage was not politically viable in the hothouse of Washington politics. The country was paying good money for intelligence activities. The Soviets were, it seemed, engaged in subversion throughout the world. The United States had to respond. Thus, the Agency's operational side and covert actions came to dominate both public perceptions of the CIA and, indeed, the "Company" (as it was sometimes called) itself. This worked for a while but also led to some major fiascoes.

If this sounds familiar, there is good reason. As an executive agency, the CIA is expected to supply the president with good, timely, nonpoliticized information. This is a rather naive expectation, and reflects a fundamental disjuncture in the American political system between *politics* and *policy* (Stone, 1997). Policy is what connects desires to outcomes. You wish to achieve a particular objective, you map out alternative strategies, you choose the one that is lowest cost or most acceptable. Policy is *instrumental*, although it does reflect political desires.

Politics, on the other hand, has to do with the debate over desires and ends, and much less with the means of getting there. Thus, in 1981, Ronald Reagan and then-DCI William Casey set out to harass the "Evil Empire," no matter what it took, as a part of their idealized political agenda. They did not want to be informed that there was no such empire to harass, or that it had fallen on hard times and no longer constituted much of a threat. The playing down of fears is no way to drum up political hysteria or support (recall the "Two Minutes Hate" in *1984*). And Robert Gates, who was at the time an assistant to Casey, wanted to keep his job. In the highly charged, anti-Communist atmosphere of the Reagan administration, he was not about to be made ineffectual by being tagged as a closet liberal. This was as true in 1947 as it is today. The notion of a nonpoliticized CIA is a nonstarter, as ridiculous in its own way as that of a nonpolitical Supreme Court.

This quandary can be seen even more clearly in the pattern of covert operations undertaken by the CIA. These covert operations had, as suggested earlier, two types of objectives. The first was to influence politics and policy in foreign countries as a means of producing outcomes more favorable to American goals. Thus, for example, during the runup to the Italian election of 1948, funds were supplied to parties such as the Christian Democrats and various other anti-Communist outlets, and attempts were made to get Italian-Americans to write their relatives in Italy that dollar remittances would cease if the Communists were to gain power. The Communists did not win in Italy in 1948, and this was ascribed, at least in part, to the CIA's activities there. Similar activities were undertaken elsewhere in Europe and Japan (Agee and Wolf, 1981; Garwood, 1985).

The second aspect of covert operations involved various types of organized activities directed against real or imagined "enemies" of the United States. Here is where imagination ran rampant. As noted above, throughout the latter half of the 1940s, U.S. intelligence agencies attempted to run anti-government military activities throughout Eastern Europe and even within the Soviet Union itself. In many instances, the groups supported by the CIA were pro-fascist, having been organized in the early days of World War II in opposition to Moscow. After the war, some of these individuals were infiltrated back into their homelands, not so much to overthrow governments as to create problems for them. Virtually all of these operations were wiped out. There was no way to supply them from the outside, and there was little sympathy for them on the inside. Such covert activities took place under the cover of what was called "plausible deniability." Technically speaking, whenever an operation was planned and launched, it was done in such a way as to allow the president to deny that he had any role in making the decision or that he even knew about it. The result was that many CIA operations took place not only without official blessing but also without much in the way of directives at all. And, in pursuit of these plausibly denied activities, the CIA often found itself in cahoots with rather disreputable people.

For instance, during the Chinese Civil War in the late 1940s, the Agency did business with various non-Communist warlords whose main trade was the running of drugs, rather than fighting Chinese Communists or providing public services. The CIA found it expedient to turn a blind eye to such activities, for several reasons. First, if they did not, their "clients" would simply not cooperate, because drugs were a great source of personal wealth. Second, such contraband was, in effect, one form of legal tender in China. Chinese money was virtually worthless, whereas drugs could be bartered for guns and other useful items (dollars were acceptable, but not of much use where barter was concerned).

Even though the warlords were driven from power in 1949, along with the Guomintang (Nationalists) who fled en masse to Taiwan, they did not disappear. Some went to Burma and Thailand, where they continued to fight Communists, participate in the local insurrections, and grow, sell, and export opium and heroin. A dozen years later, the CIA would find the connections established during the Chinese Civil War useful in conducting secret wars throughout Southeast Asia (Renard, 1996). There is considerable evidence to indicate that such activities continued during the Central

American wars of the 1980s (Scott and Marshall, 1998). A similar dynamic may be establishing itself in parts of South America today.

Another partnership cultivated by the CIA was with the Mafia. This, too, was based on expediency, rather than principle. During World War II, the Mafia in Italy proved useful in engineering anti-Axis operations. Conveniently, the Mafia was also virulently anti-Communist, inasmuch as Communists were intolerant of any corrupt activities they did not control. The wartime relationship led to various associations between the Mafia and CIA in later decades, when the American branch of the former was enlisted by the latter in the various plots to assassinate Cuban leader Fidel Castro (these are described in Church Committee, 1975).

Out of the Office and into the Streets

In many ways, the CIA reached its apogee during the Eisenhower years. Truman used the CIA, to be sure, but "psywar" (psychological warfare) and covert operations were an integral part of Eisenhower's "New Look," his attempt to economize on containment. Covert techniques were much less costly than overt ones—especially the kind that took place in Korea and was developing in Vietnam—and plausible deniability, when combined with secrecy, meant that Congress did not have to be consulted. Still, the apparent CIA successes of the Eisenhower years had their costs for the agency and the country, with the Bay of Pigs in 1961 and the Cuban Missile Crisis of 1962 being two of the less profitable endeavors. After the 1960s, the Agency was never the same.

Between 1948 and 1952, the CIA was already hard at work. In addition to its activities in Europe, as noted earlier, it developed an extensive intelligence network throughout Asia. It was instrumental in putting down the Huk rebellion in the Philippines and placing Raymond Magsaysay in the presidency of that country (Lansdale, 1972). It stirred the pot in the Middle East. In an effort to reduce anti-Western feelings, inflamed by the establishment of Israel, the CIA supported coups in countries such as Syria and Egypt. And it tried to recruit agents throughout Eastern Europe as part of the effort to discover what was going on in the USSR.

Most of these activities were, in any event, low profile ones, as they were intended to be. At home, and not knowing much about these activities, many on the political Right regarded the Agency as a haven for liberals and crypto-Communists. Today this might seem a bit odd but, in 1951, it was not. Many members of the CIA staff had been recruited from the wartime OSS, whose primary target had been fascism. Before and during World War II, it was the right wing that thought to make common cause with Germany against Soviet Russia (although Allen Dulles's OSS office in Switzerland was notorious for its dealings with Nazi Germany during the war). The agency therefore recruited heavily among those with more liberal political leanings. The various failures in U.S. intelligence—the Soviet atomic bomb, the "loss" of China, the invasion of South Korea—led many conservatives to suspect that all was not right in the Agency.

It was partly with these suspicions in mind that Allen Dulles was made director of central intelligence in 1951, even before Truman left office. He had the appropriate credentials and his brother was John Foster Dulles, who was busy campaigning for the position of secretary of state. Foster Dulles's anti-communism helped Allen Dulles to establish his *bona fides* as well as restore confidence in the CIA. During the Eisenhower administration, the CIA would be involved in many covert operations. The best known, however—in Iran, Guatemala, and Cuba—were hardly covert at all.

Iran

Iran had been viewed as a problem by Washington ever since World War II, when it was jointly occupied by the United States, Britain, and the Soviet Union. The country sits in a sensitive geostrategic location, at the head of the Persian Gulf. It controls a vast amount of oil. According to the conventional wisdom, access to the gulf has always been a goal of Moscow, under both czars and commissars. In 1951, a nationalist government under the leadership of Mohammed Mossadeq took over the Anglo-Iranian Oil Company (later renamed British Petroleum) from its British owners (among whom was the British government) and refused to give it back.

For three years, the British and Americans haggled with Mossadeq, trying to find terms for a compromise that would not be opposed by the Iranian *Majlis* (Parliament) or provide a pretext for radical attempts to overthrow the pro-Western Shah, Mohammed Reza Pahlevi (the same Shah who fled the country in 1978 in the face of the Islamic Revolution). The British, it should be noted, had economic reasons for wanting their oil back: the UK was close to bankruptcy again. The U.S. government was much more concerned about the possibility that the *Tudeh*—the local Communist party—might gain influence over Mossadeq and take Iran into the Soviet orbit. The oil companies were concerned lest a successful nationalization by Iran were to set a precedent for similar takeovers by other oil-producing countries, an eventuality they were anxious to avoid at all costs. As time passed, the stakes rose. Prevented from selling its oil on world markets due to an embargo imposed by the West, Mossadeq's government asked the Soviet Union for economic assistance. This was a red flag to the American bull. The CIA and MI-5 began to plot Mossadeq's removal from office and the elevation of the Shah—to a position of real power and authority.

The operation took place in 1953. It was run by Kermit Roosevelt (a cousin of Franklin Roosevelt), who was then head of the CIA's Middle East activities. Brigadier General H. Norman Schwartzkopf (father of the Norman Schwartzkopf who was in charge of the 1991 Gulf War) also played a major role. The elder Norman had earlier helped to set up the Iranian National Police and knew the lay of the land. In mid-August 1953, the Shah's advisers convinced him not only that Mossadeq had driven the country into the ground but also that he was preparing to take full power and overthrow the Shah. It was time, his advisers said, to appoint a new prime minister (which was one of his few constitutional prerogatives). The Shah did this and then left (or fled) Iran, leaving to the commander of his royal forces the task of delivering a letter of dismissal to Mossadeq.

On receipt of the missive, Mossadeq had ordered the Shah's emissary arrested. When this became known, pro-Mossadeq street demonstrations broke out, but got somewhat out of hand. Counterdemonstrations were organized with CIA help. Here the story becomes somewhat confused and not a little bizarre. As Roosevelt told it in his memoirs, the counterdemonstrations were begun by a group of tumblers and wrestlers whom he had paid to parade through the streets chanting pro-Shah slogans. As the procession moved through the city, spectators joined in. Eventually, street fighting began. The pro-Shah forces gained the upper hand, surrounded Mossadeq's residence, and arrested him. According to the stories that emerged later on, the entire operation cost only a few million dollars—something strenuously denied by Allen Dulles, of course—and saved Iran from communism. After the restoration, the Shah supposedly told Roosevelt, "I owe my throne to God, my people, and you" (Roosevelt, 1979).

Was the Iran operation a success? Where you stand depends on where you sit. Following the coup, the Shah moved to consolidate his power. He was assisted in this effort by the CIA and the Israeli Mossad, both of which helped to set up his secret police, the SAVAK. More than that, Iran became a major recipient of U.S. military assistance and police training. And against whom was this power directed? Some years later, it is said, Senator Hubert Humphrey asked a colleague, "Do you know what the head of the Iranian Army told one of our people? He said the Army was in good shape, thanks to U.S. aid—it was now capable of coping with the civilian population. That Army isn't going to fight the Russians. It's planning to fight the Iranian people" (Blum, 1986: 76).

In his efforts to build Iran into a regional power, and to quash all political opposition from the Muslim mullahs, the businessmen in the bazaars, and the emerging, educated middle class, the Shah went too far. Twenty-four years after the coup against Mossadeq, he lost his throne for good. But he left behind his mark. The Shah was also a major force behind the oil price hikes of the 1970s and the rise of OPEC (chapter 8). What looked like an almost cost-free operation in 1953 does not look so cheap with the hindsight of fifty years, although there is no way, of course, that Eisenhower, the Dulles brothers, or anyone else could have known this.[1]

Guatemala

The immediate sequel to the coup in Iran came in 1954, when the CIA intervened in Guatemala. There, a democratically elected government under President Jacobo Arbenz Guzman decided to implement a land-reform program for landless peasants. Even then, Guatemala was a desperately poor country: 70 per cent of the land was owned by 2.2 per cent of the population. It was one of the original "banana republics," for all practical purposes ruled by the United Fruit Company (UF). UF owned the country's telephone and telegraph systems and almost all of its railroad tracks. UF ran the only important Atlantic harbor and monopolized Guatemala's banana exports, the country's major source of foreign exchange. UF had powerful friends in Washington, too: the Dulles brothers, the husband of President Eisenhower's personal secretary, and the undersecretary of state—and former CIA director—Walter Bedell Smith. They would protect the company's interests.

Arbenz was viewed with suspicion by the United States even before Eisenhower took office; the first plan to overthrow him was formulated in 1952, the final year of the Truman administration. In the view of many in Washington and in the media, Arbenz's development plans smacked of communism. The political support he received from the tiny Communist party in Guatemala only served to reinforce this impression. But the straw that broke the camel's back came when Arbenz decided to take over some undeveloped land owned by UF. The government offered $525,000 to UF in compensation, while the company claimed the property was worth $16 million.

Why the discrepancy? For the purpose of paying taxes, UF had reported the land as being worth the lower figure; now it was screaming "murder!" and complaining that it was being cheated by being paid that amount. This was of concern in Washington, but there was more. Guatemala was in "America's backyard," not far from the Panama Canal. On the one hand, this made the supposed Communist threat more plausible, for wouldn't the Soviets be looking to strike at the American jugular, which the canal most certainly was? On the other hand, the "backyard" argument legitimized the American reaction against any hint of leftist sentiment in Central America. Finally, inasmuch as it was taken for granted that the

Soviets were active in the region, it was necessary to find threats that demonstrated such activity. The tautology inherent in these claims went unnoticed.

Throughout 1953, the CIA laid the groundwork for a coup. It cultivated disgruntled army officers. It trained a rebel force in Florida, to be airlifted to Nicaragua and then moved into Guatemala. Honduras became another staging point for the invasion, and a small air force was established there. Sabotage was undertaken as well as a full-blown psywar operation aimed at both the Guatemalan and American publics. Arbenz, stymied in his efforts to acquire weapons to defend against the CIA-engineered plan, finally turned to Czechoslovakia for arms. When a Czech ship carrying weapons docked in Guatemala, the pressure, publicity, and preparations for the coup were turned up to full volume.

On June 18, 1954, the offensive began. Planes dropped leaflets demanding that Arbenz resign and promising to return with bombs if he did not. Air attacks commenced and continued for some time thereafter. A "Voice of Liberation" radio began to broadcast reports of rebel advances through the country—even as the CIA-trained force was, in reality, making precious little progress. Efforts by Arbenz to calm the populace or convince the United States to call off the attack came to naught.

The success of the coup effort came to rest on the air force, such as it was, of the invaders. These few planes were supplied by the United States; indeed, they were sent with presidential approval when it was determined that they would be critical to the whole operation. It seems to have been this last move that, in the end, convinced Arbenz to resign and leave the country. He was replaced by a hand-picked military officer who, in the name of anti-communism, initiated a civil war aimed primarily against the country's indigenous people that, during the following forty years, resulted in hundreds of thousands of deaths (Jonas, 1991).

In the United States, the propaganda mills ground on relentlessly throughout. All kinds of evidence were either adduced or created to demonstrate that, if Arbenz was not a card-carrying Communist, he was certainly under the thumb of the Soviets. In retrospect, the evidence was all quite flimsy; at the time, in the midst of domestic anti-Red hysteria, the substance of the claims hardly mattered to the American government, public, or media. Many point to the tight connections between the Eisenhower administration and UF as proof that what was really at stake in Guatemala were economic interests, and that anti-communism was only a cover for much baser stuff. In fact, the CIA coup against Arbenz should be seen not as a unique incident for the time but, rather, for its "demonstration effects" (much as Iraq has become in our day; see Lipschutz, 2000). The operation was meant to suggest to other Latin American countries that there were clear, and quite minimal, limits to the social reforms that would be acceptable to Washington. Because *any* social reform was tantamount to challenging the political power of the upper classes, whose interests usually coincided with those of the United States, even talk of change was enough to galvanize America into action.

Cuba

The third noteworthy CIA intervention came in Cuba, but that project became an embarrassing failure. When the social pot began to boil in Cuba during the second half of the 1950s, the CIA pulled out its old plans for Guatemala, thinking to repeat the earlier success. This time, however, the Agency badly miscalculated. Cuba looked similar, but it was not. American policymakers and CIA analysts failed to appreciate both the degree of antagonism against the Cuban dictator, Fulgencio Batista, and the growing strength of the guerilla army led by Fidel Castro. While the Americans had little love for Batista, whose machinations threatened the substantial American investments in Cuba, they were not terribly impressed by Castro, his army, or their prospects, either.

Thus, when Castro and his forces marched into Havana on January 1, 1959—ten years after the Chinese Communists marched into Beijing—Washington was, once again, as surprised as anybody. At that point, the issue became whether the people and leaders of the United States could live with Castro. Within a year, they decided they could not, although whether the United States had any right to ask such a question was never seriously considered.

In 1960, Castro came to the United States and met with various officials of the Eisenhower administration. He impressed them all as a source of likely trouble (for them). His actions at home, oriented toward social justice and equity, troubled them more. But when all is said and done, Castro's political options were limited. Bowing to American wishes would have meant continuation of domestic misery and U.S. domination. Trying to deal with the United States as Arbenz had done ran the risk of permitting Castro's opponents to organize with the help of the CIA. And any efforts to break with the United States would surely generate a hostile reaction. This was no way to run a revolution and, so, Castro turned East. The timing was right; the Soviets were forthcoming. Castro's programs triggered an exodus of his most likely opponents to Miami, thereby eliminating much internal opposition. The USSR, seeking liberation movements to help, were willing to entertain a political, economic, and military relationship, to buy Cuban sugar and supply it with weapons and oil, and to provide some security guarantees to Cuba.

Needless to say, Castro's move to the left scared and enraged Washington. The CIA began to plan its invasion, fully expecting to find sympathetic allies within Cuba. Forces drawn largely from the Cuban exile community were trained in Florida and Honduras. Landing craft were procured and air cover was promised. John Kennedy inherited the operation from Eisenhower. Fearing that, were he to cancel it, he would find himself in domestic political trouble, Kennedy gave it the green light, against his better judgement (or, so it is said).

The resulting fiasco was called the Bay of Pigs. CIA intelligence suggested that the area of the planned landing was lightly settled and close to mountains that would provide refuge to the invaders. Neither was the case. The sympathetic allies did not appear, the populace did not rise up against Castro, and the expected air cover was cancelled by Kennedy when the operation began to go sour. Over 1,000 invaders were captured. They were returned only after the United States paid a ransom of $60 million in humanitarian goods (Higgins, 1987). The Bay of Pigs became a classic example of how not to run an intervention, providing valuable lessons for the future (some of which were applied during the 1980s, when the United States supported Nicaraguan Contras against the Sandinista government).

Still, in spite of such visible failures, the temptation to use covert methods, primarily in order to avoid congressional oversight, public opposition, and foreign disgust, remained overwhelming, and this remains the case even today. The result has been that most CIA activities have remained unknown or the subject of mere rumor. Indeed, the mark of a successful action is that it never becomes public and, to this extent, there is little way of knowing just how pervasive have been CIA interventions in the affairs of other countries. William Blum, author of a volume titled *The CIA—A Forgotten History* (1986), lists CIA involvement in approximately forty-five countries in addition to Cuba. Many of them were U.S. allies and, undoubtedly, his list is not a complete one. It includes China, the Philippines, Korea, Albania, Eastern Europe and the Soviet Union, both Germanys, Iran, Guatemala, Costa Rica, Syria, the Middle East more generally, Indonesia, Western Europe (including Greece, Italy, and France), British Guyana, Indochina, Haiti, Ecuador, the Congo, Brazil, Peru, Dominican Republic, Ghana, Chile, Bolivia, Iraq, Australia, Angola, Jamaica, Seychelles, Grenada, Morocco, Suriname, El Salvador, and Nicaragua. All of this leads one to wonder how the history of the past forty-five years might have looked without the CIA trying to manage the world?

≈≈

Hot Stuff!

Kiss Me Deadly (United Artists/Parklane, 1955, 105 min.)
Director: Robert Aldrich
Cast: Ralph Meeker, Albert Dekker, Cloris Leachman, Paul Stewart, Maxine Cooper, Gaby Rogers

Spies were working not only for the CIA, of course; the enemy employed them in droves, too (recall, for instance, the spy scene in *The Big Lift*). But there were spies and there were spies. Some were "moles," working for the enemy (mostly the Soviets) in the American bureaucracy, although their numbers were never very large.[2] Others tried to ferret out secrets from contacts within the scientific, military, and bureaucratic establishments. The most famous spy rings involved those chasing after atomic secrets; Julius and Ethel Rosenberg were executed for their supposed role in such a spy ring, although some of those who had actually been involved in atomic espionage, such as Klaus Fuchs, were able to escape from the United States without ever being caught (Williams, 1987).

Kiss Me Deadly is about atomic spies, although as one of the last and best known of the *films noir* of the 1950s, it is also about the degeneracy and corruption of American society during that decade. *Film noir*—literally "black movie"—was a genre that emerged in the 1940s, flourished during the late 1940s and early 1950s, and pretty much disappeared by the 1960s (although since that time, it has gone through pseudo-revivals and satirization). These films, we are told, reflected the moral disarray and disillusionment of a generation reaching maturity during World War II and under the shadow of the atomic bomb. Indeed, nihilism was a conspicuous element of *film noir*, and the race to self-annihilation a common theme (O'Brien, 1991; Shadoian, 1977). What better subject for the genre, then, than a film about a search for "the great whatsit," the thing no one can name, but which everyone wants?

As the film opens, we hear heavy breathing and see a pair of legs running down the middle of a very dark highway not far from Los Angeles; the camera pans back to reveal a young woman—Christina Bailey (Leachman). She is trying to escape unnamed pursuers by flagging down a ride, and she is having little success. Finally, Christina throws herself in front of a sports car driven by Mike Hammer (Meeker), who reluctantly picks her up. During the next few minutes, both are kidnapped by thugs and rendered unconscious. Christina is tortured to death, and then she and Hammer are loaded into his car and sent rolling down a cliff, in order to kill him and make their deaths appear accidental.

Hammer does not die; he lives to pursue the case, which turns out to have national security implications (although what kind are not made immediately clear). Everyone thinks Hammer knows something—as soon as he leaves the hospital, he is brought in for questioning by the "Interstate Crime

Commission"—but, in fact, he does not. All he does know is that the unnamed object of such concern to thugs and the authorities—the great whatsit—must be very valuable. If so many people want it, so does Hammer. The search for the great whatsit turns out to be quite deadly. Those who know what it is, or where it is, die. Even some whose links to it are quite peripheral, such as Hammer's auto mechanic, are killed. Hammer's secretary and love interest, Velda Wakeman (Cooper), is kidnapped by the bad guys so they can find out what Hammer knows. And the mysterious Dr. Soberin (Dekker), whose name and accent are not only foreign but also redolent of sobriety and poison gas, will stop at nothing to obtain the whatsit. He takes Velda hostage at his beach cottage and threatens to kill her if Hammer does not give him the goods.

The great whatsit turns out to be a box of very hot, highly radioactive atomic material. Indeed, even momentary exposure leads to severe radiation burns, as Hammer discovers. But what the whatsit is good for is never made clear. Eventually, Soberin comes into possession of the box, helped by Gabrielle (Rogers). Masquerading as Christina's roommate, Lily Carver (whose body has been found floating in the bay), and with Hammer's unintentional assistance, Gabrielle finds the whatsit.

But she is no patsy. She wants her share of the riches and she wants to leave the country with Soberin. He refuses her, saying "Where I am going you cannot come." In a rage, Gabrielle kills Soberin and prepares to look into the box. At that moment, Hammer bursts into the room, looking for Velda. Gabrielle shoots him and slowly opens the whatsit. In a scene later copied by Steven Spielberg in *Raiders of the Lost Ark*, an unnatural glow, accompanied by an unearthly roaring, emanates from the box. Gabrielle screams in horror and, as she does so, begins to smoke, ignites, and bursts into flame. We last see her as a pillar of fire.

Hammer, though wounded, escapes from the atomic conflagration and finds Velda in an adjoining bedroom. As they try to escape from the house, it too begins to burn. In the last scene, the house explodes and is incinerated in a mushroom cloud. As with other films of the '50s, *Kiss Me Deadly* has two endings. In one version, Hammer and Velda are incinerated along with the house (and the world?). A happier ending shows them escaping and huddling on the beach as the house blows up behind them.

Me, Me, Me, Me. Me!

The Mike Hammer character was a creation of Micky Spillane who, in his time, was a notorious anti-Communist. Director Robert Aldrich and his screenwriter changed the plot of Spillane's 1949 novel of the same name considerably, eschewing the original focus on drugs and the Mafia. In dealing with the atomic issue, the film becomes much bleaker than the novel, suggesting that not only is morality in short supply but so is the future.

Hammer is a distasteful and unsympathetic character (not unlike Harry Lime in *The Third Man*, but without the charm). From the very outset of the film, when he is flagged down against his will by the soon-to-be dead Christina, his constant refrain is "What's in it for me?" As Christina looks Hammer over, she tells him, "You have only one true love—you." Not until Velda's life is in the balance does he begin to think about someone else. By then, it is too late. But the pursuit of the unknown—even when it is quite evidently deadly—is too tempting. Hammer's police buddy tells him that he's gotten mixed up in atomic espionage, and Hammer stammers, "I didn't know." Replies his friend, "Would it have made any difference if you had known?"

The atomic spy's job is to discover what his or her side does not know; the atomic scientist's job is to discover what no one knows. And why? For self-interest, of course, regardless of the consequences. In the anarchic self-help world of international politics, as well as the market world of the individual man-on-the-make, the only real interest is the self. One can justify any type of behavior so long as that interest is served. But, in a world without moral restraints, where are the limits to self-serving behavior? Where are the concerns for others? Where is an evaluation of the consequences? This is a question we encounter again and again in film, fiction, and politics.

Kiss Me Deadly suggests that the 1950s were a decade of boundless self-interest not only at home but also abroad. Hammer's quest for "the great whatsit"—his Holy Grail—is successful but, having found it, he does not know what to do with it and must let it go. And, even though he does not risk looking upon the face of God, the law of unintended consequences kicks in, and Hammer runs out of luck. In the search for secrets that would give us an advantage over others, we were even willing to consider destroying the world, just as Hammer's behavior ends up destroying him. Even where American efforts were "successful," as in Iran and Guatemala, they later had consequences that were as deadly for many as nuclear holocaust would have been for us.

〰〰

Out of the Freezer, into the Frying Pan

Mike Hammer's life, at the very least, has some glamour about it. He lives in an apartment with all of the latest technology, drives a fancy sports car ("Va-va-voom!" as Nick, his soon-to-die mechanic, says), and hangs out at hip jazz clubs. Alec Leamas's life and fate are much the more accurate. He has few such perks. And there is a final irony in all of this: to what end do these sacrifices occur? What is the nature of the valuable information provided to the West through the good offices of Dieter Mundt? Minutes of the meetings of the Presidium of the Party. A schematic of lines of authority in the East German Abteilung. Nothing about bombs or Russians or the world's end. Details, details. To die for.

∿
∿

Chapter 5

Nukes!

End of Days

Imagine the following scenario: You live in Kansas City. The year is 1983. The news is bad: another crisis is brewing over Berlin and the superpowers are rattling their sabers. You pay no attention because it has happened before and will happen again. Lots of noise, no action. But you are downtown the following day, walking along, and you hear a tremendous roar—one you have never heard before. It sounds like a thousand jet engines somewhere off beyond the edges of the city.

As you look off to the horizon, you see long, thin objects—dozens, perhaps hundreds—rising slowly into the sky, on clouds of smoke and flame. And what you never expected has happened. The End is Near. They are Minuteman missiles. They are aimed at the Soviet Union. They will arrive at their targets in 30 minutes. And you know that, by then, their Soviet counterparts will have fallen around Kansas City. Your life and your civilization will be over, finished, cast into history's dustbin.

This was the premise of a made-for-television film, *The Day After*, which appeared on ABC in 1983, during the height of the "Second Cold War." The film was a controversial one, for some thought it would make Americans even more afraid of nuclear war than they already were and undermine public support for confrontation with the Soviet Union. The showing of *The Day After* on national television provided the occasion for an unprecedented public debate about nuclear war, nuclear deterrence, and the morality of threatening nuclear annihilation in order to "keep the peace."

The uproar did not take place in a vacuum. Between 1981 and 1985, various members of the Reagan administration suggested that, under certain circumstances, nuclear weapons might be detonated as a "warning" to the Soviet Union. Earlier in 1983, Reagan had proposed launching the "Strategic Defense Initiative" (SDI, aka "Star Wars") as a way of making nuclear weapons "impotent and obsolete" (Wirls, 1992). While SDI never fulfilled Reagan's dream—and probably never will, despite the decisions of both the Clinton and Bush administrations to proceed with a more limited version of ballistic missile defense—its technological wizardry and space-age artists' conceptions did much to calm public fears.

This brouhaha over nuclear weapons was hardly new; it had been going on in one form or another ever since the beginning of the Atomic Age. The core problem facing the country was, however, ontological rather than technical: How do we deal with an advanced technology that we control but whose very existence on Earth seems to threaten our survival? Inasmuch as coming to grips with this existential dilemma—abolition or international control—would have required achieving a political consensus with the Enemy, the only domestically acceptable solution seemed to be more and better technology.

More to the point, keeping nuclear war at bay, according to nuclear strategists, required that we make believable and bellicose threats to launch should conditions seem to make this necessary. Fear of destruction would make the Enemy cautious and unwilling to engage in aggressive activities (Freedman, 1983). But such a strategy of nuclear deterrence seemed to be fundamentally flawed. After all, how credible is the threat to destroy the world in order to preserve one's liberty and security? Was it "better to be dead than Red?"

The answer to the dilemma appeared to lie in one of two directions. Either nuclear weapons had to be "domesticated" by making them usable, which would involve reducing their destructiveness to levels that would make them just another battlefield weapon. Or, a means of protecting targets from their devastating power—that is, an effective strategic defense—must be invented to guard the Nation against destruction. The only other alternative was faith: Faith in the rationality of men (and all of the decisionmakers were men)—a faint hope, given human nature and human history—or faith in intervention by God. That the answer to the nuclear threat might be found in politics (and negotiations) rather than technology *or* faith was, for the most part, never taken seriously (and this remains very much the case today, as seen in U.S. relations with North Korea and China). Technology was *always* preferable to faith or politics.

Between 1945 and 1955, American science was (or appeared to be) the most advanced and innovative in the world, and the example of the Manhattan Project led people to believe—and political and scientific elites to argue—that there was nothing science and technology could not accomplish. Some dissident voices were heard but, because they relied on fallible human nature, rather than apparently infallible technology—remember, this was long before Three Mile Island, Chernobyl, the Challenger explosion, Bhopal, or the Florida election cockup, all of which were blamed on "human error"—those who counseled caution were largely marginalized. Thus, film and fiction tended to reflect two perspectives only. Either nuclear war would be fought and whomever was left alive—preferably American—would pick up the pieces and rebuild (the theme of Robert Heinlein's book *Farnham's Freehold*). Or by some equivalent of a miracle, war would be avoided (as in *Red Alert* or *Fail-Safe*), and the severely chastened survivors would take on the task of improving the technology so that the mistake could never happen again. Sometimes, as in *A Canticle for Leibowitz*, a 1959 novel by Walter Miller, Jr., both wars and miracles took place, but the Earth was nonetheless lost. *Red Planet Mars*, an obscure film released in 1952 and seen during subsequent decades only on late-night television, and *Fail-Safe* (1962) did preach the limits of technology and the need for human agency if nuclear war were to be avoided (although the former relied on a rather peculiar Christian deus ex machina, while the latter drew on the Bible for its solution). In the sardonic *Dr. Strangelove, or How I Learned to Stop Worrying and Love the Bomb*, possibly the best of Stanley Kubrick's films, there is clearly nothing to be gained from saving anyone.

"A Smoking, Radiating Ruin in Two Hours"

The main problem with the atomic bomb was that it effectively eliminated military strategy as an element of international relations. When one country with an effectively unlimited supply of nuclear weapons could simply continue to bomb its enemy until the latter ceased to exist as a viable society—even as it was being similarly smashed into oblivion—there were few, if any, social objectives worth a world war. Of course, any number of social philosophers and political pundits argued that there were fates worse than death (see, e.g., Freedman, 1983: 201-7), and that freedom was more important than life. Nonetheless, Charles de Gaulle's challenge—would the United States sacrifice New York for Paris?—put the problematic nicely.

The first atomic bombs were not very large, but neither were they very discriminating. Bombers might be able to drop them precisely on target, but the resulting blast would lay waste an area one or more miles in diameter. Inasmuch as many military targets were in or near urban areas, atomic war would inevitably mean war on civilians.

The first thermonuclear weapons (the hydrogen, "H-bomb," or super) were much larger—500 to 1,000 times the explosive power of the Hiroshima bomb. Robert Oppenheimer, director of the Manhattan Project, thought them useless as weapons. He was not opposed to atomic weapons—after all, he had all but birthed them—but he favored development of small, tactical devices that could be used on the battlefield, and not cause too much "collateral damage" to civilians and cities. The atomic scientists and designers put their heads together and came up with a variety of bombs that could, they claimed, be used just as though they were conventional weapons.

There were, for example, nuclear artillery shells with yields from 0.1 to ten kilotons (the Hiroshima bomb was the equivalent of about fifteen kilotons—each kiloton equal to 1000 tons of TNT equivalent), which could be fired from mobile guns, tanks, and howitzers. There were ADMs— "atomic demolition munitions"—some of less than one kiloton yield, others as powerful as the Hiroshima bomb—meant to lie in wait for tanks and massed armies on or under the ground. And there were even "Dial-a-yield" short-range Honest John missiles, whose warheads could be adjusted to produce a blast ranging from a fraction of a kiloton up to twenty.[1] No one ever actually tried to use these devices either on the battlefield or in war games, although they were tested in Nevada. But on a number of occasions, soldiers on both sides were made to march through newly bombed radioactive environments in order to see whether they would hold up and if they could still fight.

Even tactical nukes were too destructive to be very useful; as one wag noted later, towns in Germany were typically "one kiloton distance" from each other,[2] so that even very small atomic devices would obliterate the landscape and all the Germans in it. Virtual experience seemed to bear out this calculation. One war game in Louisiana imagined seventy bombs, each of not more than forty kilotons yield, dropped on military targets. At that point, the game ended because the umpires ruled that all life in the state had "ceased to exist" (Freedman, 1983: 109).

Nevertheless, such tactical atomic devices came to play a central role in American support of the rearmament of Western Europe and, in particular, West Germany during the 1950s. NATO (the North Atlantic Treaty Alliance) was never very confident of its ability to outgun the Red Army and the Warsaw Pact (WTO) in actual warfare. It was clearly outnumbered by the Soviets and their East European allies (whom, it was always assumed in the event of war, would shoot westward toward NATO, and not at the Soviet forces behind them, to the east). Tactical and theater nuclear weapons were felt to provide the margin that would make "victory" possible. What "victory" might look like was left to science fiction films and novels; NATO strategists did not want to think very much about it.

But the Eisenhower administration's "New Look," put in place in 1953, was not premised on war in Europe; rather, it was based on keeping the Soviets at bay through what Eisenhower's fiercely anti-Communist secretary of state, John Foster Dulles, called "Massive Retaliation." The term was meant to suggest that, should Communist forces threaten or invade some part of the "Free World"—which generally included everything outside of the direct Soviet sphere of influence—the United States would launch a full-scale nuclear counterattack, "at a time and place of its own choosing."

As was the case some thirty years later, when Reagan administration officials intimated a similar strategy, Massive Retaliation made many people nervous, and led to the emergence of the first antinuclear peace movement (Hinton, 1989; Lieberman, 2000). It also led, eventually, to "Flexible Response," a strategic doctrine tested in Vietnam and found wanting but nonetheless adopted by NATO. Whereas the public was scared and the strategists skeptical of Massive Retaliation, the military was only too happy to work out the details of bombing Russia into oblivion (Rosenberg, 1983).

The years following the outbreak of the Korean War saw what Eisenhower later called the "military-industrial complex" come into full flower. The United States was, in effect, put onto something approaching wartime mobilization, albeit without the rationing, destruction, and loss of lives that would accompany a "hot" war. While plans were made for a drawn-out World War III, most did not think it would last much beyond a few weeks.

Indeed, the strategic plan for war with the Soviet Union that emerged during this period was fairly simple. It relied on a large-scale attack by nuclear-armed American bombers flying from North America over the North Pole and bases in Europe and Asia. The long-distance bomber, which was first developed during World War II, had evolved very rapidly between 1945 and 1955, and the B-52 became the backbone of the strategic bomber force in 1955. Because it was so reliable and because its successor, the B-57 "Valkyrie," was a failure (and the B-1 and the B-2 "Stealth" bombers have never been produced in large numbers or lived up to expectations), some 300 B-52s have since been overhauled a number of times and are still in service. Most are expected to remain in service well into the twenty-first century.

The bomber fleet was organized into the "Strategic Air Command" (SAC), immortalized in several films, critiqued in at least two novels, and parodied in at least one film. Under the command of Air Force general Curtis LeMay, who was notorious for wanting to attack Russia while the United States still had an advantage, SAC was deployed at airfields around the country. As the system developed, at the first sign of an attack, relayed from the growing array of radar stations built around the periphery of North America, the bombers would take off and head for their "fail-safe" points along the Soviet borders. There, the bombers would circle, sometimes for hours, awaiting instructions to return or attack (see below).

If the alert were a real one, orders communicated by secure, encrypted radio would send them winging on their way into the Soviet Union, there to attack strategic targets. These would include command centers, bases, railroad junctions, highways, canals, dams, power plants, factories, and cities. There was no apparent limit to the required level of destruction. As strategic planners found more and more potential targets within the Soviet Union, the number of bombs delivered to the Air Force rose accordingly; as the production lines turned out more and more bombs, the number of strategic targets grew. In 1948, as noted earlier, there were fifteen atomic bombs, all of them American; by 1958, the United States had at least 30,000, and the USSR more than 10,000.

The speed and flashiness of the bomber fleet said nothing, however, about the reliability of the whole arrangement. In the beginning, only the United States had planes able to carry atomic bombs halfway around the world; the Soviets soon caught up on this account. But it also became apparent in the mid-1950s that bombers on the ground were extremely vulnerable to preemptive or surprise attacks. While there might be enough warning to get some of the planes off the ground, many were sure to be incinerated on the tarmac (Freedman, 1983:158-63; *Killian Report*, 1955; *Gathier Report*, 1957). More to the point, once the Soviets could get their bombers past U.S. defenses and over North America—and assuming they carried more bombs than there were SAC bases—cities, as the sites of industrial facilities, rail junctions, and so on—would be the next to be hit.[3]

And what were the bombers to do once they had arrived over their targets? According to the SIOP or "Single Integrated Operational Plan" declassified in the 1980s, they were to turn the Soviet Union into "a smoking radiating ruin in two hours" (Rosenberg, 1983). That was the goal, no more and no less. When the Kennedy administration came into office and the new secretary of defense, Robert McNamara, got a good look at the Eisenhower SIOP, he was appalled at the level of destruction it entailed and the complete absence of any strategy behind it. McNamara immediately ordered his underlings to revise the SIOP, so that there were a number of "options" available should an attack on the Soviets be initiated. McNamara himself devised an elaborate calculus to rationalize the magnitude of America's nuclear capabilities.

Using the statistical reasoning for which he was so famous as president of the Ford Motor Company, McNamara decided that 400 megatons of nuclear firepower would be sufficient to end the USSR as a functioning society. This was, at the time, the equivalent of 400 of the new Minuteman I solid-fuelled intercontinental ballistic missiles (ICBM) that were just replacing the old liquid-fuelled Atlas and Titan ICBMs. Each Minuteman carried the destructiveness equivalent to about seventy Hiroshima-sized bombs. The older missiles had taken hours to prepare for launch, while the new ones were ready to be let loose in very short order. Just to be on the safe side, since some missiles and bombers would be destroyed before they got off the ground, McNamara multiplied his criterion by three and got 1200 megatons. Four hundred would be on missiles, 400 on bombers, and

400 on submarines. This was enough for any circumstance, or so he thought.

Not that the number mattered. When the decision was bruited about as to how many Minuteman missiles to deploy, a few people thought 100 would be sufficient, inasmuch as SAC still had all of its bombs, and the Navy was beginning to deploy nuclear missiles on nuclear-powered Polaris submarines. The Air Force took the view that one could never have enough missiles and asked for 10,000. So, according to the now-apocryphal story, McNamara split the difference and ordered 1,000. This number acquired magical qualities and was, for a long time after, enshrined as sacred in the successive arms control treaties negotiated by the two superpowers (the most recent U.S.-Russian agreements no longer hew to this precise number).

This scale of nuclear armament came to be called "overkill." Overkill measured how many times could America's weapons kill the entire population of the USSR and, indeed, the world, and how many times the Soviets could do the same. By the end of the 1960s, the overkill factor was well above ten and perhaps as high as fifty.

All of this strategic mysticism might not have mattered had the United States been more careful about publicizing its nuclear might. The American public did not really want to know very much about the prospects of atomic holocaust, but there was political hay to be made by exaggerating the threat from the Soviets and the robustness of U.S. preparations in response. This was one of the purposes of atmospheric testing, intended not only to make sure the "devices" worked but also to send messages to both the Soviets *and* the Western publics (and, sometimes, unintended radiation doses to residents of Utah and Nevada, as they eventually discovered). Such tests, it was argued, conveyed the determination of the United States to oppose the Soviet threat. Anything that might indicate retreat on this account—for example, a ban on atmospheric testing—was, for a long time, political anathema in Washington and the weapons laboratories in Livermore and Los Alamos.

At the same time, the public was becoming increasingly nervous. The nuclear-tipped NIKE missiles devised to shield American cities from Soviet bombers were obsolete even before they became operational—they could not protect against the new ballistic missiles that were soon to be deployed. In 1957, the USSR launched its first Earth-orbiting satellite, Sputnik. That brought home a new fact of life, one that had never been a concern before: the United States was now vulnerable to attack by a foreign power and was virtually powerless to prevent it. All of this was most unsettling to the American polity. Indeed, there was even some discussion of whether it would be better, in the event of war, to surrender immediately, so as to avoid the possibility of nuclear annihilation. The authors of this proposal

were hauled before congressional committees and told never to speak
again of such an idea. What could restore public confidence?

~~~

Nuclear Madness

The deterrence dilemma, posing all of the difficulties of politics, morality, and
life became the focus of numerous novels and films. Some treated the issue
with great seriousness, some with great fatalism, and one or two with black
humor. Now that men could initiate Armageddon at the flick of a switch, how
could they be restrained from doing so? For some, human nature made such
actions inevitable; for others, the inherent unreliability of technology made
failure inevitable. In either case, the consequences would be horrendous.

Red Alert, Peter Bryant (New York: Ace, 1958)
Fail-Safe, Eugene Burdick and Harvey Wheeler (New York: McGraw-Hill,
   1962)
***Doctor Strangelove, or How I Learned to Stop Worrying and Love
   the Bomb*** (Columbia, 1963, 93 min.)
Director: Stanley Kubrick
Cast: Peter Sellers, George C. Scott, Sterling Hayden, Keenan Wynn,
   Slim Pickens, James Earl Jones

In *Red Alert,* Brigadier General Quinten, about to be relieved and promoted
from his command at Sonora Air Force base in Texas, orders SAC's 843rd
Wing of B-52 bombers to attack the Soviet Union. Quinten has been
diagnosed with inoperable cancer and, in a fit of either madness or insight,
has determined to make the world safe from communism for his
grandchildren. Of course, Washington and the Pentagon are taken
completely by surprise and soon discover that (1) they have no way to recall
the bombers without the appropriate code and (2) that the only person who
knows the code, General Quinten, has cut off all communications with the
outside world (and will soon shoot himself, in any case).

In the War Room, the president and Joint Chiefs discuss the situation.
The military sees this as an opportunity to get rid of a nagging problem, and
favors sending the rest of the bomber fleet in after the 843rd to finish off the
Russians. But the president knows something the Joint Chiefs don't: The
Russians have buried at least twenty H-bombs, jacketed with cobalt, in the
Ural Mountains. As soon as the Soviets face defeat or destruction, they will
detonate the bombs. The world will soon be covered by a radioactive cloud.
Within a year, the Earth will be dead.

Fortunately, the recall code for the bombers is discovered and all but
one of the planes change course and head back to the United States. That

one bomber, however, continues on its mission to destroy its targets. All Russian efforts to shoot it down prove unsuccessful. The president and the Soviet premier agree that triggering of the twenty H-bombs must not be allowed to happen but, at the same time, the nuclear destruction of a Russian city cannot go unavenged. The president agrees that the Russians may launch a missile at Atlantic City in exchange for the Russian city. At the last moment, the bomber misses its target, and Atlantic City is saved. But the lesson both sides learn is not a political one; rather, they recognize that as soon as both sides have operational intercontinental ballistic missile systems, "war becomes profitless." Mutually Assured Destruction (MAD, although Bryant does not call it this) will keep "peace on earth." (Similar logic was offered in *The Day the Earth Stood Still*.)

If the story sounds familiar, there is good reason. Allowing peace to rely on human nature seemed the height of folly; a technological solution would not be affected by emotion or insanity. It would be "fail safe." Or would it? The next version of the story appeared as *Fail-Safe*.

In *Fail-Safe*, the president of the United States sacrifices New York for Moscow. The cause of failure in this story is a minor electronic glitch—a blown capacitor—which causes an incorrect message to be sent to a strategic bomber group on a routine alert. As a result, the group flies past its "fail-safe" point and heads on toward Russia, where it is programmed to drop 20-megaton hydrogen bombs on Moscow. There are three major characters in the novel besides the president. These are Peter Buck, the president's Russian-speaking translator, Air Force general Warren Black, an old friend and confidant of the president, and Dr. Walter Groteschele, once a German refugee and now a Harvard professor whose specialization is nuclear strategy.

Groteschele (who seems to have been modeled primarily on Henry Kissinger and, to a lesser degree, on Herman Kahn, discussed below), has provided the administration with the intellectual rationale for a robust nuclear capacity. He revels in thinking about how the nuclear force might be used for coercive political purposes. Fortunately, there are numerous technical and organizational safeguards on the nuclear system—General Black has played a major role in seeing these put into place, although he has serious doubts about their reliability—that prevent the weapons from being launched except under conditions of absolute certainty that an attack is underway. Once the approach of the Soviet bombers has been verified, however, the system can be shut off only by a direct order of the president, communicated through an elaborate system of electronic signaling devices.

On the particular day of our story, things go wrong. An unidentified object is picked up by U.S. radar, which triggers an alert that sends the "Vindicator" strategic nuclear bombers into the air. Within a few minutes, the bogey is identified as a commercial airliner with engine trouble. Unbeknownst to anybody, however, the technological safeguards have failed: The blown capacitor prevents one of the bomber groups from receiving the message to return to base. To complicate matters, the Soviets have been jamming certain radio channels as part of a deliberate effort to prevent the U.S. military from communicating with the bombers. The Soviets try to shoot down the errant planes but, despite American attempts to help, two get through and destroy Moscow.

At this point, the president is faced with a momentous decision. The Soviet premier will not accept mere assurances that a mistake has been made, and his generals are demanding full-scale retaliation. Some of the president's advisers, including Groteschele, also believe that the only viable followup is a comprehensive nuclear attack on the Soviet Union in order to prevent the United States from being leveled. What will convince the Soviets and silence the Americans?

The president falls back on an old biblical dictum. He orders General Black to take a loaded strategic nuclear bomber into the air over New York City—where, not coincidentally, Black's family lives and which, on that day, the president's wife is visiting—and drop four 20-megaton bombs. Black follows the president's orders and then commits suicide. Buck reflects on world peace. Groteschele contemplates a new career. Justice is served and peace is preserved.

A film version of *Fail-Safe* was released in 1964, starring Henry Fonda as the president, Walter Matthau as Groteschele, and Larry Hagman as General Black. This film is generally considered to convey the stark seriousness of the nuclear issue, although it is rather dull. More to the point, Matthau is miscast as Groteschele, who is really the only character of any interest in the novel. A year earlier, a much better version of this story was released by Hollywood, as *Doctor Strangelove, or How I Learned to Stop Worrying and Love the Bomb.*

The screenplay for *Dr. Strangelove* was based on Peter Bryant's *Red Alert,* but there are so many similarities to *Fail-Safe* that the reader/viewer might think the screenwriters borrowed from the latter novel (it is probably more the case that Burdick and Wheeler borrowed from *Red Alert,* which was published by a minor science fiction publisher, Ace). The major difference is that *Dr. Strangelove* is black comedy.

General Jack D. Ripper (Hayden), the commander of Burpleson Air Force Base, orders a bomber wing to proceed beyond its fail-safe point and attack the Soviet Union. Ripper is certifiably nuts, and keeps talking about fluoridation and the contamination of "precious bodily fluids." Or as he says to his aide, Group Leader Lionel Mandrake (Sellers, in one of three roles), who is on loan from the British military, "I can no longer sit back and allow Communist infiltration, Communist indoctrination, Communist subversion, and the international Communist conspiracy to sap and impurify all of our precious bodily fluids."

Once Ripper is found out, President Merkin Muffly (Sellers) is urged by his advisers to follow through with a massive nuclear strike. He resists and, inviting Soviet ambassador De Sadesky into the War Room, places a call to the Soviet premier, who is—how shall we put it—otherwise occupied and not a little drunk. The president gently tells the premier that there is a "little problem with the bomb."

A complication arises: the Soviets, behind in the "arms race, the space race, and the peace race" have built and deployed a "Doomsday Device" in order to save money. The device is an enormous H-bomb jacketed with "cobal-thorium G" that, when detonated, will encircle the Earth with a deadly radioactive shroud that will kill all life. Moreover, the device will trigger automatically should a nuclear blast be detected within the boundaries of the USSR. Finally, there is no way to turn it off. As the Soviet Ambassador explains, the decision to deploy the Doomsday Device was made when the Soviets learned that the United States was considering the same step. The president protests that he knows of no such plan, but Ambassador De Sadesky replies slyly, "We read it in the *New York Times*."

Muffly turns to his nuclear strategist, Dr. Strangelove (Sellers), to ask if such a device is possible. "Of course," replies Strangelove. "When all you need to do is to bury a bomb, there is no limit to its size." A study of such a device was commissioned by the "Bland Corporation," notes Strangelove, but "based on the findings of the report, I concluded that such a device would not be a practical deterrent for reasons which, at this moment, must seem all too obvious."

For a moment, Strangelove admires the idea of such a foolproof deterrent, but then turns to De Sadesky and berates him: "Why didn't you announce it? The whole point is lost if the world does not know about it!"

The ambassador apologizes: "The premier was going to announce it at the next Party Congress. You know how he loves surprises" (this in the aftermath of the Cuban missile crisis, which came as a surprise to almost everyone).

The film continues along the lines of *Red Alert*. General Ripper commits suicide, but Mandrake is able to decipher the general's last scribblings, and all of the bombers but one are recalled. That bomber proceeds to its destination despite everyone's efforts to shoot it down. When the bomb gets jammed in the bomb bay, the pilot (Pickens) climbs down and releases it manually. Astride the phallic projectile, he rides it down to its target at a Soviet nuclear missile base, waving his cowboy hat in the best tradition of the Western bronc busters.

Meanwhile, back in the War Room, the assembled contemplate the end of the world. Dr. Strangelove suggests that the country's leaders might repair to some deep mines, which, if stocked with sufficient supplies and women, would permit them to wait out the 100-year period of deadly radioactivity. As the men discuss this option, one of their number begins to worry about the Russians doing the same, stockpiling nuclear bombs, and attacking the Americans when everyone emerges from the mines. He decries the possibility of a "mineshaft gap" as the film ends with shots of mushroom clouds and the British World War II tune "We'll meet again."

≈

They Must Believe That We Believe That They Believe

Into a growing breach of faith stepped the new generation of nuclear strategists, including Herman Kahn and Henry Kissinger. Before these two came to public attention, there had been considerable discussion about nuclear deterrence, but only at a fairly fundamental level. Many strategists held the view that, even in the event of a sizable surprise atomic attack on the United States by the Soviet Union—the Japanese attack on Pearl Harbor was still taken as the model for war initiation—a sufficient number of strategic bombers would get away and make it to their targets, thereby making the costs to the Soviets unbearably high. This, they reasoned, would be enough to make the Soviets think twice about launching such an attack.

Others contended that reading the minds of the people in Moscow was a fragile reed and an insufficient hedge on which to base America's security and survival. Only by being prepared to wage *offensive* war against the Soviets—and there were some who even went so far as to argue for a preemptive surprise attack, as indicated in the films and novels—could the Kremlin be made to realize that the costs of war were far greater than any marginal benefits that might result. Therefore, American preparations for nuclear war should be visible, loud, and certain, so as to make Moscow doubly cautious. But, as discussed earlier, there was a more fundamental problem here that was, for the most part, mentioned only *sotto voce*: Could the United States actually be relied upon to respond if the Soviets used nuclear weapons at anything less than the all-out level? This was the New York for Paris question, once again.

Such a concern grew out of the nature of the American commitment to the defense of Western Europe. In exchange for an implicit understanding that its NATO allies, and especially West Germany, would not develop nuclear weapons—an understanding broken in the 1950s and 1960s by France and the United Kingdom—the United States would provide a "nuclear umbrella" to deter Soviet aggression. What this meant was that, in the event of a Soviet-led attack on Western Europe, the United States would, if necessary, use nuclear weapons to repel the invasion. But in order to keep such a scenario from escalating from battlefield and theater nuclear attacks to missile barrages against European cities, the United States would also have to threaten nuclear attacks on *Soviet* cities far behind the front lines. This might lead, in turn, to retaliatory strikes against *American* cities, also distant from the actual hostilities. Having worked through this scenario, some feared, the Americans might think twice about initiating nuclear war at all, thereby obviating the deterrent effect of having the weapons and the umbrella. It was this that led de Gaulle to ask his (in)famous question and the French to develop what they called their force de frappe.

Both Kissinger and Kahn took on this dilemma in their written work and public pronouncements. Kissinger, in *Nuclear Weapons and Foreign Policy*, published in 1957, argued that the promise (or threat) of all-out nuclear war was simply not a credible one. He proposed that the United States think seriously about, and prepare for, both limited objectives and limited war. Indeed, Kissinger went so far as to propose *detaching* war from territory. In his version of limited nuclear war, "[S]elf-contained units with great firepower [would] gradually gain the upper hand by destroying their enemy counterparts without physically occupying territory or establishing a front line" (cited in Freedman, 1983: 107).

Evocative of the floating fortresses in Orwell's *1984*, these units would be self-sufficient and use tactical nuclear weapons against the enemy. Because they would not depend on supply lines to and through urban production centers, the collateral damage to civilians and cities could be limited. If the voting public could be left largely unscathed, Kissinger reasoned, the policymakers might gain free rein to engage in war once again.

Herman Kahn, in books entitled *On Thermonuclear War* (1960) and *On Escalation* (1965), grappled with the question of how to keep war between the superpowers from escalating into a full-scale nuclear "spasm." The ability to constrain such conflict would allow war to retain at least some political utility, he argued. But Kahn, unlike Kissinger, tended toward rhetorical extremes in order to illustrate his premises and conclusions. He became notorious for minimizing the potential costs of nuclear war. It was Kahn who suggested that losses of 20-50 million might not be so bad (a line repeated by General Buck Turgidson—George C. Scott—in *Dr. Strangelove*), and asked "Would the survivors envy the dead? Kahn's answer was "no." Deep shelters would protect the survivors, allow them to live reasonably comfortable lives, and enable them to rebuild the United States in a matter of decades (another position parodied in the "shelter race" at the end of *Dr. Strangelove*). Kahn mapped out some forty intermediate steps on a "ladder of escalation" between peace and thermonuclear war that would provide bargaining leverage in a crisis. Some of the upper steps did involve the use of nuclear weapons, but in restricted numbers. Only at the top of the ladder did full-scale war break out (Kaplan, 1983).

The problem was that, academics notwithstanding, it was difficult to convince the public that such restraint was possible. Once the first atomic bomb had been lobbed, wouldn't the recipient have a strong incentive to reply in kind? And, having received a nuclear reply, would not the initiator then lob back another one or two or five or fifty? At some point, whether earlier or later, there would be no limits to speak of, and the world would come to an end (hence the reason for arguments that, if someone were to survive, better it be an American than a Russian). Given this logic, reminiscent of the automaticity of the "domino theory" and redolent of the "Doomsday Machine," the concept of a limited nuclear war appeared as something of an oxymoron. It was in response to this dilemma that the doctrine of flexible response was offered, which became the strategic doctrine of the Kennedy administration and its successors (chapter 7).

It's All a Game, See?

If nuclear weapons could not be used in a literal sense—and no one wanted to experiment with them—perhaps they could be used in a symbolic one. To return to the initial problem of nuclear deterrence, how could you make a credible threat to go nuclear if you actually never wanted to follow through on the threat? The answer, as illustrated in *Dr. Strangelove* (and the James Dean film *Rebel without a Cause*) was to play the game of "Chicken." Thomas Schelling, at the time another Harvard strategist and one of the best-known analysts of "game theory," put it thus: "Cold War politics have been likened . . . to the game of 'chicken.' This is described as a game in which two teen-age motorists head for each other on a highway—usually late at night, with their gangs and girlfriends looking on—to see which of the two will first swerve aside" (Schelling, 1966: 116).

The "rational" driver would, of course, save his life by swerving aside at the last moment, but the objective of Chicken is to impress the other driver, and the watching gangs and girls, with one's determination by *not* swerving. Hence, the more commitment to not swerving that one can convey, the more convincing one's determination will be, and the more likely it is that the other driver will swerve. The ultimate commitment would be, as some have suggested, to throw the steering wheel out the window, thus making it impossible to swerve and threatening automatic death for both if the other driver doesn't chicken out (Freedman, 1983: 188).[4]

The nuclear strategy equivalent of automotive Chicken is a system that, given the appropriate signal, would automatically launch a nuclear attack against the enemy. Because such a system would be meant to *prevent* a nuclear war from occurring, the system would have to assure the enemy that nuclear retaliation was guaranteed absolutely in the event of a unprovoked attack. Inasmuch as any human involvement in such an arrangement would introduce the possibility of *not* retaliating, the system would have to be fully automated. Hence, the Doomsday Machine of *Dr. Strangelove*. Of course, as Dr. Strangelove points out in the film, a deterrent is no good if you don't know about it; a Doomsday Machine would require a good deal of publicity if it were to fulfill its role of preventing nuclear war as intended.

While the idea of such a device was discussed in the late 1950s and early 1960s, it seems never to have been built (although there was some evidence, reported in the *New York Times* in 1994, that the Soviets *had* built such a system, which they called the "Dead Hand"). The United States preferred to rely on arrangements that suggested it was prepared for almost automatic retaliation in the event of an attack ("launch on warning") but which nonetheless incorporated numerous safeguards that would allow an attack to be called off at the very last moment. This became somewhat more problematic as missiles replaced bombers as the mainstay of the nuclear force, because they, once launched, cannot be recalled (a point over which President Reagan once stumbled).

A few strategists thought even this very small degree of human intervention to be too much. During the latter half of the 1970s, for example, hard-line analysts such as Paul Nitze argued that the Soviet Union had acquired a large enough number of highly accurate ICBMs to allow it to launch a surprise attack against the United States. In the process, the Soviets could destroy virtually all of the United States's land-based retaliatory force, yet still hold enough ICBMs in reserve to threaten another precise attack on U.S. targets and cities *after an American retaliatory strike*. Inasmuch as bombers and sea-based missiles were not sufficiently accurate to destroy the remaining Soviet ICBMs, the United States would have no choice but to surrender, without war, to a simple Soviet *threat* to attack with its missiles (Nitze, 1976-77).

For such skeptics, the answer was to build a "hard-target first strike capability" that would communicate to the Soviet Union the American ability—if not the intent—to match Moscow threat-for-threat. The instrument of this strategy was what was first called the "MX"—for "Missile Experimental"—and later dubbed the "Peacekeeper" by the Reagan administration.[6] Each MX was designed to carry ten nuclear warheads of sufficient accuracy and yield to destroy Soviet ICBMs in their silos, thereby placing the Soviet missile force at risk. Putting so many eggs into one basket meant, however, that the MX missiles could not be held back for retaliatory purposes. They would be quickly destroyed in a nuclear first strike by Soviet ICBMs.

This apparent vulnerability led to yet another dilemma. Strong political opposition emerged to a deterrent strategy premised on a hair-trigger threat. The proffered solution was, therefore, to make it more difficult to target and destroy the MX missiles. Either they would be put in silos that were highly resistant to nuclear blast—something almost impossible to accomplish—or they would be mobile so that, in a crisis, they could be moved around with their location unobservable by satellite (something like the B-52s on airborne alert).

The Carter administration opted for mobility, and proposed to put the MX on railcars or truck trailers that could be shuttled around special "race-tracks" built in Nevada and Utah. Needless to say, the solution was not a very elegant one, and the citizens of those two states were not very enamoured of the idea. In the end, the problem of MX vulnerability could not be solved at reasonable political or monetary cost, and the missiles were put into vulnerable Minuteman III silos scattered around the Great Plains, where many remain to this day.

And what became of nuclear deterrence? Because the technology would not cooperate, the Reagan administration found it necessary to fall back on rhetoric. In place of deploying nuclear weapons in a threatening fashion, members of the Reagan administration were deployed to engage in threatening nuclear discourse. For example, testifying before the Senate Foreign Relations Committee in 1982, Secretary of Defense Casper Weinberger argued that

⨍ To deter successfully, we must be able—*and must be seen to be able*—to retaliate against any potential aggressor in such a manner that the costs we will exact will substantially exceed any gains he might hope to achieve through aggression. We, for our part, are under no illusions about the consequences of a nuclear war: we believe there would be no winners in such a war. But this recognition on *our* part is not sufficient to ensure effective deterrence or to prevent the outbreak of war: it is essential that the Soviet leadership understands this as well (Weinberger, 1982: 2-3; first emphasis added).

People such as T. K. Jones, a briefly notorious Boeing engineer, then-vice president George Bush, and other politicians, policymakers, and pundits spoke of nuclear war as something that could be fought and survived (Scheer, 1982). Some tried to give the impression, as well, that nuclear war was a viable option in the event of conflict with the Soviet Union. They argued that the Kremlin valued its weapons more than its people and would have no qualms about using rather than losing its nukes (Gray and Payne, 1980). It was no wonder that the American public became nervous, or that films depicting the onset and consequences of nuclear war stirred so much controversy.

~~~
~~~

Will the Survivors Envy the Dead?

The Day After (ABC Television, 1983, 126 min.)
Director: Nicholas Meyer
Cast: Jason Robards, JoBeth Williams, John Lithgow, Steve Gutenberg

Testament (Entertainment Events/American Playhouse, 1983, 90 min.)
Director: Lynn Littman
Cast: Jane Alexander, William Devane, Kevin Costner, Rebecca De Mornay

Berlin is heating up again, only this time there are uprisings, riots, and, finally, war between East and West. *The Day After,* set largely in Lawrence, Kansas, amid fields of wheat and nuclear-armed intercontinental ballistic missiles, is as loud, graphic, and chilling a nuclear war film as one is ever likely to see. The special effects are impressive. People are vaporized, buildings incinerated, cars thrown through the air, cities leveled (much of this is, by now, a familiar special effects staple of end-of-the-world films; it was not in 1983). Most of the movie, broadcast as a two-part mini-series on network television, tells the stories of Dr. Russell Oaks (Robards) and others as they struggle to come through the aftermath of a nuclear attack. Many of the survivors die and those who are not are horribly injured. The film ends with Russell returning to the radioactive rubble of his home in Kansas City. There he is welcomed by squatters warming themselves in front of what is left of his fireplace. Russell, we are left to assume, is not long for the world. Whether anyone else will live to envy the dead is left to the viewer's imagination.

By contrast, *Testament* is a quiet film and offers no special effects at all (indeed, the only indication of a nuclear detonation is a brilliant flash seen through a living room window). The story is set in a small California town somewhere north of San Francisco. The central characters constitute an ordinary family of five. Catastrophe strikes without warning or explanation; it simply happens. One day, as the mother (Alexander) and children are watching TV, transmission from the East Coast ceases. A few minutes later, the blinding light appears and San Francisco goes off the air. And then, for a few moments, things return (almost) to normal.

Neighbors wander into the street, asking each other "what has happened?" even though it is pretty obvious. The rest of the film shows how life continues, and ends, under a radioactive cloud. The father (Devane), delayed in the city, is dead. One by one, the town's residents die of radiation poisoning. The mother loses two of her children. The viewer is left to wonder whether or not she and her remaining son will survive.

Although *Testament* was released in theaters, and was a superior piece of work (Alexander received an Academy Award nomination for her role), it garnered much less attention than *The Day After*, which was heavily publicized on TV. Perhaps *Testament* was too introspective; perhaps it was too close to home. In *The Day After*, there are survivors and heroes, but the sheer desperation of the living occupies the mind. In *Testament*, there are no heroes. Just people, whose loved ones die, one by one. Makes you think. No one, it seems, likes depressing movies.

∿∿∿

Who, Then, Will Save Us?

For more than forty-five years, the nuclear dilemma left people grasping for answers. Throughout the decades of Cold War, there was a gut feeling that, sooner or later, nuclear weapons *would* be used. After all, there were so many of them and so few restraints on using them—or so it seemed. Yet, amid all of the many discussions that took place within successive U.S. administrations, the decision to use nukes was never made. Not that the temptation didn't arise. Years after the event, President Eisenhower's Air Force chief of staff, Nathan Twining, recalled ferocious debates over whether or not to relieve the besieged French garrison at Dien Bien Phu in North Vietnam (chapter 7):

> I still think it would have been a good idea [to have taken] three small tactical A-bombs—it's a fairly isolated area, Dien Bien Phu—no great town around there, only Communists and their supplies. You could take all day to drop a bomb, make sure you put it in the right place. No opposition. And clean those Commies out of there and the band could play the Marseillaise and the French would come marching out of Dien Bien Phu in fine shape. And those Commies would say, "Well, those guys might do this again to us. We'd better be careful." And we might not have had this problem we're facing in Vietman now had we dropped those small "A" weapons (quoted in Gaddis, 1982).

The weapons were not used then, nor during the several Berlin crises or in Korea or during the crises over Quemoy and Matsu or during the 1956 war in the Sinai or the 1962 Cuban Missile Crisis or in Vietnam or the 1973 Middle East war or at any other time. One might be forgiven for thinking that nuclear deterrence actually worked, that, as Thomas Hobbes claimed, men feared death more than anything else. But one might also think that there was an unreasonable degree of faith operating here, faith that human reason would always trump fear and loathing. Not everyone was so convinced; some sought solace in a different kind of faith.

~~~

God *Is* with Us!

Red Planet Mars (United Artists, 1952, 87 min.)
Director: Harry Horner
Cast: Herbert Berghof, Peter Graves, Andrea King, Marvin Miller

Red Planet Mars was based on a Broadway play of 1950. It is set in 1957. Chris Cronyn (Graves), an earnest young scientist, and his wife, Linda (King), are collaborators on a project to establish radio contact with Mars, using a device called the "hydrogen valve." This, according to Cronyn, "amplifies sound waves a thousand times" and thus makes it possible to broadcast over the thirty-five million miles separating the two planets (the screenwriters' grasp of physics is not a strong point of the film; sound cannot propagate through the interplanetary vacuum, and radio waves are electromagnetic). The hydrogen valve—obviously meant to echo the "hydrogen bomb"—is the design of a Nazi scientist, Franz Kaldor (Berghof). After the war, Kaldor was jailed by the Americans but escaped with the help of the Soviets. Cronyn found the diagrams for the valve "at Nuremberg."

As the film begins, the Cronyns have just seen photos of Mars, taken through the Mount Palomar telescope. The photos show the famous (non-existent) canals and the polar ice cap. Over the course of five days, the ice cap has melted and the canals filled with water. The photos clearly indicate the presence of a powerful civilization on Mars (although why, if they are so advanced, it has taken them until 1957 to get around to melting the icecaps is never made clear). Seeing the photos, Linda, who is also the mother of two young boys, becomes very worried about the consequences for humanity of making contact with Mars. She points out that, so far, science has simply made it possible for humans to destroy themselves. Chris, on the other hand, seeing nothing but scientific gain, dismisses her concerns. The Cronyns return to their lab in the San Diego Mountains to continue their work.

They have managed to contact Mars—they think—but have not yet found a way to send messages back and forth. Eventually they succeed, but the messages are so fantastic in their implications—Martians live 300 years, their agriculture is super-efficient, they derive all their energy needs from "cosmic radiation"—that the economy of the "Free World" collapses. Insurance companies cancel policies, farm prices collapse, coal mines close, steel mills stop operating, and unemployment soars. As the secretary of defense tells Cronyn, "you've done more damage to the Free World in a few days than the Communists have done in years."

But the situation is not so simple and the film is far from over. Franz Kaldor is still alive, in the pay of the Soviet Union, operating a radio transmitter high in the Andes. While he has not managed to contact Mars, he is able to hear the messages sent to and from the lab in California, and to send them on to his masters in the Kremlin. There, the Politburo debates whether to launch a nuclear attack on the West while it is in disarray. Unfortunately for the Soviets, the Martians are not yet finished with their messages.

After some days, during which the messages coming in cannot be translated, one arrives whose content bears a striking resemblance to Jesus' Sermon on the Mount. Successive messages also contain religious admonitions. As word of the messages' contents spreads throughout the world, a religious revival takes place. In the Soviet Union, aided and abetted by the Voice of America and clandestine radio sets, an uprising takes place. The Soviet government is overthrown, the Orthodox Patriarch becomes head of a provisional government, and Russia withdraws all its troops from Eastern Europe. The world gives thanks for this new era of hope and peace.

There is more. Chris and Linda, filled with new hope, return to their lab to try to reestablish contact with Mars after a nine-day silence. Suddenly, Franz Kaldor appears. His hut and equipment have been destroyed (nine days earlier) in an avalanche. He, however, has dug himself out and sneaked into the United States. He reveals to the Cronyns that the messages they received did not come from Mars, as everyone thought, but from him. He shows them his notebook as evidence. Kaldor, it seems, has been engaged in an elaborate plot to undermine the United States and the USSR, the two countries that he, as an unrepentant Nazi, hates the most. Crowing about his success, he compares himself to Lucifer in *Paradise Lost*, having defeated God where others failed.

As his final act of destruction—setting the two countries at each others' throats once again—he intends to reveal the fraud to the press, whom he has summoned to the lab. But Linda, looking at the notebook, points out to Kaldor that, although the initial messages were indeed fake, the later religious ones do not correspond to what is written in his notebook. Therefore, they must be from Mars. Kaldor shrugs this off, suggesting that the codebreakers in Washington fabricated the religious messages that which, in any event, were much more effective in undermining the Soviets than those he actually sent.

The Cronyns, seeing the chance of world peace slipping away, decide to blow up their lab, taking Kaldor and his secret with them. Linda opens the valve to a tank of hydrogen and asks Chris to light her cigarette. Before he does, a final message from Mars arrives, proving that the religious messages are, indeed, authentic. Kaldor is so enraged by this that he shoots the video screen. The hydrogen detonates and both Cronyns and Kaldor are killed. But the religious messages remain, and the world undergoes a spiritual transformation that ends the threat of nuclear annihilation.

(*Red Planet Mars* has never been remade but, for a close parallel, see *Contact*, directed by and starring Jodie Foster. *Contact* is based on a novel by Carl Sagan, who must have seen *Red Planet Mars* during the 1950s.)

Science or Salvation?

Given that nuclear use seemed inevitable to almost everyone (even if they did try to ignore the possibility), and that nuclear deterrence might fail, who or what could prevent the weapons from being used? *Red Planet Mars* offered one possibility. While the story seems absurd and not a little embarrassing to secular humanists, what is striking about *RPM* is the juxtaposition of the search for ultimate truths in either science or religion (a topic also explored in Walter Miller's 1959 novel, *A Canticle for Leibowitz*). Chris Cronyn is the epitome of the American scientist, a kind of con-temporary Thomas Edison. He is a lone inventor, working only with his wife (whose actual role in the operation, aside from throwing levers and mothering their children, is not very clear). Cronyn's primary allegiance is to the accumulation of knowledge, in the hope that it will lead to the betterment of mankind. For him, contact with Mars can provide only positive results.

Linda, his wife, has a different view of the matter. Even though she has worked with Chris for years, she has second thoughts about science in light of the development of nuclear weapons. For her, science has brought the world to the edge of the abyss, and further research is only likely to push it over. She believes that contact with Mars is folly and that only faith can provide a way out of the nuclear dilemma. More than this, she represents herself as the archetype of women around the world, whose primary concern is the safety of their children, and not the power or primacy of nations or the pursuit of knowledge. In the end, of course, Linda is proved right, although both she and Chris sacrifice themselves for their children and the greater good.

Ironically, perhaps, these two apparently conflicting perspectives— science vs. faith—are not as far apart as the authors, playwrights, and screenwriters might have us think. Chris Cronyn is searching for a set of scientific rules or laws that not only will solve the problems of humanity but also make them conduct their affairs in an orderly and predictable manner. If only people would follow science in their everyday lives, he seems to suggest, they would behave in a logical and rational manner. Harmony—akin to the "harmony of the spheres"—would automatically follow. Advanced civilizations can be based only on science and, therefore, they must know these rules. Certainly, having refrained from blowing themselves up for so many years, even though they use "cosmic" energy, the Martians must have discovered some scientific principle that prevents such an outcome.[6] The revelation of this principle should, instantaneously, bring peace and prosperity to Earth.

Linda, in contrast to Chris, believes that science cannot change what lies at the root of conflict and war: human nature. Hence, it is only through changing people's beliefs—consciousness raising, if you will—that they will change the way they behave. Nations, however, have cast their lot with science and ceased to believe in the eternal verities. The religious messages thus play the role of a literal deus ex machina—"god in the machine"— delivered through the devilish invention of Lucifer embodied in the Nazi Franz Kaldor. The revelation of *these* principles does, almost instantaneously, bring peace to Earth—the peace of the grave.

While *Fail-Safe* does not bring God into the picture, groundless faith nonetheless is central to the book, which centers on the whole issue of human responsibility in the nuclear age. The president argues that the accidental elimination of Moscow is the fault of the fail-safe system, but observes that

> This disappearance of human responsibility is one of the most disturbing aspects of the whole thing. It's as if human beings had evaporated, and their place was taken by computers. And all day you and I have sat here, fighting, not each other, but rather this big rebellious computerized system, struggling to keep it from blowing up the world . . . Somehow these computerized systems have got to be brought under control.

Khrushchev agrees and a new day of peace dawns.

It would be too simplistic, however, to leave it at that. As we saw earlier, it was (and is) precisely the automaticity of the system that, according to the strategic analysts, helps to reinforce nuclear deterrence. More than that, the risk of triggering an event such as that depicted in *Fail-Safe* is an integral part of the doctrine. Indeed, not only does the system work as intended, it works almost too well. But there is more to it than even this: The reliance on technology to reinforce nuclear deterrence also helps to "naturalize" the doctrine and eliminate all political considerations. Paradoxically, then, the destruction of the two cities in *Fail-Safe* virtually becomes an "act of Nature" (or God).

By treating deterrence as something akin to a physical "law," we attribute to it clocklike characteristics with which we cannot, and should not, interfere, except at great costs to our security (precisely Hobbes's argument in *Leviathan*). At that point, all politics, all conflict over means and ends, all debates about morality disappear and any questions about whether we should threaten nuclear war as a means of "keeping the peace" are silenced by the very existence of the system. Created by men, it is now greater than men (see D. F. Jones, *Colossus*). Should we question it, we signal a less-than-full determination to resist the enemy and thereby undermine our commitment to wage nuclear war should it become "necessary."

Such a process of "naturalization" is not limited only to questions of nuclear deterrence, of course; arguing that markets, left to themselves, operate at greatest efficiency and produce the most desirable outcomes, is another means of avoiding difficult political questions. In letting "Nature" run its course, we are doing nothing else than putting our faith in forces beyond our power to influence or change, and hoping that no one will argue with the outcome.

Watching *Red Planet Mars* from the perspective of a half-century later, we laugh at the seemingly naive and simplistic notion of Jesus on Mars; reading *Fail-Safe*, we quail at the thought of applying biblical injunctions to horrific accidents. Yet, the complexity of the nuclear dilemma—and the apparent unacceptability of political compromise with the Soviets—made the search for solutions, whether scientific or religious, all the more poignant and pointless. Ronald Reagan's promise of a shield that would make ballistic missiles impotent—a shield whose realization was dependent on the discovery of scientific (natural) principles as yet unrevealed—was no more and no less than an appeal to the same kind of faith.

There is nothing new about this; it is a hope that goes back thousands of years. Gershon Scholem once observed that the followers of orthodox Judaism relied on laws and tradition for social stability and progress, while believers of what he called the "messianic impulse" hoped for "[T]ran-scendence breaking in upon history, an intrusion in which history itself perishes, transformed into ruins because it is struck by a beam of light shining into it from an outside source (Scholem, 1971:10, quoted in Lilla, 1995: 38). So it would seem to be with nukes. Whether the laws come from science *or* religion, the goal remains a sort of "naturalized" salvation that converts through its irresistible logic and renders politics irrelevant.

The fear of global nuclear holocaust has, to a large degree, vanished since 1991. Although their numbers are declining, both the United States and Russia still possess large stocks of nuclear missiles ready to launch at a moment's notice. Still, we are much less obsessed with the robustness of our nuclear deterrence or concerned with our nuclear credibility being undermined by questions about our commitment. Instead, our leaders warn us of nuclear "rogues" and "terrorists" who, if they acquire the bomb, will hardly hesitate to use it, as if they lack control, discrimination, and comprehension (Lipschutz, 1999). Such people are, quite naturally, un-controlled, unpredictable, and probably crazy. We talk about defenses against the missiles sent off by these countries and individuals, but we also worry about truck and suitcase bombs. If these worries have any basis in reality, who will save us from them?

Chapter 6

The Final Frontier

Who You Calling Ugly?

Ever since the film version of *The Ugly American* was released in the early 1960s, the term has been used to describe a type of especially odious U.S. citizen who travels abroad, speaks loudly, and exhibits high levels of insensitivity to the feelings and cultural mores of non-Americans. It is of some interest to note, therefore, that the eponymous hero of the 1958 book of the same name, written by William Lederer and Eugene Burdick (the latter a co-author of *Fail-Safe*), *was* ugly. He was also ingenious, insightful, and sensitive although, as he and others like him were to discover, these elements of character were not highly valued by the representatives of American power in foreign lands.

Constantin Costa-Gavras's film *State of Siege* was released in 1972. The central character in that movie *was* an American, although, played by Yves Montand, he was far from ugly. Still, the activities in which he engaged, on behalf of the United States, were quite ugly. And he had a particularly ugly way of shrugging off responsibility for the things he had done.

The Lederer and Burdick book was largely fictional, albeit "based on fact," according to the authors. It suggested that Americans could and should have at heart the best interests of those whom they had come to help. This was the best way, the authors argued through their vignettes, to prevent the spread of communism in Asia and defeat it where it had already appeared. The Costa-Gavras film was based on a true incident, and it indicated exactly whose interests the United States was concerned about when it became involved in the Third World.

In a sense, these two works span the period during which American concerns about the Third World were most intense but the least sensitive. It was also approximately the period during which the attitudes of the American public went from idealism to cynicism, from the New Frontier to

Watergate. In his inaugural address in 1961, President Kennedy pointed to developing countries as the central arena of global politics and called on Americans to help these countries help themselves; by 1973, as we saw earlier, President Nixon's secretary of state, Henry Kissinger, could say about the CIA-assisted coup in Chile, "I don't see why we need stand by and watch a country go communist due to the irresponsibility of its own government" (quoted in McCormick, 1989: 186).

Between these years the disaster in Vietnam took place (it is the subject of chapter 7). There was, of course, no shortage of U.S. interventions during the 1960s, but it was also the era of the Peace Corps, the Alliance for Progress, and a kind of hope for the country's and world's prospects that, in the United States at least, has not been seen since. The American relationship to the developing countries (or "rising peoples," as Kennedy put it) was not of much concern to the popular media, although it was reported regularly in the news. The question that was never satisfactorily answered—then as now—was why need there be a relationship at all? Why did developing countries matter? And what would happen if the United States did not pay attention to them? To account for this interest, we need to go back to the late 1940s, to be "present at the creation," as Dean Acheson put it in the title of his memoirs (Acheson, 1969).

Development for Whom?

In his inaugural address on January 20, 1949, President Truman proposed what was to become known as "Point Four" (it was the fourth point in his speech). As Julius Caesar did with Gaul, Truman divided the world into three parts: Free, Communist, and "underdeveloped." He said

> We must embark on a bold new program making the benefits of our scientific advances and industrial programs available for the improvement and growth of underdeveloped areas. . . . The old imperialism—exploitation for foreign profits—has no place in our plans. What we envisage is a program of development based on the concepts of democratic fair dealing (quoted in Esteva, 1992: 6).[1]

Truman's concern, as well as that of his advisers and the entire American economic and political elite, was that the world not collapse back into the Depression of the 1930s, which many still feared might happen. More than this, the United States wanted to prevent a return to a situation in which much of the world outside of Europe and North America came under the control of European empires, as had been the case before World

War II. Were the imperial powers to fully reclaim their rule over their colonies, the United States might well be denied access to their raw materials and markets, which were essential to American as well as global prosperity.

The reasons for European expansion into what was later called the "Third World" were, to a large degree, economic (although imperial glory was not irrelevant). The raw materials and commodities needed for industrial expansion, including rubber, tin, tungsten, oil, copra, and sisal, came in growing quantities from colonies in various regions, especially Asia. The potential markets in these colonies were also seen as important. This is what inspired Western penetration of China and Southeast Asia in the nineteenth century, and it remains true today. One hundred years ago, the belief was that, if it were possible to sell each Chinese a pin, a thimble, a button, or a spool of thread, one could become fabulously wealthy (today, the items are computers, VCRs, CDs, and software).

Looking to the future, China could become an immense market for manufactured goods from Europe and America. This would help to reduce the problem of surplus capacity that, at the turn of the nineteenth century, was beginning to bedevil relations within Europe. Nonetheless, while Britain, France, Germany, Russia, and other Western countries established commercial concessions in China under treaties of extraterritoriality during the late 1800s, China's market potential never came to fruition. This did not, of course, prevent the West from continuing to think of China in such terms—although today it is China that sells buttons, thimbles, and VCRs to the rest of the world.

If the economic importance of the colonial world was built on the foundations of Western activities in those regions during the century prior to 1914, the bases for the Cold War responses were put in place during the 1930s. During that decade, for example, Japan sought to create an economic domain in East Asia, the Greater East Asia Co-Prosperity Sphere (Feis, 1950). The establishment of a Japanese puppet state in Chinese Manchuria—called Manchukuo by Japan—was seen in Europe and the United States as the second element (after Korea and Taiwan) in an Asian empire that would, ultimately, exclude the Western powers from all of Asia (a fear that is today projected onto the People's Republic of China).

All of the imperial powers, including the United States, had a real or imagined stake in preventing this. The Europeans, in particular, depended heavily on commodities from their Asian colonies as a means of earning dollars from the United States via "triangular trade." Japan's program of military and economic expansion threatened *their* empires. In the end, war came and Japan lost.

Having invested so much blood and money defeating Japan, there was no way that the United States would walk away from Asia after the end of World War II. Asia, rife with instability and conflict, was not, however, the same place it had been in 1930. There was a civil war underway in China, between the Guomintang, or Nationalists, and the Communists. The two had been temporary allies for the purpose of fighting Japan, but they were now at each other's throats (Tuchman, 1970; Pepper, 1999). There were insurrections throughout the European colonial territories, in India, Burma, British Malaya, Indochina, and the Philippines. All were aimed at driving out the colonial powers and achieving independence. It was in these areas that the European powers were showing themselves most insensitive to the political consequences of colonialism. And the United States, given the choice between "self-determination" for a colony and support for a European ally, rarely failed to choose the latter.

Finally, it was in Asia that communism appeared to be making major inroads. The anti-imperial revolts in the colonies were often described, somewhat inaccurately, as "communist-inspired." While it is true that Communist groups of one sort or another were often deeply involved in the rebellions, this was not the main reason that they were taking place. There was little interest in Moscow, either strategic or ideological, for supporting these revolts if they were not under Soviet control.

By 1950, therefore, the "underdeveloped areas" were seen as crucial in the developing global battle between East and West, but the American response was framed in economic, rather than political, terms. Poverty and revolution were inextricably linked in this view; as Dwight Eisenhower wrote in his wartime memoirs, "Wherever popular discontent is found or group oppression or mass poverty or the hunger of children, there Communism may stage an offensive that arms cannot counter. Discontent can be fanned into revolution, and revolution into social chaos" (Eisenhower, 1948: 476-77, quoted in Lipschutz, 1989: 138).

The solution, according to this line of thought, was to foster the conditions under which foreign investment and development could take place without the political inconvenience of independence. Once this happened, and economic growth was taking off throughout a society, went the argument, people would have enough to eat, a place to live, a job, and the opportunity to purchase goods and gadgets—made in the United States, of course. Finding themselves in a position to emulate American lifestyles, the peoples of the underdeveloped regions would automatically choose to ally with the West. As a 1951 study by the National Security Council put it,

> Point IV is not only a significant economic program, but also must be regarded as an important political and psychological measure on the theory that economic progress and better living conditions as well as the cooper-

ative methods of technical assistance at the "village level" by which these results are sought, will promote political stability and popular morale, create attitudes favorable to the United States and render the people of the underdeveloped countries less susceptible to communist subversion (NSC, 1951: 2-3, quoted in Lipschutz, 1989: 125).

Up to this point—circa 1950—the Western response to colonial rebellions had been to meet force with force. The United States was itself faced with such a rebellion in the Philippines, a former colony. The archipelago was granted independence in 1946, but remained a strategic dependency in respect to the twenty-three military bases (under ninety-nine-year leases) that the United States retained there. During the late 1940s, a Communist-led uprising, under the Hukbalahaps, swept through the islands. Filipino army and police forces were unable to suppress the revolt, inasmuch as many local authorities and military personnel were either affiliated with or sympathetic to the Huks. Many in the United States believed a Huk victory would be a disaster; as a 1950 report from the U.S. Joint Chiefs of Staff put it:

> From the viewpoint of the USSR, the Philippine Islands could be the key to Soviet control of the Far East inasmuch as Soviet domination of these islands would, in all probability, be followed by the rapid disintegration of the entire structure of anti-Communist defenses in Southeast Asia and their offshore island chain, including Japan. Therefore, the situation in the Philippines cannot be viewed as a local problem, since Soviet domination over these islands would endanger the United States [sic] military position in the Western Pacific and the Far East (NSC-84, 1950: 2-3, quoted in Lipschutz, 1989: 103).

It seems not to have occurred to the authors of this document that the Huks might have no connections at all with the Soviets.

In 1950, the CIA sent an Air Force intelligence officer, Colonel Edward Lansdale, into the Philippines with orders to set the situation right. Lansdale developed a close relationship with Ramón Magsaysay, an articulate and, by most accounts, honest individual who had accepted the position of Philippine secretary of defense at this most inopportune moment. Under Lansdale's tutelage, Magsaysay turned the military into a much more efficient institution, reduced its internal corruption, and convinced much of the country's population that the government could serve the people's interests. By 1953, with Lansdale's advice and U.S. assistance, the Huk rebellion was broken (Lansdale, 1972). A few years later, Magsaysay was elected president of the country, but he died in a plane crash not long after that. Subsequently, the Philippines went back to being what it had been. New insurgencies developed, and they continue until the present day.

Thus, even as the CIA covertly helped to engineer coups in Iran and Guatemala, the tactics pioneered by Lansdale were offered as a low-cost alternative to direct intervention. And while the restoration of "order" in the Philippines was by no means a nonviolent affair, it was accomplished largely through the offices of domestic actors rather than foreign ones. This approach was especially attractive to Washington. Not only was it less costly, it did not require the commitment of U.S. troops to battle. Still, while the Philippines seemed secure, the rest of Asia was not and, when Lansdale's approach to "nation-building" was tried in South Vietnam, it failed (chapter 7).

In the final analysis, and in spite of the lofty pronouncements of Point Four and associated agencies of economic development, the 1950s were much more the Decade of Europe than the Third World. It was during this period that the Marshall Plan became the "Mutual Security Agency," whose primary function was the provision of military arms and aid to America's European allies (making major contributions to the dollar-gold dilemma described in chapter 4). Not until late in the decade, when many of Europe's colonial territories had or were about to gain their independence, and Southeast Asia was beginning to heat up, did the "underdeveloped areas" appear, once again, on the American radar screen.

⋙

Ugly Is in the Eye of the Beholder

The Ugly American, William Lederer and Eugene Burdick (New York: Norton, 1958)

The Ugly American presents a series of semifictional vignettes about the experiences of Americans in Southeast Asia—Burma, Vietnam, and a mythical country called "Sarkhan," a thinly disguised version of Thailand—during the 1950s. All three countries are described as targets of the Communists. Vietnam, having been the focus of a war between the French colonial forces and the Viet Minh, is threatened once again by the same forces. Burma is subject to internal subversion. Sarkhan seems to be menaced by both domestic forces and external ones. Lederer and Burdick juxtapose blundering, foolish American diplomats, military officers, and journalists—most of whom they describe as mediocre and "second-rate"—against manipulative, sensitive Russian ones, who are careful to learn the languages and cultural practices of the countries to which they are posted. In this matchup, the

Russians win hands down.

But there is another kind of American, according to the authors, one who might not be as well trained as his or her Russian counterpart, but whose Yankee ingenuity and honesty cannot help but impress the "natives." These are engineers who build their own machines, farmers who get their hands dirty, priests who go out into the "boondocks" to deal directly with the people, and soldiers who carefully read Mao in order to successfully confront the Communist guerillas. Each in his own way trusts the people with whom he deals, and each is trusted in return. Such Americans are the greatest threat to Communist blandishments, claim Lederer and Burdick, for their efforts demonstrate that the Communists seek only power and control, while the Americans are concerned for people's health, welfare, and happiness (i.e., life, liberty, and property).

At every turn, however, these "common" Americans are undone, not by their Communist opponents *but by their own countrymen.* The diplomats remain isolated in their embassies and refuse to learn the local language or eat the local food. They do not want to sweat or get out of their automobiles. They do not want to upset the government authorities or cause political trouble. They do not want to support small, cheap projects that improve locals' well-being. They do want to support the big, visible projects requiring large quantities of American capital but which benefit only the rich, powerful, and corrupt.

Chapters 1, 5, and 8 relate the story of "Lucky, Lucky Lou" Sears, an ex-congressman who is now U.S. ambassador to Sarkhan. Sears is highly insensitive to the locals and only seeks a cushy sinecure until such time as he can snare a judgeship back in the United States. In chapter 1, we also meet John Colvin, a believer in powdered milk, who runs afoul of the local Communists but refuses to surrender. Chapter 2 is about another "Lucky, Lucky Lou." This one is Louis Krupitzyn, the Russian ambassador to Sarkhan, who represents the best the Soviets have to offer. Not only does he speak the language, he also respects the religion (unheard of for Communists!). And he is a true subversive, using his position to put the Americans in the worst possible light.

In chapter 3, we read about Father Finian, who organizes an anti-Communist campaign in rural Burma. Chapter 4 introduces us to Ruth Jyoti, a crusading Southeast Asian newspaper editor and publisher. She is sent on an all-expenses-paid trip to the United States, where she is less than overwhelmed by Americans' apparent naiveté about Asia. Chapters 6 and 7 offer an object lesson on the low quality of the women and men recruited to work in U.S. embassies. Chapter 9 and 21 are about Lucky Lou Sears's replacement as U.S. ambassador to Sarkhan, Gilbert MacWhite. He learns that the local Chinese, and especially his servants, may be spies for the Communists in Beijing. In spite of his desire to do good, MacWhite is eventually recalled to the United States for his efforts.

Chapter 10 introduces the reader to Colonel "Edwin B. Hillendale," modeled on Edward Lansdale and his successful efforts to suppress the Huk rebellion in the Philippines. Hillendale reappears in chapter 15, as well, trying to repeat his Philippine success in Sarkhan. Chapters 11 to 12 are about the French failure in North Vietnam, and the authors recommend that the U.S. military read Mao very carefully before taking up the fight in South Vietnam. Chapter 13 relates a dinner conversation between an U Maung Swe, a Burmese journalist, and an unidentified American, in which U.S. failures in the region are discussed. Chapters 14, 16, and 20 relate the good intentions of visiting American engineers, military men, and politicians, and the ways in which they are foiled in their efforts by local American bureaucrats. Finally, Chapters 17, 18, and 19 are about the "Ugly American," his wife, and a Sarkhanese colleague, who successfully develop cheap, inexpensive methods of doing age-old painful tasks, but whose successes generally go unnoticed.

Got Milk?

The Ugly American appeared only a few years after the establishment of South Vietnam in 1956, during a period when the Eisenhower administration's commitment to protecting that country was beginning to come under question (see chapter 7). The book represented Lederer and Burdick's effort to illustrate to the American public how the United States might successfully stop communism in Asia, and it purported to explain why, without a change in approach, failure was a certainty. "[I]f such things [as we describe in this book] continue to happen," warn Lederer and Burdick in "A Factual Epilogue," "they will multiply into a pattern of disaster" (1958: 271).

Funding big projects would not be enough, they argue. Such showcases attract publicity but, if they do not benefit the people, they will not be of much use in the campaign to defeat communism. Yet, in their observations, the authors reveal a surprising lack of political insight:

> The result [of our current policies] is that we often develop huge technical complexes which some day may pay dividends but which at this moment in Asian development are neither needed nor wanted *except by a few local politicians who see such projects as a means to power and wealth.* . . . We pay for huge highways through jungles in Asian lands where there is no transport except bicycle and foot. We finance dams where the greatest immediate need is a portable pump. We provide many millions of dollars' worth of military equipment which wins no wars and raises no standard of living (Lederer and Burdick, 1958: 281-82; emphasis added).

That the United States might have an *economic* interest in such projects, that influential American corporations might be highly dependent on these grandiose projects, rather than small, helpful ones, is suggested only in passing.

> If the only price we are willing to pay is the dollar price, then we might as well pull out before we're thrown out. If we are not prepared to pay the human price, we had better retreat to our shores, build Fortress America, lean to live without international trade and communications, and accept the mediocrity, the low standard of living, and the loom [sic] of world Communism which would accompany such a move (Lederer and Burdick, 1958: 284).

Curiously, the authors never clearly articulate the rationale for an American commitment of the type they propose, except that the failure to do so will lead, inevitably, to the victory of communism. There is a sense, moreover, in which, in the telling of their stories, they invert liberal arguments on behalf of democracy and markets and turn dialectical materialism on its head: The Communists advocate powerful ideas, while the Americans provide only needed material goods. Thus, when John Colvin, the powdered milk man, struggles with his wartime Sarkhanese friend Deong, he says "I'm not in politics, I'm just trying to organize a milk distribution center for your country."

To this, Deong replies, "John, powdered milk and cattle are part of politics and therefore part of history. . . . If you get this crazy milk and cattle scheme of yours going, it could in time change the economic balance in Sarkhan."

"What's wrong with that?" asks Colvin. "That's what I want to do." To this, Deong replies that Colvin is "the wrong person," since he is an American. Colvin realizes suddenly that Deong is a Communist.

When Colvin asks why his friend has "gone over," Deong replies that the Americans can't win: "You've done nothing but lose since the end of the war. And for a simple reason: *you don't know the power of an idea*. The clerks you send over here try to buy us like cattle" (Lederer and Burdick, 1958: 23-24; emphasis added).

In the chapter that follows this one, Lederer and Burdick try to illustrate why "ideas" are more powerful than material well-being. There, Father Finian organizes a small group of Burmese peasants in a propaganda campaign against the local Communist organization. Why are so many Burmese enthralled by this foreign ideology, he wonders? Not because the ideas are powerful but, according to Finian's followers "[M]any Burmese are for the Communists because they think the Communists will do good things for the people . . . for the peasants and cheap-pay workers. Give us land and more food and maybe automobiles and radios and cheap medicine."

Father Finian, who believes that communism is "the face of the devil . . . put on earth to test again the morality of men," convinces his followers that the most important thing is not food but, "a country where any man may worship and live as he wishes" (Lederer and Burdick, 1958: 57, 47, 55). And, so, they go to work to subvert the Communists. Yet, the entire message of the book is that it is the "little things," the material necessities that, supplied through cheap and inventive means, will win over the hearts and minds of the Asian masses (recall thimbles, spools, and shoelaces).

In the final analysis, although Lederer and Burdick's message was widely received in the United States—as of 1965, the book had sold over three million copies—it was as confused as anything coming out of Washington. If we truly believed in the power of ideas, why did we have the right to impose our ideas on other people and invade when they did not accept those ideas (as Kissinger appeared to believe)? And if we truly believed that the way to a person's vote was through his or her stomach, did it really matter what anyone believed? In the end, the United States came to believe, the power of persuasion could not match the power of the gun.

$$\stackrel{\sim\sim\sim}{\sim\sim\sim}$$

To the "Lands of the Rising People"

On January 21, 1961, a mere twelve years after Truman's proclamation of Point Four, the American public listened to John F. Kennedy issue *his* call to arms. As Kennedy put it in his inaugural address, "Let every nation know, whether it wishes us well or ill, that we shall pay any price, bear any burden, meet any hardship, support any friend, oppose any foe, in order to assure the survival and success of liberty" (quoted in Ambrose, 1991: 181).

For Kennedy, the Third World was the critical arena of ideological competition. On January 1, 1959, insurgent forces under the leadership of Fidel Castro entered Havana, replacing the old, corrupt pro-American regime of Fulgencio Batista and, eventually, confiscating U.S.-owned properties. Not long after, the Chinese Communists had made clear their belief that "revolutionary wars" would sweep through the Third World. And, on January 6, 1961, Premier Khrushchev, in competition with the Peoples Republic of China, declared that the Soviet Union would actively support "wars of national liberation" in the developing world, too.[2] In Washington, his speech was seen as a gauntlet thrown down, a challenge that must be met lest the United States show itself to be, as the Chinese later claimed, a "paper tiger."

Ten days later, in his first State of the Union Address, Kennedy pinpointed developing countries as the place where East-West confrontation would occur: "The great battleground for the defense and expansion of freedom today is the whole southern half of the globe . . . the lands of the rising people" (quoted in Ambrose, 1991: 183). Ten weeks later, the world watched the CIA-sponsored debacle at the Bay of Pigs. It was a failure not only so far as its immediate objective—the overthrow of Castro—was concerned but also a disaster in terms of U.S. diplomacy toward the rest of Latin America. Relations had nowhere to go but up, but, after the Bay of Pigs, they immediately went down.

The American relationship with Latin America had long been an uncomfortable one; as the old saying went, "Ah, poor Mexico: so far from God, so close to the United States!" During World War II, the United States made no bones about these countries being both critical and secure sources of strategic materials as well as the location of the Panama Canal and a southern bulwark of America's Caribbean defense. Any Latin American country that made even the slightest overtures toward the Axis powers instantly came under U.S. scrutiny and pressure. Little changed in this regard after 1945. As the Cold War developed, the strategic/economic relationship between Latin America and the United States remained central, with Americans on the lookout for any incipient radicalism that might threaten U.S. investments there (as seen in chapter 4).

Given foreign investment, the demand for raw materials, and the availability of various market opportunities, the Latin American economies grew. But as the economies of the Latin American countries grew, so did the domestic gap between rich and poor. Emulating the American system of higher education, the university system was expanded. This led, however, to rapid growth in the size of the intelligentsia. Between the poor and the young educated classes, there was ample fuel for the fires of leftist radicalism.[3]

Progress for Whom?

In 1958, Vice President Nixon and his wife, on a visit to Caracas, Venezuela, and several other countries in the region, were set upon by angry mobs and attacked with stones and eggs. The level of rage at the United States throughout Latin America came as a complete surprise to Washington, which had not been paying much attention to the region. In an effort to defuse further outbreaks of violence, and in response to a proposal earlier made by the president of Brazil, President Eisenhower quickly agreed to the establishment of an Inter-American Development Bank, capitalized at $1 billion. The bank would provide loans throughout the region that would, it was hoped, foster greater economic growth and stifle demands for radical change. Even in the late 1950s, however, $1 billion did not go very far. Furthermore, investment and economic growth would not begin to address the structural inequities that fostered revolution in countries such as Cuba.

Thus, by the time he took office, Kennedy faced the prospect of revolution spreading throughout Latin America. He, too, placed his faith in economics and markets (although he also invested in regional militaries). In March 1961, he announced the establishment of the "Alliance for Progress," intended solely for the Western Hemisphere. To this program, proclaimed Kennedy, the United States would commit $20 billion over a ten-year period, to be matched by $80 billion in investment from within the Latin American countries during the same ten years (LaFeber, 1993: 215). The American funds would be provided through the newly established U.S. Agency for International Development (USAID), successor to the old Mutual Security Agency. The expectation was that such investment would increase the economic growth rate and address growing popular dissatisfactions that threatened political stability throughout the region (Packenham, 1973).

Alas, this was not to be. Not only did the Alliance for Progress fail in its economic goals but it also proved unsuccessful in its political ones. Between 1961 and 1966, nine Latin American regimes were overthrown by their militaries (LaFeber, 1993: 216), generally under the claim that they were dallying with communism. In some countries, such as Brazil, the coups took place with American connivance. In 1965, the U.S. Marines intervened in fighting in the Dominican Republic to ensure, as claimed by President Johnson and others, that elements "friendly" to Castro did not take power. Finally, the financial contribution promised to the Alliance for Progress by the United States was never delivered in its entirety, nor were the Latin American countries able to provide their commitment.

As has often been the case with such aid schemes, moreover, the Alliance for Progress proved to be more of a boon to the already rich than to the poor. Its funds were made available as loans and investment capital, rather than as outright grants. Therefore, access to them was dependent on an individual's or corporation's credit rating or political connections, rather than need or rate of return. Beyond this, there was ample opportunity to tap into the flow of funds through a variety of extra-legal and illegal methods, with the inevitable result that much of the money was never applied where it was intended or needed. Consequently, the gap between rich and poor only got wider. And this, in turn, simply exacerbated the precarious political situations in these countries and fostered further challenges.

~~~
~~~

Siege of State

State of Siege (Cinema 5, 1972, 119 min.)
Director: (Constantin) Costa-Gavras
Cast: Yves Montand, O. E. Hasse

State of Siege is what would today be called a "docudrama." As noted in this chapter's introduction, the film draws on real events and is only fictionalized in terms of dialogue and the insertion of characters. One of these is the veteran newspaperman Carlos Ducas (Hasse, who plays the German spy in *The Big Lift*), spokesman and interrogator for a kind of journalistic Greek chorus. Set in Montevideo, Uruguay, the film tells the story of the kidnapping and execution of USAID official, Philip Michael Santoré (Montand) by the Tupamaros, an urban guerilla movement made up largely of middle-class intellectuals and blue-collar workers. Santoré is modeled on Dan A. Mitrone, an actual USAID official who was kidnapped and executed by the Tupamaros in 1970.

As the film begins, Santoré is found dead in the back seat of a stolen car. In a series of flashbacks, the film shows how he is kidnapped and spirited to a Tupamaro hideout, the "People's Prison," where he is interrogated by one of the guerillas. During the questioning, Santoré claims that he is assigned to work with local police on "traffic" problems. As the interrogation proceeds, however, we discover that he has had an extended career of advising police in other countries—such as Brazil and the Dominican Republic—where military coups have taken place.

It soon becomes clear that, not only is Santoré not a traffic cop, he has been deeply involved in training Latin American police in tactics of repression and torture, all for the purpose of imposing and maintaining civil order in those countries. And why? As Santoré puts it to Hugo, his interrogator, "You are subversive. You're Communists. You work for the ruination of our society, the values that uphold civilization and Christianity, the Free World's very way of life. You're enemies to be fought and beaten in every way."

The Tupamaros attempt to exchange Santoré's safety and freedom for that of several of their fellows, held as political prisoners in Uruguayan jails. But the capture of a number of Tupamaros and the execution of several others put paid to this plan. Finally, Santoré is condemned by a tribunal of guerillas. Rather than endanger themselves by meeting together, each tribunal member climbs aboard a city bus, casts his or her vote, and then gets off at the next stop (one of the tribunal members is a policeman). The film closes with

Santoré's replacement arriving at the Montevideo airport under the watchful eyes of workers who, we presume, are also members of the movement.

Das Kapital Punishment

The relative failure of the ideals of the Alliance for Progress was the context for *State of Siege*. Because capital requires a stable and reliable political order if it is not to flee from one country into the banks of another—indeed, if it is to flow into a country at all—the mechanisms for maintaining domestic law and order become as important as those for ensuring the external security of the nation. To be sure, USAID provided the funds for a wide range of projects dealing with development, welfare, health, education, and so on. But, as Costa-Gavras and many others before and since have shown (Levinson and de Onis, 1970; Latham, 2000), it was a favorable climate for investment and profit that was the most important goal. Hence, provision of technical aid and training to the police departments of Latin American countries, to enable them to anticipate and suppress domestic dissent and unrest, was a natural outgrowth of the overall objectives of the Alliance for Progress.

Costa-Gavras's goal in the film was not only to illuminate the way in which U.S. economic interests were served both by the political and elite structures of the Latin American countries but also the ways in which the Americans intervened in the domestic affairs of those countries, albeit under the cover of what appeared to be good intentions. The search for and punishment of Communists was, ultimately, about maintenance of a domestic order necessary for economic interests to thrive, oblivious to the impoverishment around them. For this, Costa-Gavras was bitterly attacked in the American press, as anti-American, as a sympathizer with communism, and as a romanticizer of the guerillas.

While the film was hailed as a critical success by many, it was not a hit at the box office. Understandably so. It presents a story that is far outside of the mainstream of American film, including films critical of various aspects of American life and politics at home and abroad. But the film is not rabidly anti-American, and is somewhat equivocal where Santoré is concerned, illustrating the peculiar compartmentalization of morality that seems to affect all such representatives of capital. He appears, on the one hand, as a dedicated father even as, on the other, he is a staunch advocate of U.S. foreign policy and is willing to do almost anything to support it. The evidence presented by the Tupumaros is all circumstantial—no one is able to actually link Santoré to specific tortures or killings—but, by the end of the film, few viewers will be left unconvinced of his complicity (and that of others) in the militarization of the lives of people in Uruguay and other Latin American countries.

Today we can, perhaps, look at *State of Siege* as a document and documentary of the past, a commentary on the stakes and tactics of the Cold War, as played out in a region just to the south of the United States. That kind of stuff is over . . . or is it? In April 1995, an article in the *San Francisco Chronicle* reported on the "School of the Americas," a U.S. Army academy at Fort Benning, Georgia, where soldiers from Latin America were trained in various techniques of both a military and civil nature. And what of the graduates, who included Panama's Manuel Noriega and the late Robert D'Aubuisson, one of Honduras's best-known right-wing sponsors of death squads? Were they rogues and thugs or not? A spokesman for the school tried to put the best face on it thusly: "Out of 59,000 students who have graduated from a variety of programs [at the Academy], less than 300 have been cited for human rights violations like torture and murder, and less than 50 have been convicted of anything" (Schmitt, 1995: A8).

In 1999, Congress began to move toward closing the school. In December, 2000, the U.S. Army responded by changing its name to the "Western Hemisphere Institute for Security Cooperation," and claiming to instruct its students in human rights. Whether "new management" and a more innocuous name can change the school's "educational culture" remains to be seen (*The Nation*, 2001).

~~~
∿∿

Chapter 7

Vietnam, Over and Over

Syndromes

The twenty years between 1955 and 1975 generated a great deal less in the way of literature or film connected to the war in Vietnam than the two decades that followed the war's end. Given the impact of Vietnam on American politics, this might seem surprising. But until the early 1960s, many Americans did not know that such a place even existed (and not much had been heard about Southeast Asia since 1955 or so).

In 1956, Graham Greene published *The Quiet American*, a book about a U.S. foreign aid official in Vietnam who is engaged in espionage on the side, so to speak. In 1965, *The Green Berets*, by Robin Moore, appeared in print, and a few years later it was turned into a film starring John Wayne. The first mildly critical work about the war appears to have been a 1967 novel, *Incident at Muc Wa*, by Daniel Ford; in 1978, it was released as the film *Go Tell the Spartans*. But there are no fictional films from the period that address directly the political basis for the American entanglement in Vietnam (except, perhaps, *Hearts and Minds*, a 1974 documentary). Most that appeared later focused on the psychological impact of the war on the U.S. public.

From the American perspective, the Vietnam War did have a great deal to do with psychology, as opposed to politics, which might be one reason why it remains so traumatic even today (especially for those who aspire to the presidency). In a curious fashion, moreover, both films and novels seem to contain what is almost an air of accusation *against* the (South) Vietnamese, who are made to seem as somehow having *enticed* the United States into the morass of Southeast Asia. Certainly, this is one image projected in Francis Ford Coppola's *Apocalypse Now*, perhaps the best-known, if not the best, film about the Vietnam War. Captain Willard (Martin Sheen), the protagonist—he can hardly be called a hero—is drawn upriver, into the jungle, by Colonel Kurtz's (Marlon Brando) almost magnetic force, one that Willard can neither resist nor comprehend. The river becomes a path to madness, from rationality to irrationality, from light to dark. (Why, as Norman Mailer entitled his 1967 novel, *are* we in Vietnam?) Yet, one can invert the equation, too. In Cambodia, at the end of the line, there is total clarity—the "diamond bullet in the forehead," as Kurtz puts it. By contrast, in Nha Trang, the starting point of Willard's journey, those who appear sane are nothing of the sort; there is only opacity; nothing is real. It is the heart of darkness.

It's Them Dominoes

How the United States came to find itself in Vietnam is almost as central to our story as what the military did once it was there, why its mission was in trouble from the start, and why it eventually withdrew. In 1950, shortly after the outbreak of the Korean War, then-NATO commander Dwight Eisenhower met with a group of American congressmen who were seeking his views on the situation in Asia. In the course of the briefing, he expounded as well on the conflict in Vietnam, and France's efforts to regain control over its breakaway colony. According to Eisenhower, the Viet Minh—the Vietnamese nationalist coalition fighting French colonialism—were part of a global picture. A French failure in Vietnam was unthinkable, he argued. If it occurred, the Communists "would be pushing in through Burma—already a hotbed of unrest and trouble—pushing on down to rubber, tin, tungsten, the Sumatra oil. . . . Then," concluded the General, "you begin to see a picture that is terrible" (quoted in Cook, 1981: 108).

A few years later, now-President Eisenhower further explained what would happen if the Communists were not stopped in Asia. As he articulated it in a press conference, if France lost,

> [M]any human beings [would] pass under a dictatorship. . . . Finally you have . . . what you would call the 'falling domino' principle. You have a row of dominoes set up, you knock over the first one, and what will happen to the last one is the certainty that it will go over very quickly (quoted in LaFeber, 1993: 162).

No great domino player he, although where dominoes were concerned, truer words were never spoken. Whether this principle of physics also applied to countries was never very evident. Still, the metaphor was a compelling one, if not entirely accurate. Not only did the "domino theory" stick, it became a central rationale for U.S. interventions around the world.

Richard Barnet once observed that Eisenhower's "testimony [about

Vietnam was] of questionable historical weight because he seemed to have only the haziest idea of what was there" (Barnet, 1973: 159-60). We are led to conclude ultimately that Eisenhower was not the only one in the dark. Few others really had much of an idea what was in Vietnam or why the United States should get involved. Even today, more than half a century after fighting broke out between French forces and the Viet Minh, the Vietnam War remains something of a mystery to most Americans. Indeed, the conflict there seems to have been less about real things than imagined ones—or, at least, about things in the mind. For that is what the Vietnam War was about, for the most part: The credibility of American commitments in the face of a conjectured threat from world communism.

How did the United States come to be involved in a war in Vietnam, a place that, as late as 1964, hardly anyone in America could find on a map?[1] As was true of many Cold War conflicts, the U.S. commitment was the consequence of decisions made during the closing days of World War II. At the Potsdam summit, in mid-1945 (the first such meeting attended by Truman after succeeding to the presidency), the Americans, Russians, and British decided that, following the Japanese surrender, Vietnam would be divided at the 16th parallel. The northern part of the French colony would be occupied by Chinese troops, the southern by British ones. As soon as possible, France would send replacement troops, reclaim Vietnam, and carry on as though it were still 1940. The French reoccupation took place in March 1946 and almost immediately precipitated what later became known as the First Indochina War, between the Vietnamese nationalists, or "Viet Minh," and French forces, many of whom were natives drafted from other French colonies. France tried to suppress the Viet Minh with force, but failed. By the end of 1946, war was general throughout Vietnam.

Why was a distant Asian colony worth yet another war so soon after the defeat of the Axis? To France, Indochina was not only a matter of imperial greatness—a dwindling asset in an era of atomic power—but also a source of national income, via the raw materials produced there and the dollars those materials earned from sale to the United States (recall that dollars were the only currency other countries would accept unconditionally). The economics of a colony consumed by war were not very favorable, however. By 1948, the French were spending three times as much on military operations in the northern part of Vietnam as they received in exports from *all* of Indochina. Moreover, this substantial drain on financial resources was beginning to tell at home, where the French economy was in dismal shape and European reconstruction had not yet begun in earnest. Paris was less and less able to finance the war.

The impacts of the First Indochina War were not limited only to France and Vietnam, either. With so much of the French army tied up in Asia, American efforts to build a military alliance in Western Europe were floundering. An anti-Soviet coalition, it became clear, would require rearming Germany, and a Germany rearmed was not viewed with great equanimity by the other nations of Western Europe. The French government was willing to countenance such a move only if it could maintain enough troops at home to counterbalance the implicit threat posed by the new German forces required by the alliance. And this was not possible so long as the war in Indochina continued.

In the late 1940s, and into the early 1950s, American policymakers viewed French policies in Vietnam with some degree of skepticism and distaste. On the one hand, they were not terribly pleased with the way the French were seeking to restore colonial rule in Southeast Asia. On the other hand, it was clear that Indochina, if pacified, *might* be an important part of the international system of triangular trade.[2] Throughout 1949, the French were being bled badly in Vietnam, and they pleaded with the Truman administration to provide support for their military efforts and their puppet emperor Bao Dai, who supposedly ruled in those parts of Vietnam not under Viet Minh control. The United States, recalling how Nationalist forces in the Chinese Civil War had been a bottomless and fruitless sink for U.S. aid, were reluctant to throw good money after bad.

But events during the second half of 1949 cast the situation in a different light and changed minds in Washington. The Soviet atomic bomb, Communist entry into Beijing, and insurrections throughout Southeast Asia tipped the balance. By the end of 1949, the United States was funneling substantial funds into the region, a flow that only grew larger after the outbreak of the Korean War. Indeed, by the end of 1950, most of the bill for the French colonial war against the Viet Minh, as well as the military buildup in metropolitan France, was being paid by the United States. Such help did not turn the tide toward the French cause. Unable to fight a guerrilla war, the French continued to lose badly and, losing continually, they also managed to transfer a substantial amount of weaponry to their adversaries (see Sheehan, 1988).

The nadir of the French effort came in 1954, at Dien Bien Phu, a remote fortress in the northern part of Vietnam, with little military importance, and far from French centers of command or supply. Here, France staked its colonial future. Dien Bien Phu was more of a symbol than a place of strategic value. The French military believed that holding the fortress would demonstrate the futility of the rebellion to the Viet Minh and induce them to give up the war or, at least, to negotiate. The challenge was made and met. In the course of a long siege, Viet Minh forces managed to squeeze the French out of Dien Bien Phu and, eventually, forced them to give up their rule over the northern half of Vietnam (as noted in chapter 5, the Eisenhower administration contemplated dropping a "small" atomic bomb near Dien Bien Phu or providing other material assistance, but decided against it). The United States, although discouraged by the French loss, did not give up on Vietnam. The stakes appeared to be too high.

After the siege of Dien Bien Phu, the French lost their stomach for colonial war in Asia (and the war in Algeria was yet to come). France wanted out, and decided to negotiate the future of Vietnam with its adversaries. The official participants at the 1954 Geneva Conference convened for this purpose included France, the Viet Minh, Russia, and China. The United States attended only as an "observer." In the final agreement, the French agreed to withdraw all of their forces in the North to the area south of the 17th parallel, while the Viet Minh agreed to withdraw its forces to the area north of the same line. A truce would be established between the French military and Ho Chi Minh's forces (although this truce would not apply to any Vietnamese government that might proclaim its rule over the area south of the seventeenth parallel). The southern part of Vietnam would stay out of regional military alliances (similar to the one the United States was trying to put together in the Middle East). Elections to unify the country under one government would be held by 1956.

With this agreement, the First Indochina War came to an end. The cost in lives was enormous. Between 250,000 and one million civilians were killed, along with 200,000 to 300,000 Viet Minh and 95,000 French colonial troops. These numbers would be dwarfed by what was yet to come.

Moreover, there was a catch. Only official attendees to the conference signed the 1954 Geneva Agreements. Not signing were the United States and Bao Dai's regime, now based in the southern city of Saigon and recognized by the United States as the government of South Vietnam. The Eisenhower administration made clear that the United States was under no obligation to observe the terms of an agreement it had not signed, and it broke those terms in short order.

Within a few months, the United States was providing military assistance directly to the new South Vietnamese government, bypassing the French. American advisers began to train a South Vietnamese army and to seek a new, more democratic leader for the South to replace the imperial Bao Dai. The requirement for elections was ignored, inasmuch as it was recognized that Ho Chi Minh would easily score an enormous victory over any and all challengers. The United States argued that its actions were the only way to preserve freedom and democracy in South Vietnam, but the real reason for avoiding elections was to make sure that communism could not score an easy victory in Asia and expose the Eisenhower administration to Democratic Party charges that it, too, was losing parts of Asia.

Our Man in Saigon

The vessel for American hopes in Vietnam was Ngo Dinh Diem. Diem was a Catholic (most Vietnamese were Buddhist), born in North Vietnam, but living in self-exile at a Maryknoll seminary in Ossining, New York. In some Vietnamese circles, Diem had acquired a minor reputation as a non-Communist nationalist, although his most noteworthy act had been his refusal to join the Bao Dai regime. Beyond that, his nationalist credentials were virtually nonexistent. But Washington hoped that Diem would be to South Vietnam what Ramon Magsaysay had been to the Philippines: an instrument of democracy in the hands of Colonel Edward Lansdale of the CIA. Diem was sent to South Vietnam to become prime minister under Bao Dai who had abdicated in the interest of "democracy." He was no longer emperor but remained the nominal head of the country. That state of affairs did not last long. In 1956, Diem held a rigged election, ensuring himself the presidency. He then sent Bao Dai packing.

Diem was neither the United States's first mistake in Vietnam nor its last, but he might have been one of the worst. The choice of Diem reflected an almost complete American obliviousness to the situation in the South and the political and religious divisions among its inhabitants. First, and foremost, as noted earlier, Diem was Catholic. This made him attractive to U.S. policymakers, but quite unpopular in the South, inasmuch as Catholics were widely disliked for collaborating with the French colonial regime. Before the North-South border was closed in 1956, about two-thirds of the Catholic minority in North Vietnam fled South at the urging of Lansdale and the CIA. In the South, they became an even smaller and more resented group. Once in power, Diem and his family relied heavily on their co-religionists for political support, knowing them better and assuming that they were more reliable than Buddhists and Vietnamese of other religions. This, as things would turn out, was a major strategic error on Diem's part.

By 1956, then, the die was cast. South Vietnam played a minor economic role in the "Free World," but it was depicted as a major domino in the stakes for Asia. In the view of U.S. policymakers, American credibility worldwide rested on this very fragile game piece, one that required support no matter what the ultimate cost. In choosing Diem to carry the mantle of democracy and the hopes of the West, the Americans thought they were putting into office a political moderate, one who loved Vietnam, abhorred communism, and could generate a nationalist ethos that would be attractive to the largely agricultural people of South Vietnam.

None of this was the case and Diem did nothing to make the job any easier. Fearing domestic opposition, he systematically began to eliminate all non-Communist competitors for power in the South, mostly religious sects and crime organizations with their own private armies. Diem saw them as a much greater threat to his rule than the North or the southern Communists. In destroying such groups, who were much more interested in local control and enrichment than politics, according to Neil Sheehan, Diem did away with "the most effective opponents of Communism in the South" (Sheehan, 1988: 177).

After eliminating his non-Communist competition, Diem's American advisers urged him to take up land reform as a means of undercutting the Communists' appeals to the peasants. Diem did so, but his program proved a failure, too, inasmuch as the result was to *undo* earlier land reforms. Prior to the country's division in 1956, the Viet Minh had carried out some land reforms in the areas they controlled south of the 17th parallel while, in other parts of the South, peasants had undertaken land reform on their own. Diem declared all such transfers invalid and promulgated a new law which transferred a great deal of property to northern Catholics newly resident in the South. He also ordered the return of much of the land confiscated by the Viet Minh and peasantry to its former owners. The result was growing antagonism toward Diem, his regime, and his religious compatriots.

But Diem's major mistake—one that unwittingly lit the fuse for the "Second Indochina War"—was his "Denunciation of Communists Campaign." Aided and abetted by American military advisers, the Diem regime began to root out and eliminate those Viet Minh cadres, and their sympathizers, who had remained in the South after the division of Vietnam. The South Vietnamese and Americans assumed that there was little or no difference between these individuals and the "real" Communists in the North, and that it was best to get rid of as many of the former as possible. In the course of the campaign, the Diem regime killed thousands of suspected Viet Minh and imprisoned many more. In their own defense, and in defiance of contrary orders from Hanoi, the "stay-behind" cadres launched an uprising against the government in the South.

The stay-behinds also found sympathizers and supporters among those groups and classes that had experienced the heavy hand of the Diems. By 1958, as a result, a major guerrilla revolt had begun. It was during this period that the appellation "Viet Cong" (VC)—short for "Vietnamese Communists"—was invented as a substitute for *Viet Minh* which, the American advisers discovered, possessed heroic connotations throughout the South. Faced with the fait accompli of a broad uprising in the South which it did not control, the Ho Chi Minh regime in the North decided to move in and take over.

In 1960, the National Liberation Front of South Vietnam, modeled on the Viet Minh League of the 1940s, was established as a front for northern involvement. Supplies and troops began to move from North to South by sea and land. This was the situation faced by the Kennedy administration upon entering office.

Who Put the "Flex" in Flexible Response?

Ever since Greece and the launch of the Truman Doctrine in 1947, U.S. policymakers saw almost all civil violence as having a common origin, in Moscow. By the same logic, they did not view the guerrilla war in South Vietnam as having a local origin but, rather, as one piece in a global Communist game plan. This belief was only buttressed by both Soviet and Communist Chinese declarations of (competing) support for wars of liberation aimed against the West. Ironically, by 1960, the Soviet Union and the Peoples Republic of China were becoming enemies—that was one reason for Khruschev's speech in 1960—but evidence of a conflict between the two Communist giants was mostly regarded in Washington as disinformation.

The initial U.S. response to the uprising was to rely on the military capacities of the South Vietnamese government to put down the guerrillas; as Eisenhower once observed, native soldiers were much less costly than Americans, in both monetary and political terms. This was also long-standing colonial policy—the metropole would provide the officers and the locals, the cannon fodder. The strategy assumed, however, that the Army of the Republic of Vietnam (ARVN) could be turned into an effective fighting force whose sympathies would lie with Diem and his government, an ill-founded belief. Diem, moreover, was less concerned about the Viet Cong than challenges from ambitious generals within the ARVN, whom he feared might launch a coup. The generals, in their turn, were more interested in accumulating wealth than seeing their troops go into battle. Finally, lower-ranking officers and troops were more concerned with staying alive than fighting for anything as vague as South Vietnam. To most of them, the country appeared more a Catholic creation than a nationalist project worth dying for.

And what about the peasantry who sheltered the Viet Cong guerrillas? Either the peasants *were* Viet Cong—just as, ten years earlier, they had been Viet Minh—or they played both ends against the middle to protect their meager property and possessions. Consequently, the Diem government found itself at war with the stay-behind cadres, northern troops, *and* the southern peasantry. This was not, as one might well imagine, a formula for success. By 1961, the fighting began to spread into Laos (although not yet Cambodia). It became clear that, unless ARVN could somehow be made to fight, South Vietnam would be lost and the dominoes might begin to fall.

The Kennedy administration thought it had a way to beat the guerrillas at their own game, through *flexible response* and *counterinsurgency*.

These were more akin to academic theories than military strategies or tactics, but this was an administration top-heavy with academics—the "best and the brightest," as David Halberstam later called them (1972). Vietnam, moreover, seemed a perfect place in which to test out ideas for defeating communism, given that such wars were turning out to be much more common than ones fought across well-defined fronts and battlefields.

"Flexible response" was the brainchild of General Maxwell Taylor. In 1958, disgusted with the Eisenhower administration's emphasis on deterrence of the Communists through heavy reliance on nuclear weapons, Taylor resigned from the Army.[3] Massive retaliation, according to the analysis offered by Taylor in his 1960 book, *The Uncertain Trumpet*, made no distinction between level of hostilities or threat. A small border incursion was treated conceptually in the same way as a massive invasion, with both to be deterred by nuclear weapons.

Taylor thought this stupid. Why threaten to destroy the world for a platoon of soldiers or minor bits of land? Men were valuable, to be sure, but such a tradeoff was hardly believable. It would make more sense to have in reserve a range of weaponry and tactics that would permit a proportionate reaction to Soviet or Red Chinese provocations (recall, moreover, that this was one reason Robert Oppenheimer had opposed development of the H-bomb in 1950). Nuclear weapons could be part of the scheme, but it would be better to have conventional options so as not to have to go nuclear early in a conflict. One might, perhaps, thereby avoid having to go nuclear at all. Flexible response grabbed JFK by the ear. Maxwell Taylor was invited into the Kennedy administration, and flexible response was the military strategy applied in both Europe (where war never broke out) and Vietnam (where it did).

In retrospect, flexible response might seem a rational way to prevent a war from going nuclear. It was (and is) also a profoundly apolitical approach to war-fighting. Flexible response relies heavily on psychology for effect and effectiveness and it presumes that an enemy deals *only* in the currency of pain. With flexible response, according to the theory, when confronted by calibrated escalation, the enemy will rationally calculate gains and losses. Sooner or later, goes the argument, the costs will clearly outweigh the benefits, the enemy will recognize the error of her ways. Then she will sue for peace or withdraw (this same logic was applied in the 1999 bombing of Serbia, with limited success). As we shall see, this calculus presumes that the enemy's concepts of rationality and costs are the same as one's own, which is not always the case in practice.

The theory of counterinsurgency was, in many ways, a mirror image of the guerrilla tactics of the Viet Minh and Viet Cong. But, whereas the Viet Cong guerrilla could, in the words of Chairman Mao, swim like fish in an ocean of sympathetic peasants (Mao, 1948), the counterinsurgent could not.

He was more like a fish out of water. (This does not mean that a successful counterinsurgency force could not have been developed, although its goals, tactics, and fighters would probably have made it indistinguishable from that of the Viet Minh. And where the United States has done this with some success, as in Afghanistan, the results have not been especially salutary.)

Inasmuch as the peasants could not be depended upon to support such a force, successful counterinsurgency required that they be brought under government control, either being resettled in special hamlets or forced to move to the cities. The American U.S. Special Forces, or "Green Berets," and the South Vietnamese Rangers thus became the counter-insurgent guerrilla force, well trained at killing but unable to turn the tide in favor of ARVN and South Vietnam. That strategy was an apolitical one, too, assuming as it did that the peasants were indifferent about who governed them, desiring, like Americans, only life, liberty, and property. How could the Communists provide this?

Counterinsurgency was a failure almost from the beginning. The South Vietnamese forces were reluctant to fight and only too ready to give up their weapons to the Viet Cong. Indeed, some of them *were* Viet Cong, enrolled in both armies. ARVN stole from the peasantry and offered nothing in return, in contrast to the Viet Cong who understood, at least, the political reasons behind the war and could explain it to the peasants. The ARVN preferred to go where the Viet Cong were not to be found, they had no great commitment to the Diem regime, and they could not explain why they were fighting the heroes of the anticolonial war against the French.

Not that the Viet Cong were paragons of virtue. They did not hesitate to make examples of collaborators and execute them if necessary. They did discriminate more than ARVN in terms of demands and punishments, offering peasants a better chance of making it through the war relatively unscathed. For the most part, however, the peasantry found itself stuck between a rock and a hard place, forced to make choices that were, at best, not very attractive.

Flexible response made little headway in winning the war, for the simple reason that nothing was being communicated through the American commitment to the South. Because the initial wave of U.S. military advisers sent in 1961 was not allowed to lead ARVN troops or, for that matter, to actively engage in battles in the field, the growing U.S. intervention was not taken seriously either by the North or the United States's allies in the South. Moreover, because the Northern effort was still fairly decentralized in 1961, Hanoi was not in a position to receive such a message and disseminate it to the cadres fighting in the South. So it soon became necessary to up the ante and increase the pressure, in the hope that the North would "get the message" and pass it on to their fighters in the South.

By early 1963, it was becoming clear to Washington that the South Vietnamese forces were in danger of losing. The Viet Cong were acquiring more influence and more modern weaponry—much of which was provided courtesy of the United States via ARVN. Heavy weapons, supplied by the Soviet Union and China, were smuggled into the South from the North. Growing numbers of men carrying growing quantities of equipment were infiltrating into the South via the Ho Chi Minh Trail and the ocean. In Saigon, meanwhile, President Diem and his henchmen remained interested only in preserving their positions of wealth and power. They were perfectly content to leave the countryside to the Viet Cong, so long as they could maintain control over the cities, where the greatest opportunities for self-aggrandizement and accumulation were to be found.

As mid-1963 passed, the growing carnage throughout much of the South, and the anti-Buddhist policies of Diem, fostered increasing opposition to the government, especially among Buddhists. This culminated in self-immolations by Buddhist monks, broadcast on American television, and mass arrests of Buddhist monks by the regime. Eventually, a U.S.-sanctioned coup by ARVN generals against Diem and his family resulted in the assassination of Diem and a new government. Here the thought was similar to, and as fruitless as, Diogenes's search for an honest man. If only a credible South Vietnamese nationalist could be found, one not so intent on personal riches but, rather, the interests of the country! The military and people would surely follow such a selfless individual, and the war could be turned around and won.

The Americans repeatedly overestimated the commitment of the military and its generals to the very idea of South Vietnam. Diem was followed by a Big Spin of generals, each less competent than his predecessor, each putting the whole project at ever-greater risk of collapse. The wheel finally stopped on one Air Marshal Nguyen Kao Ky. In spite of his cowboy/ aerobaticist image, Ky was able to maintain a modicum of stability and put a halt to the procession of presidents. A few years later, there was even a credible presidential election, in which General Nguyen Van Thieu, vice president under Ky, won election to the presidency of South Vietnam. Ky, in turn, became vice president. The two managed to remain in office until the bitter end, in 1975.[4]

≈≈

Fighting Soldiers from the Sky

The Green Berets, Robin Moore (New York: Crown, 1965)
Incident at Muc Wa, Daniel Ford (Garden City, N.Y.: Doubleday, 1967)

Although many books have been written about the Vietnam War, unlike these, most appeared after 1970. Both are about the U.S. Special Forces in Southeast Asia although, where Moore's is deadly serious, Ford's book is something of a black comedy. Both books were also turned into films. *The Green Berets* is a turgid piece of moviemaking starring John Wayne and David Jansen. *Go Tell the Spartans*, the film version of *Muc Wa*, stars Burt Lancaster but does not do real justice to Ford's novel. The first film is the much better known of the two, and the hit single of the same name is, for better or worse, unforgettable.

The Green Berets presents a series of fictionalized vignettes about Special Forces activities in Vietnam circa 1964, when they had become part of the U.S. Military Assistance Advisory Group (MAAG), assigned to advise ARVN but to stay out of combat. Moore narrates the stories. A free-lance journalist, he writes that, at age thirty-eight, he went through the rigorous training required of all Special Forces candidates so that he could tell the "true" story of Vietnam. Following completion of training, Moore (Jansen in the film) travels to South Vietnam. There, his military connections serve him well and he is accepted as a "civilian" military man, and permitted to visit various Green Beret outposts and go out on search and destroy missions.

Moore wrote *The Green Berets* as a paean to the U.S. Special Forces. Much of the book is devoted to their military exploits, but he also describes "civic action projects" intended to endear these men to the locals, such as "digging wells for villagers, establishing schools and hospitals, and even helping remote peoples improve their economic standards [sic]" (p. 7). Nevertheless, the stories he tells reveal that, for the Green Berets, victory was much more important than the morality they often avowed. Moore, himself, is firmly convinced of the need for counterinsurgency forces in order to "Keep the perimeter of the free world from shrinking further" (p. 13). This is best done by "keep[ing the Green Berets] out of politics," as one colonel puts it, although politics always seemed to be intruding into their activities (Clausewitz notwithstanding). Moore sympathizes with officers in the field, who believe the command is always getting in the way because SOPs (standard operating procedures) are more important than results.

In many ways, the most graphic of the chapters is the first, which de-scribes Moore's experiences at Phan Chau, a fort in the Mekong Delta near the Cambodian border. Manned by Green Berets and South Vietnamese

Rangers, the fort is close to completion when Moore arrives on the scene. But it is under imminent threat from the Viet Cong. Although the delta was far south of the border region with North Vietnam, in the early 1960s it was heavily contested turf. During the day, the government controlled the cities and the rural roads; at night, much of the delta was guerrilla territory.

Moore recounts how the men in the fort prepare for and repel the VC attack when it occurs, through a variety of stratagems, including incursions into Cambodia (a violation of international law), blowing up of parts of the fort in order to kill VC infiltrators among the Vietnamese Rangers (a violation of SOP), and murder and torture to extract information (a violation of orders). Moore is relatively nonjudgmental about such activities, believing them to be necessary in order to win the war as well as hearts and minds. His conclusion: "Whatever the outcome in Vietnam will be is anybody's guess, but whatever happens, Special Forces men will continue to fight Communism and make friends for America in the underdeveloped nations that are the targets of Communist expansion (p. 338)."

Incident at Muc Wa presents a rather different picture. Reading it side-by-side with *The Green Berets,* one might even think that the first book was meant as a satire of the second (according to Ford, he reviewed Moore's book for *The Nation* but it did not influence what he wrote[5]). The story occurs in 1964 in an unnamed Southeast Asian country, one clearly modeled on South Vietnam. The two main characters are Rebecca Shaw and Stephen Courcey. Shaw is a young, attractive, Jewish, freelance journalist for *The Liberal* (a journal like *The Nation*, to which Ford reported on *his* travels in Vietnam). Courcey is a corporal and demolitions expert in the "Raiders." He has fallen in love with Shaw and, when she rejects him, Courcey enlists for a tour in Southeast Asia. On arrival, he is sent to a base near "Penang." The base commander, Major Barker, has little use for either Courcey or his colleague, Second Lieutenant Ray Hamilton.

Not long after Courcey's arrival at the base, the generals in the capital, "Thaitan," order Barker to prepare a position paper on Muc Wa. It is an abandoned French outpost near the border. There are no villages nearby and the place has no obvious strategic value. But, in order to get the generals off his back, Barker has his assistant fabricate a report about the site's importance. His plan backfires, and the generals order Barker to set up a base at Muc Wa. Feeling that the entire project is a waste of time and men, Barker decides to use his most useless troops for the mission and sends Courcey, Hamilton, and two other Americans, along with a force of native Raiders.

The Raiders arrive at the location marked on the map and there they find nothing but an old French graveyard with a weathered wooden arch. On the arch is written, in French, a quote from the men who held the Persians off at Thermopylae in 480 B.C., and whose heroism is recorded in that noblest of epitaphs: "Go, stranger, and tell the Spartans that we lie here in obedience to their laws."

The Raiders begin to build their fort and, as they do so, they gradually begin to attract the attention of "Charlie Romeo," the guerrilla enemy in the bush. After a couple of months, when the base is more or less complete, it comes under growing attack from the enemy's 507th Battalion. This, it turns out, is the same force that, ten years earlier, helped to drive the French out of the country.

Shaw visits Muc Wa in order to write an exposé of the American intervention for *The Liberal* (her father has paid for the trip). She hopes to see Courcey, but he is out in the field with a platoon, preparing to fake an attack on the fort in order to impress a visiting general. Courcey's force is ambushed by men from the 507th, and the fake attack turns out to be a real one. Enemy pressure on Muc Wa increases, much to the bewilderment of Barker and his Captain:

> "I don't know why Charlie wants Muc Wa so bad, but he's damned well not going to get it . . . Al?"
> "Sir?"
> "Draw up a contingency plan for reinforcing Muc Wa."
> Captain Olivetti lurched and almost fell. "But, sir," he said. "Muc Wa is a waste of time."
> "Couldn't be, or Charlie wouldn't be committing five hundred men to knock it off."
> "Well . . ."
> "*Five hundred men,* Al!" Major Barker cracked his knuckles. "Think of it! Charlie's throwing a whole battalion against Muc Wa—would he be doing that if it wasn't important to him?"
> "Well, sir, maybe he's thinking the same thing. Maybe he's throwing men in there because he thinks it's important to us."
> "Nonsense!" the major said. "Charlie wouldn't be such a damn fool as that, now would he?" (pp. 173-74).

Ultimately, the Americans "exfiltrate" from Muc Wa and abandon the native Raiders. Courcey, however, has fallen in love with this useless place. He remains behind and he dies when the fort is overrun and destroyed by Charlie Romeo. To Shaw, who does not know any better, Courcey is a hero.

Predictably, *The Green Berets* made a much bigger impression in 1965 than *Incident at Muc Wa* did in 1967 (the latter has just been reprinted). The American battle with global communism still made sense to many, Vietnam was still far away, and victory was still guaranteed by the military. Moore took it for granted that South Vietnam was part of the big picture, and that every fort was a "nail" whose loss would reverberate around the world. The "generals," he claimed, were hostages to the politicians who had no idea what was going on or what was truly at stake. Hence, the Green Berets would fight the war on their terms and tactics and, paying no attention to the rules and regulations, would win it.

Through his novel, Ford suggested that there was much less clarity in the situation than was widely supposed. Ford offered the possibility that the whole Vietnam effort might be something of an illusion. His Major Barker is concerned only with protecting himself and getting back home alive, something that would be threatened if his soldiers have to go out and *fight*. The generals and civilians, who never bother to go out in the field and have no idea what is going on, keep coming up with new ideas for measuring success and sending useless men to do unnecessary jobs. But the search for a mission must continue. Even useless places like Muc Wa, which had not seen anyone from either side in ten years, could be turned into strategic linchpins. Without retrospectively reading too much into Ford's novel, that Muc Wa could be abandoned without anyone (except Shaw) caring very much implied, perhaps, that the same thing could happen with South Vietnam as a whole.[6]

〰〰

All the Way with LBJ!

On a trip to Dallas in 1963, President Kennedy was shot and killed. Would JFK have expanded U.S. involvement in Southeast Asia? Would he have withdrawn American troops? Does it matter? In 1964, his successor Lyndon Johnson ran as the "peace" candidate—a peace many assumed included Vietnam. LBJ charged that the Republican presidential nominee, Senator Barry Goldwater of Arizona, would be bad for peace. He would enlarge the war, claimed Johnson, and send American boys to die, once again, in Asia.

But, even as this came from one side of his mouth, LBJ was speaking to his advisers about ordering in U.S. troops with the other side. The administration had already concluded that the war could not be won by Saigon. American credibility was at stake, too, they believed. A U.S. failure to act in Vietnam would lead its allies to devalue American commitments. Moreover, according to Johnson, a loss in Vietnam would lead to Red Chinese coming ashore in Honolulu and San Francisco.

Notwithstanding publication of the Cox Report in 1999, and charges of supposed Chinese theft of American nuclear weapons designs, it is difficult today to imagine fears of a Chinese invasion carrying any credence (however ridiculous, such fears date back to the late nineteenth century). It helps to recall that, in 1964, the Peoples Republic of China (PRC) had just detonated its first nuclear device (U.S. policymakers apparently discussed the possibility of a preemptive strike against Chinese nuclear facilities around that time; a few years later, the Soviets proposed a similar strike; see Burr and Richelson, 2000). The PRC was providing active support to guerrilla wars in Asia and Africa. There was trouble brewing in Indonesia, which some thought was linked to the PRC. In 1965, General Suharto and his army (with input from the CIA) killed 500,000 people—mostly Chinese—accused of belonging to the Indonesian Communist Party (Kwitny, 1986: 278-81; Kolko, 1988: 173-85). The split with the Soviets was still not taken seriously, and no one anticipated that China would soon be convulsed by the Cultural Revolution and largely out of the strategic picture.

Johnson was elected in a landslide. Citing authorization under the Tonkin Gulf Resolution passed by Congress, his administration began the process that would have some 540,000 troops fighting in Vietnam by 1968 as well as the bombing effort whose destructive tonnage would soon exceed the total dropped on Europe during World War II (Harrison, 1989: 249-50). This was, supposedly, flexible response in action. Troop numbers were gradually increased, the American military became more involved in fighting on the ground, and firepower was applied to growing numbers of targets. Eventually, believed the White House brain trust, North Vietnam would cry "uncle!" Each incremental increase in troops and bombing was judged by the generals and the "Whiz Kids" in the Pentagon and White House to be enough, if not to bring the war to an end, at least to bring the North to the negotiating table. Each incremental increase failed to do the trick.

The Johnson strategy continued for four long years, during which the light was visible at the end of the tunnel but the train was stopped dead in its tracks. Each American general sent to oversee the war thought he could win with only a few more troops, and each was wrong. The bombardment of the North, in the "Arc Light" and "Rolling Thunder" campaigns, was supposed to demonstrate to Hanoi that the United States could continue to turn up the pressure far more than the North Vietnamese could tolerate. But flexible response failed in almost all respects.

Discrimination in targeting was not easy at the altitudes preferred by the B-52 programmers and pilots, and so the leadership in Hanoi could not be decapitated. As a result, North Vietnamese civilians suffered a great deal and died in large numbers, but this only led them to support the war all the more. One major assumption about bombing that turned out to be incorrect was the belief that destroying the North's industries would make it unable to continue the war. The fact was that the North was not very industrialized and not at all democratic. Factories and fuel tanks could be destroyed, but weapons and oil could be replaced by imports from China and the USSR. And public pressure to give in simply could not develop.

Absent the external patrons of North and South, the war could not have continued as long as it did; with the superpowers and China supplying each side, it went on much longer than necessary. Finally, the United States and South Vietnam would not carry the ground war into the

North—to do so would be to court Chinese intervention, as had happened during the Korean War—all that counted were hearts, minds, and land in the South. There, the civilian population found itself being treated like an enemy. The Americans could not tell friend from foe, and the ARVN troops did not seem to care.

By 1968, the war no longer bore any resemblance to the guerrilla uprising of the late 1950s or the northern intervention of the early 1960s. North Vietnamese main forces, well armed and strongly committed, were playing a central role in the fight, confronting their adversaries not in the set battlefield confrontations preferred by the Americans but in jungle warfare. There was growing opposition to the war in the United States as well as emerging doubts in Washington about whether the war could be won.

Now it became a matter of finding a way to exit gracefully. Senator George Aiken of Vermont suggested that the United States simply declare victory and leave. A few people advocated suing for peace. Most policymakers were more concerned about credibility and honor—about the psychology of allies who, seeing the United States fail a client, might join the Soviet "bandwagon"—than minimizing losses. They carried the day. The war continued.

Was there a turning point in the war, a point at which it was lost? In 1968, during the Tet Lunar New Year, guerrillas and North Vietnamese regulars were able to infiltrate troops into the South's major cities and launch a coordinated attack on strongpoints within them. Many of the cadres involved in this effort had, until Tet, lived lives of relative quietude, waiting for orders to come from the leadership. The orders came and even the U.S. embassy in Saigon came under fire from the enemy before the attack was beaten off. The Tet Offensive, as it came to be called, was a military defeat for the North and the National Liberation Front, but a psychological victory for the Communists and a sobering experience for the United States and ARVN. It showed not only that the Communists were able to fight a war the Americans could not but also that the entire society of South Vietnam was so riddled by agents and sympathizers that victory was an almost meaningless concept. Victory against whom? And to what end? The dilemma was best articulated by the U.S. officer who told about having to destroy a village in order to save it (a tactic dramatized metaphorically, but perhaps unintentionally, in the 1971 Clint Eastwood film, *High Plains Drifter*).

In 1968, LBJ, fearing that he could not be reelected after a scare from Senator Eugene McCarthy in the New Hampshire primary, announced that he would not run for reelection. In 1968, Robert Kennedy promised to end the war but was assassinated. In 1968, demonstrations against the war were larger than ever. In 1968, the Democratic National Convention in

Chicago was besieged by protests in the streets but nominated Hubert Humphrey as its candidate (Mailer, 1968). And in 1968, Richard Nixon ran for president, promising a "secret plan" to end the war. As the American public discovered after he was elected, Nixon was again selling used cars. He had a plan to end the war, to be sure, but it consisted largely of more of the same.

By 1968, too, the original rationale for the American involvement in Vietnam had been lost, as had been memory of the almost twenty-year history of U.S. involvement. The commitment was pursued, all the same. While Nixon had already been in Congress when that original commitment was made to France, he no longer saw it as the reason for staying in Indochina. What he did see was that, first, the United States was being bled to death in Vietnam, and that this could not continue due to both cost and domestic opposition. But Nixon also thought (along with Henry Kissinger) that to withdraw would undercut American credibility. Having given up on this commitment, who would trust the United States to fulfill its promises in the future? (This was a theme raised, once again, during the 1991 Gulf War, the 1996 Taiwan Straits crisis, and the 1999 bombing of Yugoslavia.)

Nixon recognized that the expenditure of so many dollars on the war, without a domestic tax increase or budget reductions, might erode America's global economic dominance. The United States was, quite literally, bleeding gold, as the dollar came under growing pressure in European currency markets. At the same time, the flood of dollars brought on by expenditures for the war was triggering a wave of inflation that would soon engulf the industrialized world.

Nixon's solution was twofold: "Vietnamization," aka the "Nixon Doctrine" and the closing of the "gold window" (chapter 8). The Nixon Doctrine involved a return to the old colonial strategy of using native cannon fodder to fight imperial wars. The United States would withdraw its ground troops from Vietnam, supply weapons to ARVN, and let the U.S. Air Force and Navy provide air cover, bombing the North into submission. The fighting on the ground would be done by South Vietnam's army. This allowed Nixon to pursue what he called "peace with honor," albeit at the cost of 30,000 additional American lives and uncountable Vietnamese ones. It was also a peace whose costs have yet to be tallied, as we shall see below.

"Peace with honor" was concluded in Paris in early 1973, when Henry Kissinger and Le Duc Tho signed the Paris Peace Accords. Since 1969, desultory negotiations had been underway between the United States and North Vietnam. Unbeknownst to these negotiators, one of whom was the U.S. secretary of state, Kissinger was conducting "back channel" talks, playing China off against the Soviet Union, escalating and pausing the bombing of the North, all in an effort to get Hanoi to sue for peace. The agreement, as finally concluded, granted to the North what it had already achieved on the battlefield, an eventual role in a future government of South Vietnam (essentially what would have been obtained had elections been held in 1956).

The South Vietnamese government of Thieu and Ky protested, but was mollified by a secret letter from Nixon promising supplies and American reentry into the war should the accords be violated. Both promises were, in any event, bald-faced lies, as subsequent events demonstrated. Kissinger and Le Duc Tho received the Nobel Peace Prize for their achievement. Le had the good taste not to accept it. Kissinger showed no such qualms.

The agreement was, in any event, violated regularly and with impunity, as South Vietnamese attacked Communists, who retaliated in kind. The Peace Accords were never more than America's means of pulling out of the Vietnamese quagmire. Although the United States continued to provide air cover to ARVN, the effort to sustain South Vietnam became increasingly hopeless. In the spring of 1975, the North Vietnamese army made several major military breakthroughs in the northern part of South Vietnam. ARVN began to disintegrate. The United States did nothing.

Within a matter of weeks, the Communists were in Saigon and, in April 1975, the brief, troubled existence of South Vietnam came to an end. By then, few thought the game worth the candle (although in the years since, there has been no end of attempts to rehabilitate the war as heroic and necessary). The expenditure of lives was enormous, and the war left behind a devastated land that has never really recovered. Someone has written that the true sign of a great nation, and a heroic act, is the ability to recognize a lost cause and give it up gracefully, as the Soviets did in Eastern Europe in 1989. By this measure, American behavior in Vietnam was neither heroic nor the response of a great nation.

≈

Apocalypse When?

Apocalypse Now (Omni Zeotrope, 1979, 153 min.)
Director: Francis Ford Coppola
Cast: Martin Sheen, Marlon Brando, Robert Duvall, Harrison Ford

Apocalypse Now is presented as the recollections of Captain Willard (Sheen), a member of the Special Forces whose expertise lies in "terminations," that is, assassinations. As the film opens, Willard is in a sleazy hotel room in Saigon, dreaming of jungles, helicopters, and war, and awaiting instructions for his next "mission." He is, quite clearly, hovering on the edge of psychosis. Summoned to a briefing in Nha Trang, Willard finds himself in a house trailer virtually indistinguishable from anything in Toledo, Ohio, his home town. There, a high-ranking general and a CIA operative brief him on the activities of one Colonel Walter Kurtz (Brando).

Kurtz, it seems, is a brilliant military man who, at the age of thirty-eight, forewent the possibility of rising to the level of general officer and, instead, enlisted in the Special Forces (the usual age for joining was eighteen or nineteen). He was then sent to Vietnam, where his methods gradually became "unsound." In particular, Kurtz's troops were coming under an unusually large number of surprise attacks by the VC and NVA. So, he ordered the execution of four South Vietnamese intelligence agents whom, he suspected, were actually working for the North and, indeed, the attacks dropped off to almost nothing. Gradually, Kurtz gathered around him a "Montagnard army" of Hmong and other highland peoples, moved across the border into Cambodia, and began to prosecute the war on his own. There, the General in Nha Trang tells Willard, Kurtz rules "like a god" over "his peoples," who will do whatever he tells them to.

To the military officers in Nha Trang, Saigon, and Washington, Kurtz has clearly "gone insane." They cannot allow an out-of-control officer to make policy, however successful he might be. Willard is, therefore, ordered to take a Navy patrol boat upriver into Cambodia, and to terminate Kurtz's command—"with extreme prejudice," as the CIA agent says, in his only line in the film.

Willard is both fascinated and repelled by Kurtz. On the one hand, he wonders, how can anyone talk about "unsound methods" or insanity in this war; on the other, what has driven Kurtz to do what he has done? And *why* do his methods, however unsound, work?

The river becomes Willard's conduit to Kurtz, and as he moves deeper into the jungle, toward his destination, the world becomes more and more senseless. To get to the mouth of the river, Willard contracts for transportation with one Captain Kilgore (Duvall) of the Air Cavalry. Kilgore has no interest whatsoever in Willard's mission or orders, at least not until he discovers that one of the men on the Navy patrol boat (PBR) transporting Willard is a world-class surfer. On learning that the surf at the mouth of the river is also world class, Kilgore decides to attack and destroy the nearby village so his men can catch some quality waves.

Further up the river, the PBR comes to a supply base where a USO show, starring recent Playboy playmates, is about to begin. The show degenerates into a mob scene as the women-starved soldiers assault the stage. In a scene modeled on the last-minute American evacuation from Saigon in 1975, the bunnies are lifted off the stage just as the mob is about to overwhelm them. A couple of especially hardy grunts grab the helicopter struts and hold on but, like the Vietnamese "friends" left behind, they fall into the water below and fail to reach paradise.

Just before reaching the Cambodian border, the PBR comes upon the bridge at Do Long. This is destroyed every night and rebuilt every day (shades of prudent Penelope!), just so the generals can say it remains open. The PBR arrives in the dark, amidst the VC's fierce (nightly) attack on the base. Willard goes ashore, looking for the commanding officer. Coming upon one crazed soldier hiding in a foxhole, he inquires who is in command. The soldier looks at him and answers, "I thought you were!" There is no CO. Willard returns to the PBR, and the journey upstream continues.

Eventually, the boat reaches Kurtz's outpost, in an ancient temple in Cambodia. Although the site is festooned with bodies and heads, it is almost peaceful by comparison with the chaos so far confronted by Willard and his colleagues (and, by this point in the film, only two of the boat's half-dozen crew members are still alive). Here we finally discover what drives Kurtz. Like the Leviathan, he rules "his people" with both love and fear. Those who obey unconditionally are loved; those who disobey are killed. Those who disobey and live—like Willard—have a mission. In this case, it is that Willard will replace Kurtz.

Kurtz's methods, as he tells Willard, are not "unsound." Rather, they are precisely the methods of the enemy. To illustrate his point, he relates a story (one that actually took place, according to screenwriter John Milius). Once, when he was still part of the "official" war, Kurtz and his men went into a village to inoculate children against polio. A short time later they were called back to the village, and discovered that the VC had followed them in and cut off all of the children's inoculated arms. The limbs were left behind in a pile as a warning to not cooperate with the Americans.

At first, Kurtz was horrified; later, he recognized that here lay real power. Kurtz has, in effect, adopted this approach: arm for arm, horror for horror, terror for terror. His methods are, perhaps, better understood as a form of flexible response but, whereas the generals in Saigon depend on B-52s, Kurtz uses nothing more sophisticated than a machete.

The end of the film comes when Willard does kill Kurtz. He foregoes, however, the opportunity to succeed Kurtz as god. And what kind of god? As Willard leaves the temple, he finds a notebook in which Kurtz has scrawled: "Drop the bomb! Exterminate them all!" Who Kurtz has in mind is not clear: the Vietnamese or the generals? Willard and the lone surviving crewman—Lance, the surfer—return to the PBR to make their way back down river and, perhaps, carry Kurtz's message and methods from the dark jungle into the light of day (as Willard says in a voiceover, early in the film, "I wanted a mission and for my sins they gave me one").

The Madness of Method

Could the United States have "won" the war in Vietnam using Kurtz's methods (or any other)? For that matter, what would have constituted "winning"? Since there was never any possibility of "conquering" the North— to do so would have risked World War III—the best to be hoped for was a stable regime in the South backed, perhaps, by a permanent garrison of American troops, as has been the case in South Korea since the early 1950s. By 1973, a Korean-type of settlement would have looked good in Washington.

What is, perhaps, less evident is that the Kennedy administration's resort to flexible response was, from the very outset, doomed to fail. The problem is that flexible response is a *psychological* approach to war and politics, and not a military one. This is quite evident in *Apocalypse Now*. But to repeat what was said earlier, the gist of the argument is as follows. Full-scale war would, inevitably, lead to the use of nuclear weapons. This, according to the classical logic of war, could have no political purpose, inasmuch as it would lead to global destruction. Therefore, to prevent escalation to full-scale war, it was necessary to convince the enemy that you would, if provoked, act irrationally *and* escalate—in other words, deter at a less-than-nuclear level. Ideally, the enemy would be unwilling to risk a destructive war and back down, with the result that one's political goals would be satisfied. In other words, the fundamental idea was to psych out your enemy, not to fight to the finish.

In the case of Vietnam, there was clearly a problem with such a strategy. The ostensible targets of flexible response were the Soviet Union and China and, for a time, the Americans thought that they pulled all of the strings in North Vietnam. This was not the case. The North Vietnamese were doing virtually all of the planning and fighting in the South, albeit under the rubric of the National Liberation Front. They could mount a full-scale war against their enemy, knowing full well that the United States could not respond to such provocation without the risk of drawing in the Soviets and Red Chinese. To wage full-scale war against North Vietnam—to "bomb them back into the Stone Age," as General Curtis LeMay, head of the Strategic Air Command in the late '50s, was wont to do—would have created an international political firestorm. The upshot was, consequently, that nothing the United States was able to do either politically or militarily could induce the North Vietnamese to sue for peace on terms acceptable to Washington.

This paradox is one subtext of *Apocalypse Now*. Although the film was not released until 1979, well after the end of the war, the original screenplay was written by John Milius in 1969, in the midst of the war (Milius, a hard-line Cold Warrior, also wrote the screenplay for *Red Dawn*; see chapter 8). The film was based, somewhat loosely, on Joseph Conrad's *Heart of Darkness*. The generals wanted to follow the rules and escalate according to a logical set of operating procedures. When the costs became too great, they believed, the enemy would sue for peace.

Kurtz recognized that the Communists' commitment to war was total and could not be deterred through an economistic rationality. Control of the hearts and minds of the people could not be achieved via abstract principles, as game theorists and military strategists argued; it had to be accomplished through punishments and rewards, one by one, person by person. How could corporate CEOs or general officers, used to issuing orders to tens of thousands at once, ever comprehend this? They never did.

As with Conrad's novel, the film can also be viewed as an exploration of the motivations of men in war. Both ask what is rational and what is irrational; what is sanity and what is insanity; what is moral and what is immoral? Both propose that, in particular settings, it becomes nearly impossible to make such distinctions. More than this, *Apocalypse Now* suggests that, in Vietnam, the effort to make such distinctions—and for what purpose?—simply blurred them to such an extent that good and evil became indistinguishable.

In Nha Trang, Kurtz's methods were deemed "unsound" because they had not been approved through standard operating procedures. In Cambodia, the American generals' methods were deemed "unsound" because they did not work. In Nha Trang, the generals' methods were sound because they were regulated through bureaucratic rules and procedures (Max Weber's "rationality"). In Cambodia, Kurtz's methods were sound because they were regulated by the "laws of the jungle." In the heart of darkness, no light was ever really visible at either end of the tunnel.

※

Sideshows?

The war extended beyond Vietnam and continued long after 1975. During the 1960s, the CIA conducted an extensive "secret" war in Laos, in which it enlisted the Meo, or Hmong, people of the highlands in a never-ending battle against the North Vietnamese and their Laotian allies, the Pathet Lao. North Vietnam transhipped men and materiel through Laos, as well as Cambodia, via the Ho Chi Minh Trail. The conviction in Washington was that a pro-Western regime in Vientiane, the Laotian capital, was necessary to stop the flow of arms and men. At the same time, there was a civil war underway within the country, with "neutralists" battling the Pathet Lao for power. This conflict was of sufficient concern to Washington that a Geneva conference on Laos was convened during the first year of the Kennedy administration.

The U.S. goal at Geneva was to legitimate a coalition government over which the West could exercise some degree of influence, but the experiment was never very successful. And the Hmong suffered badly for their trust in the United States. At the beginning of the 1960s, there were more than 100,000 of them in the hills and mountains of Laos; by 1975, fewer than 20,000 remained. Many of those fled to the United States and a large fraction now lives in California. In 1975, not long after the fall of South Vietnam, the Pathet Lao took power in Laos.

Arguably, Cambodia suffered even more than Vietnam. Throughout the 1960s, a more-or-less neutral regime under Prince Norodom Sihanouk held power in Phnom Penh. Sihanouk tried to play both ends against the middle, accepting aid from the West while tolerating the presence of the NVA and Viet Cong in Cambodian territory. In 1969, with the connivance of the Nixon administration, Sihanouk was tossed out of office by one of his pro-U.S. generals, Lon Nol. The unexpected result was a shot in the arm for the Cambodian Communists—the Khmer Rouge—who, until that time, had played a fairly insignificant role in the country's politics and were few in number. Throughout this period, it should be noted, the United States was regularly bombing the Ho Chi Minh trail in Cambodia and Laos.

Lon Nol proved unable to get the North Vietnamese out of Cambodia and in the spring of 1970, Nixon ordered a massive U.S. invasion of that country. His goal was to cut the flow of men and materiel down the trail and wipe out a supposed NVA/VC command headquarters located there. The invasion led to an explosion of protest around the world, inasmuch as it seemed an expansion of the war rather than the withdrawal promised by Nixon.

In the long run, the invasion proved a failure, and, like the fabled village, it had the ultimate effect of destroying Cambodia, rather than saving it (Shawcross, 1979). In order to weaken the Lon Nol regime, the North Vietnamese began to support the Khmer Rouge, providing the military wherewithal that made them a force to be reckoned with. In 1975, North Vietnam allowed its Khmer Rouge allies to take power in Cambodia. In the attempt to return the country to "Year Zero," the Khmer Rouge laid waste to the land and people (Greenfield and Locke, 1984; Shawcross, 1984).

Relations between the two Communist countries deteriorated rapidly—the Khmer Rouge were killing not only ethnic Cambodians but ethnic Vietnamese Cambodians in large numbers, too. In 1979, Vietnam invaded Cambodia in a drive to oust the Khmer Rouge from power and eliminate the threat to Vietnam and the Vietnamese Cambodians. A Vietnamese-led regime was put in place. In spite of UN-led programs to restore some form of democracy in Cambodia, the leader of that regime retains dominant power even today. And, although Cambodia is at peace, from time to time war threatens to break out between factions struggling over control of the state.

While promises of aid to the North were made as a secret side-agreement to the 1973 Paris Peace Accords, none has been forthcoming. Since 1975, the United States has maintained normal diplomatic relations with Laos but not until 1995 did it drop its embargo against Vietnam and begin to move toward normalization of relations. Until the early 1990s, Washington refused all dealings with the regime installed in Phnom Penh by Vietnam, continuing to recognize the ousted Khmer Rouge regime as the legitimate occupant of Cambodia's seat in the UN. Such are the oddities of *realpolitik* and international diplomacy.

The result of these policies was the further impoverishment of both Cambodia and Vietnam, although marketization and the recent revival of diplomatic relations between the United States and Vietnam has lead to a gradual improvement of conditions in both. The southern half of Vietnam generally remains better off than the northern part, even though it was the North that won the war. The reconstruction of Cambodia that is now underway is shaky, at best, and is taking place with very little in the way of financial commitments from the United States.

With the end of the Cold War, the United States has had even less interest in the fate of Indochina than it did in the years following the fall of the South. The Russians have abandoned the Soviet naval base at Cam Ranh Bay, and the U.S. bases in the Philippines have been evacuated. U.S. relations with the PRC are relatively convivial, although they have their ups and downs. There are no other evident military threats to U.S. interests in the region, unless one counts the internal stability of countries such as Indonesia. For that matter, U.S. strategic interests in East Asia remain unclear.

Should the United States play a "peacekeeping" role, and try to keep China, India, and others from struggling for military dominance? Will the United States have to intervene in the event of a war over the oil-rich Spratley Islands in the South China Sea, claimed by five nations? Might North Korea, in desperation, attack the South or Japan (a possibility that seems ever more remote)? Is it important to remain in Asia so as to reassure Japan against China and North Korea? The United States has economic interests in the region, to be sure, but how might military power help to protect these, especially when Japan, Taiwan, and the PRC are so economically important there? After decades of struggle to retain Asia within the American "sphere of influence"—especially the economic one—the area is no longer the United States's to retain.

Coda

The Vietnam War was never declared and in many ways it has not yet ended. To be sure, American military intervention in Southeast Asia concluded long ago, and all that remains behind are the bodies of several thousand MIAs whose burial sites are unknown. But at some point, the *psychological* war moved from Indochina to the homeland, where it has been waged ever since, albeit in an episodic and desultory fashion ("Governor, did you serve in Vietnam? Did you dodge the draft? Why did you teach business law? Whom did you bomb while in the National

Guard?"). And why? Some observers have suggested that it was the experience of "losing" that was traumatic; others have contrasted Vietnam with World War II, the "good war," in which friend and enemy were clearly differentiated and the United States won (Terkel, 1984). I think neither fully accounts for the staying power of this particular trauma; to explain that, we need to look at the more general crisis of ideology and legitimacy.

Vietnam, as a "syndrome," has little to do with the actual war. Instead, it has become an indicator of faith in America's "exceptionalism" as well as a question of loyalty to that ideology. Inasmuch as the North could not have defeated the Americans via raw military power, the loss must have been the work of "traitors" to the faith, in Washington and the body politic at large (hence, the famous bumper sticker: "America: Love it or leave it"). Had everyone kept the faith, the United States could not have lost the war. Moreover, those who did lose the faith and betrayed America are still among us—indeed, according to some cultural conservatives, such as William Bennett (1998), President Clinton was such an individual—and such people must be purged from the body politic (see chapter 10). This is why presidential candidates are always called to account for their behavior between 1960 and 1975 (even though they do not always answer).

What *did* you do in the Cold War, Daddy?

∿
∿

Chapter 8

Renewing the Cold War

Is It Cold in Here, or Is It Just Me?

The First Cold War never really came to an end, so it is something of a conceptual error to speak of "renewing" it. Still, there is no gainsaying the fact that, during the first half of the 1970s, there was a tempering of antagonisms between the United States and the Soviet Union as a result of the joint diplomacy of President Nixon and Henry Kissinger. This led some to think that full normalization of relations was a possibility, followed by an end to the Cold War. Even American military and financial aid to South Vietnam did not really stand in the way of what was called *détente*. In 1977, Jimmy Carter entered the Oval Office determined to pursue full peace between the two superpowers; in 1980, he left a fully reconstructed Cold Warrior, having put in place what would later become known as the "Reagan military buildup." Ronald Reagan brought anti-Soviet Cold War rhetoric to a level not seen since the 1950s, only to give it up before leaving office in 1989.

[margin handwritten note: Rhetoric that worked. Destroyed the U.S.S.R. July, 1989. The wall came down]

How might we explain the revival of the Cold War during the 1980s? Was there a renewed threat from Soviet communism? Was global conquest, once again, on the agenda? Or was something else going on?

What did occur was that, during the 1970s, U.S. economic domination of the "West and the Rest" came under increasing pressure as a consequence of both domestic and foreign factors. The fallout hit hard. Inflation, the energy crisis, and economic competition from allies all had their effects. These, in turn, led directly to the feeling that America was a prisoner of Third World countries, dissed by its allies, and threatened by others. The widely held sense of insecurity that resulted was only temporarily held at bay by Ronald Reagan's battle with what he called the "Evil Empire."

To be sure, for many a new Cold War was justified by what they saw

145

as the renewed aggressiveness of the Soviet Union, made possible by the growing power and accuracy of its nuclear missiles, and evidenced by its support for Marxist revolutionaries in Africa and its invasion of Afghanistan in 1979. But it was the combination of insecurity and perceived threat together that proved to be a political jackpot.

A veritable torrent of related books and films appeared during the first half of the 1980s, building on Washington's efforts to restore American confidence as well as to purge the real or imagined weaknesses of the 1970s. In response to heightened tensions between the United States and the USSR, especially over Europe, numerous cultural products took up the theme of war. The second Rambo film, *First Blood, Part II*, remains the most notorious of these, but films starring Chuck Norris and other patriotic kick boxers, as well as the depiction of teenage guerillas, as in *Red Dawn*, all proved quite popular. The techno-twit novels of Tom Clancy and his imitators also attracted much attention. War, after all, remained the ultimate act of purification. Not only could it—in theory, anyway—sweep Marxism into the "dustbin of history," as Reagan suggested, it could also redeem the shame of Vietnam and Teheran. To explain the entire cycle, however, we will have to go back to the early 1970s and examine both gold and oil. But, first, a preview.

≈

This Time, *We* Get to Win!

Rambo: First Blood, Part II (Anabasis Investments, 1985, 92 min.)
Director: Sylvester Stallone
Cast: Sylvester Stallone, Richard Crenna, Charles Napier, Julia Nickson

[handwritten: wrong state]

John Rambo (Stallone) is a Vietnam veteran, a former Green Beret, Congressional Medal of Honor winner, and itinerant, who has been sent to prison after going berserk in a small Tennessee town and killing dozens (see Morrell, 1972). At the beginning of *Rambo II*, his old Green Beret commander, Colonel Trautmann (Crenna), comes to the prison quarry where Rambo is smashing rocks to offer him a deal he cannot refuse. If Rambo will parachute into Vietnam and search for evidence of American POWs, all will be forgiven and he will receive a presidential pardon. Rambo, always thoughtful and slow to speak, ponders the offer for a moment. Then he asks "Do we get to win this time?"

Rambo's mission is rigged, of course. He is ordered to take photographs, leave no footprints, and then get out of the country. Under no circumstances is he to bring back any missing Americans (and no one believes that he will find any). Rambo is flown to a secret CIA installation in Thailand, where he is fitted out with all kinds of advanced military and espionage equipment (worthy of James Bond, in fact). He will be closely monitored, too. But when Rambo jumps out of the plane over Vietnam, he gets snagged by a strap on his pack. He must cut off his materiel and parachute in with only a knife, a bow, and a quiver of explosive arrows.

Almost immediately, Rambo meets up with his in-country contact, a young Eurasian woman (Nickson). Together, they seek out the prison camp which, they discover, is still occupied. Rambo is determined to bring out at least one POW and, with the predictable degree of violence, manages to bring one to the pickup site. But, spotting Rambo, his female colleague, and his prize, the Vietnamese military give pursuit. The pilot of the arriving helicopter is ordered to abort the mission. Rambo flees with his newly found love, but she is shot and killed, and he is captured.

Rambo is then returned to the prison camp, where he is tortured by both Vietnamese and Russians (who are dressed and presented so as to evoke memories of World War II film images of Japanese and German soldiers). Once again, of course, Rambo escapes, taking along all the POWs, blowing up the prison camp, and generally creating havoc. He hijacks a Russian heli-copter and returns with his treasure to the CIA base in Thailand. In a final act of defiance and mayhem, Rambo destroys all of the CIA's monitoring equipment. Man beats machine (and Washington). America beats Russia and Vietnam. The world is whole again.

~~~

Economics 101: Cheap Gold and Dear Gas

The 1970s dawned with a twin resource crisis. The United States was, quite literally, running out of cheap gold *and* oil. It was gold that backed the dollar and made it legal tender around the world, and it was the dollar that kept the United States on top. The origins of the gold drain, as explained in earlier chapters, were to be found in the military policies of presidents Truman, Eisenhower, Kennedy and, most of all, Johnson. LBJ had two major goals for his administration: to win the war in Vietnam and to create the "Great Society." The latter was to be his legacy to posterity, at home. Neither came cheaply—the total cost of the Vietnam War was about $200 billion in then-current dollars (or $20 billion per year) and the Great Society certainly ran upward of ten billion dollars each year (putting men on the moon was not inexpensive, either).

In retrospect, both projects seem rather cheap, but they were part of a federal budget that, at the time, was around $200 billion per year (perhaps five or more times as much in current inflated dollars). Rather than exact these added costs from taxpayers, LBJ paid for the programs by printing dollars. The result was, on the one hand, the start of a domestic inflation that was further exacerbated by the oil shocks of the 1970s and, on the other hand, a new flood of dollars into the international system, added to that of the 1950s and early 1960s. This tended to cheapen those dollars held in lieu of gold by foreign governments.

Thus, when Richard Nixon took office in 1969, exchange pressures on the dollar were intense and growing. Because exchange rates among Western currencies were fixed by the Bretton Woods rules, it was not possible, as it is now, for currency speculators to profit by selling one for another.[1] Governments kept relatively firm to their commitment not to convert dollars into other currencies and to support the fixed price of gold, at $35 per ounce. But whereas American citizens were not allowed to own gold, Europeans could, and some speculated against the dollar in European gold markets. This had the effect of raising the "free" price of gold relative to the dollar—it began to take more dollars to buy an ounce of gold—and devaluing the dollar holdings of the Europeans and their governments.

Throughout the 1960s, the French government had been increasingly unhappy with this state of affairs. It began to demand gold in exchange for its dollars, which it had the right to do. This drained U.S. gold reserves in Fort Knox, and meant there was less gold to back each dollar in circulation overseas (thus was the plot of *Goldfinger* made manifest). By 1971, pressure on the dollar was so strong that Nixon was forced to devalue it and suspend its convertibility into gold. This was followed not long after by a second devaluation, the "closing of the gold window"—the end of convertibility of the dollar to gold (Gowa, 1983)—and the shift to floating currencies which continues today (although no longer within the European Union after adoption of the Euro).

Nixon recognized that devaluation and going off gold were not enough to maintain a stable dollar and he sought other ways to reduce U.S. government spending and the outflow of dollars into the international economy.[2] One convenient synergy was to be found at the intersection of security, energy, and economic policy, through application of the "Nixon Doctrine." As discussed in chapter 7, the Nixon Doctrine was first applied in Vietnam, where it was called "Vietnamization," but it was also extended to other regions, including the Persian Gulf. The problem in the Gulf was, essentially, the playing out of the drama that had begun with the British note about Greece in 1947 that launched the Truman Doctrine. Oil supplies there were seen as highly vulnerable to disruption by both internal and external forces. Islamism was not yet an issue, but Arab socialism was. Egypt, for example, was supporting rebel troops in a civil war in Yemen, at the southern end of the Arabian Peninsula, and some feared it might try to move into Saudi Arabia where the bulk of known Middle East oil reserves were found.

The solution to this dilemma had been, in the eyes of Western power(s), to keep troops garrisoned in the region. Throughout much of the twentieth century, Great Britain had supplied the forces but, in 1969, London announced that it was withdrawing its last troop garrisons from east of the Suez Canal. This, some feared, would leave a so-called power vacuum in the region and numerous opportunities for radical trouble-making. All of these factors might well pose a threat to stable oil production and prices (Yergin, 1991).

At the same time, the United States was running up against the limits of its domestic oil resources. Under legislation passed during the Eisenhower administration, the import of cheap Persian Gulf oil into the United States was restricted by oil import quotas. This system had been put in place to protect domestic oil companies, especially small ones, whose production costs at the wellhead were much higher than those in Saudi Arabia ($1.00 per barrel vs. 10¢ per barrel). By 1969, however, as domestic reserves tightened, the cost of gasoline began to creep upward.

Then, as now, rising prices at the gas pump were politically problematic. Letting cheaper supplies into the country would reduce the pressure on prices at the pump and from voters at the polls. Better yet, if prices in the Middle East could be made to rise a small amount, the Europeans, who had been getting the benefit of cheap oil for many years (but charging heavy taxes), would have to pay more—in dollars. This would help the United States recover some of those dollars, inasmuch as five of the Seven Sisters (aka, "Big Oil") were American. But how to do it?

In the midst of the Vietnam War, and facing a gold crisis, the Nixon administration was in no position to send the U.S. military to the Middle East. Nor was there any apparent way to leverage a modest increase in oil prices that would satisfy the domestic U.S. producers while also getting them to agree to permit increased imports. American policymakers began, therefore, to think about ways to get around this problem.

The Nixon Doctrine, intentionally or not, provided the answer. The United States could sell military equipment and provide training to Persian Gulf armies—for dollars—but military responsibilities would be taken on by the Gulf countries themselves. These countries would use dollars to buy arms, dollars that they were getting from Europe in exchange for their oil. Completing the virtuous circle, the dollars would come home, Americans would be employed in the manufacturing of the weapons, and no U.S. soldiers need be shipped to the Middle East.

In the Persian Gulf, the beneficiaries of the Nixon Doctrine were Iran and Saudi Arabia, as the two largest Western-oriented countries in the region. The latter, with a population below ten million, could not provide the manpower to adequately secure the Gulf, whereas the former, with many more people, could. The only real problem was how Iran would pay for the weapons, because oil revenues were, at the time, sufficient only for domestic development and *baksheesh* (bribes and corruption). The answer was to engineer a small increase in the price of oil and use the added revenues for arms purchases.

The Sisters and the States Get the Shaft

To understand how this problem was solved, we have to consider, for a moment, Libya. In contrast to most of the Middle East oil states, production in Libya involved not only what were then the Seven Sisters (Texaco, Gulf, Chevron/Socal, Esso/Exxon, Mobil, British Petroleum, and Royal Dutch/Shell) but also a whole raft of independent American and European producers. The Seven Sisters had oil concessions all over the world, while the independents in Libya, for the most part, had concessions nowhere else. In 1969, King Idris of Libya was overthrown by a group of young colonels, one of whom was Muammar Gadhafi (yes, the same one).[3]

Within a very short period of time, the colonels evinced an interest in earning more royalties from Libya's oil than were being received, as well as reducing the country's dependence on the United States and Europe. They began to put pressure on the oil companies, threatening to cancel their concessions if they did not pay higher royalties. The Seven Sisters refused, but they had oil in other countries. The independents did not. This pressure eventually forced Occidental Oil—the company founded by Armand Hammer—to break ranks with the Sisters and pay higher royalties to the Libyan government. Other oil-producing governments demanded equal treatment, and began to get it.

The Seven Sisters did not approve of this price ratcheting. At their behest, in an effort to stop it, in 1971 Western governments agreed to meet with the oil-producing governments to discuss prices. Two sets of negotiations were scheduled, one in Tripoli, Libya, the other in Teheran, Iran. The major oil companies agreed to attend the meetings, thinking they had little to lose. They also had received a commitment from the U.S. government to prevent any price increases.

But the Sisters were betrayed. The Nixon administration recognized that higher prices would provide Middle Eastern countries—in particular, Iran—with the revenues they would need to pay for American armaments. In both meetings, the oil companies were double-crossed by Washington. And the American government was fooled, too.

The Nixon administration thought that the oil producers would be satisfied with a relatively small price increase—on the order of a dollar a barrel (a few cents per gallon). Once the price of oil began to rise, however, there was little to stop it from rising to what the market would bear and producing countries could arrange. And, as it became apparent that consumers would pay large sums of money for a tank of gas, the Shah of Iran realized that there was a lot of money to be made from oil. He was transformed from an American proxy into a "price hawk." The final blow came in 1973 when, in the wake of an oil embargo and panic engendered by the Arab-Israeli October War, oil prices were hiked from $4 to $12 a barrel. And not long after that, the properties of the Seven Sisters were taken over by the oil-producing governments. Western control of oil was at an end (Schurmann, 1987).

The price hikes and the oil embargo were not taken lightly by Western politicians. When it became clear that the Organization of Petroleum Exporting Countries (OPEC)—a group that had been founded in 1961, but which hardly anyone knew existed (Yergin, 1995)—had its hands around the West's "jugular vein," the issue of national security rapidly came to the fore. Foreign policy analysts warned that loss of Western control not only constituted an unacceptable taking of "our oil" but also posed an intolerable threat to America's freedom, safety, and prosperity. Some went so far as to propose military occupation of the oil fields (Sampson, 1991: 323). Worse yet, other countries followed the lead of OPEC, forming raw materials cartels that they hoped would allow them to control production, restrict supplies, raise prices, and get rich, too.

The runup in prices coincided with—and, indeed, was driven by—a period of both rapid economic growth and growing inflation throughout the West. Demand for raw materials and commodities rose to very high levels. Long lines formed at the gas pump. Tempers flared. As people cast about for explanations for this dilemma, they came upon a book called *The Limits to Growth* (Meadows, et al., 1972), prepared at the Massachusetts Institute of Technology and sponsored by the Club of Rome (at the time, another unfamiliar organization). According to the computer models used for the study, raw materials would become increasingly costly and scarce over the following 100 years, and this could lead to the collapse of civilization if immediate action weren't taken. A cottage industry emerged to attack the study and its methods, but the basic message, correct or not, had been broadcast: The United States and the world were running out of oil!

Over the next six years, as "energy crisis" became a household word, Americans would become obsessed with the cost of gasoline and angered at the way OPEC kept leading Washington on, making promises that it could not and would not keep. Prices rose, inflation ravaged Western economies, and no one could do very much about it. Few imagined that American pandering to the Shah of Iran in 1971 would lead, almost directly, to the establishment of the Islamic Republic of Iran only eight years later.[4]

The Enemy of My Enemy Is . . . Whom Did You Say It Was?

To Shah Mohammed Pahlevi, the newly found wealth accompanying the West's energy crisis provided the chance to revive his "White Revolution" of the 1960s and "develop" Iran to Western standards, by establishing the infrastructural base for economic growth after the oil would run out. That, along with the weapons bought with oil revenues would, he thought, make Iran a power to be reckoned with, not only in the Gulf but elsewhere, too. Unfortunately for his own future, the Shah ignored politics at home. While pouring funds into the Iranian economy favored the growing middle class as well as the Shah's family and cronies, he neglected and offended the mullahs in the mosques and the merchants in the markets (Yergin, 1991: 564, 626, 674-75).

They had never forgiven the Shah for his complicity in the 1953 CIA coup against the Mossadeq government, and now they blamed him for their society falling victim to Western immorality and economics. In 1971, the Shah held a massive celebration of the 2,500th anniversary of Persia at a specially constructed city at Persepolis. He invited thousands of guests to the event—including then-U.S. vice president Spiro Agnew—and spent between $100 and $200 million in self-glorification (Yergin, 1991: 563-64). Many Iranians regarded the Shah's attempt to connect himself with the ancient kings of Persia as a repudiation of Islam.

A vigorous opposition to his rule began to develop during the 1970s, much of it among Iranian college students in the United States. They began to publicize the Shah's unsavory secret police, SAVAK, and they were able to generate considerable Western sympathy. SAVAK had been established with CIA and Israeli help and, by the 1970s, had acquired an especially vicious reputation for torture of dissidents and gross violations of human rights. Paradoxically, perhaps, the newly found wealth flowing into the country also helped to create business for SAVAK. Many middle-class Iranians went abroad to study, where they became targets for the secret police, either as spies for the regime or as opponents to it. The dissidents began to build alliances with the Islamic opposition, organized around the Ayatollah Khomeini. He was, by then, living in France, after being expelled from Iraq as the result of an agreement between the Shah and

Saddam Hussein (which was, thereafter, the source of Khomeini's eternal enmity toward Iraq and one factor behind the Iran-Iraq War of the 1980s).

As 1978 began, no one in Washington imagined that the Shah might be overthrown, but his days as Iran's ruler were already numbered. Even to the last moment, the United States sought ways of keeping him in power in the face of the Islamic-liberal coalition that was determined to see him off. In the end, the Shah had no choice but to flee the country and seek refuge elsewhere. In his place, an interim government composed of both liberals and Islamists was established. It soon gave way to a Shi'ia Islamic theocracy intent, it seemed, on spreading Islamic revolution throughout the Middle East.

The Islamic Republic of Iran was a new type of state. It fit into no category known to Washington. Right-wing dictators and left-wing radicals were familiar and could be dealt with, but a theocracy—in the late twentieth century!—was a political anomaly. President Carter's national security adviser, Zbigniew Brzezinski, and others were convinced that it was the first piece in an Islamic "crescent of crisis," extending from the Horn of Africa at one end to Pakistan at the other. They were sure that Khomeini and his mullahs would spread their particular brand of Shi'ism throughout the Middle East even as they were inevitably co-opted by communists under direction from Moscow.

This fear was further exacerbated by events farther east. In 1979, a Soviet client regime in Afghanistan came apart. There, a Communist government, established several years earlier after the Afghani king was deposed by his cousin, was brought down by a gun battle during a cabinet meeting. The Soviets invaded in an effort, they claimed, to reestablish stability and protect an ally. The West did not believe a word, convinced that the Soviet Union was on the way south, to the Indian Ocean and the Persian Gulf (this was explained by noting that the Russians had wanted a warm-water port ever since the days of the czars).

President Carter warned that the United States would countenance no threats to Gulf oil, from either Communists or others, and established the "Rapid Deployment Force" (RDF). The RDF existed only on paper, but its mission was to serve as a nuclear tripwire in the event of a southward thrust by Moscow toward the oil fields. Why the Soviets might want Gulf oil was never made very clear although, as we shall see, Tom Clancy's *Red Storm Rising* made a somewhat implausible case for such desire. The RDF was renamed the Central Command, but it did not see action until 1990 when the plans were pulled off the shelf and it was sent to Saudi Arabia to deter Iraq from moving beyond Kuwait. But that is another story and another book (Lipschutz, 1992).

For the United States, worse was yet to come. The Shah found refuge in Panama, but was found to be dying of cancer and could not receive adequate medical care there. Two of his old, well-placed friends, David Rockefeller and Henry Kissinger, interceded with President Carter, asking him to allow the Shah to go to New York for treatment. The affront to the Islamic Republic was total. Students occupied the U.S. embassy, took some fifty employees hostage, and thumbed their noses at the "Great Satan" on nightly television. Negotiations commenced, hopes were raised and dashed over and over, and all efforts came to naught. An attempt to free the hostages by sending helicopter-borne troops into Teheran failed miserably when the craft crashed in a desert sandstorm, killing a number of would-be rescuers.

The hostages were not released before 400-plus days passed, after Jimmy Carter had been defeated in his bid for a second term and Ronald Reagan was about to take the oath of office. "America Held Hostage," the daily late-night report on ABC, captured the feeling of the nation during those fourteen-odd months. It was left to Reagan to do something about those feelings.

∿
∿

World War Three Meets the Wild, Wild West

Red Dawn (MGM-United Artists, 1983, 114 min.)
Director: John Milius
Cast: Patrick Swayze, Harry Dean Stanton, Charlie Sheen, Jennifer Grey, Ron O'Neal

Calumet is a typical Front Range Colorado town. Its primary source of income seems to be ranching and its primary interest appears to be football. As the story opens, Calumet is about to become the front line in World War III. The film's only black character, a teacher, is lecturing on the war-fighting tactics of Ghengis Khan, a subject that is clearly boring the students to death. Suddenly, the class's attention is diverted to the windows as paratroopers drop from the sky. The teacher, irritated by the interruption and determined to get to the bottom of this outrage, stalks out of the building. To the students' great shock, he is machine-gunned and falls dead.

Thereafter, events move rapidly. A group of teenage boys, under the leadership of a recent high-school graduate (Swayze, playing a one-time football hero who failed in the clutch during the big game), escapes from the town as it is being occupied by Cuban, Nicaraguan, and Soviet troops. The boys head for the mountains, and name themselves "Wolverines," after their high school mascot. From their high-country redoubt, they launch guerrilla attacks against the enemy.

As the plot develops, the boys are joined by two teenage girls and betrayed by one of their number, whom they execute. Midway through the film, the group rescues a downed American fighter pilot, who tells them about the progress of "World War III." The Europeans are sitting it out, Washington has been vaporized, the Midwest is occupied, Denver is under siege, and the people are eating rats. But there are "half-a-billion screaming Chinamen on America's side" (the other 500 million are, apparently, dead). The pilot also explains how the invasion happened. It seems that illegal immigrants from Central America, masquerading as tourists on charter flights, were able to come in and take over.

Before the pilot is killed while single-handedly attacking a Soviet tank, he advises the Wolverines on their tactics, thereby greatly enhancing their capabilities. Each successive victory liberates more equipment, increases the Wolverines' confidence, and allows them to engage in more serious actions. Eventually, all of the enemy's energies are directed toward wiping out this valiant band of freedom fighters, even to the point of flying in one of the USSR's premier antiterrorist experts. He is no more successful in capturing or killing the teenagers than anyone else.

Ultimately, the band is defeated, but not before it has wreaked havoc with the morale of the occupiers, especially Bella (O'Neal), the Cuban leader of the forces in Calumet. Bella bemoans the fact that, until now, he has always been on the side of the insurgents. In Calumet, he is no better than a common policeman. At the end of the film, after all of the Wolverines but two are killed and the war is over, one of the survivors tells us that the United States has triumphed and driven out the invader, with no help from anyone else, least of all the perfidious Europeans.

~~~

My Nukes or Yours?

On taking office, Richard Nixon faced two other major problems besides gold, oil, and Vietnam, and both reemerged during the 1980s. The first was responding to growing Soviet power and capabilities, especially in the nuclear realm. The second was dealing with the People's Republic of China, with which the United States had never had diplomatic relations. Nixon's strategy was crafted largely by Henry Kissinger, who had jumped from Nelson Rockefeller's 1968 presidential run to Nixon's after the former failed to win the Republican nomination. Kissinger's ideas were drawn directly from the school of nineteenth-century European realpolitik, which subscribed to statecraft, diplomacy, and negotiation, rather than the American school of realism, which claimed to view interstate relations in terms of power and national interests (Kissinger, 1957; Schurmann, 1987).

Whereas American realists paid lip service to the classical concepts of realpolitik, they were actually quite ideological when it came to the Cold War. They were less concerned about interests than defeating communism and, consequently, the Soviet Union loomed very, very large in their calculations. Kissinger preferred to see the Soviet Union as a traditional "Great Power," one less devoted to propagating its ideology than in getting its due in terms of the perks deserved by a large, powerful country. Kissinger reasoned that, if the Soviet Union could be drawn into a web of complex economic and political relations with the West, these would constrain it while, at the same time, giving it some of those perks. Consequently, the task of containment would be made that much easier (Gaddis, 1982). As a side benefit, if the Soviets had enough at stake in this web of relations, they might also be willing to withdraw support from their North Vietnamese allies, thereby reducing military pressure on the South and allowing the Americans to withdraw gracefully under the pretense of "Vietnamization."

The Kissingerian web of relations with the Soviets included several elements. There were Strategic Arms Limitations Treaties (SALT), which were meant to moderate U.S.-Soviet nuclear competition. Nixon and Kissinger sought to grant Most-Favored Nation (MFN) status to the Soviet Union in order to increase trade opportunities, although this was not finally accomplished until 1991 because of what was called the Jackson-Vanik Amendment, which required free emigration from the USSR as a precondition. Several other agreements on nuclear weapons testing and permissible activities in peripheral regions were signed. Under a new four-power agreement over Germany, there emerged the *Ostpolitik* of the Brandt government in West Germany. This was meant to establish all sorts of ties with East Germany, a new understanding over Berlin, and the diplomatic recognition of the German Democratic Republic. By 1972, détente seemed to be delivering what Kissinger had promised.

Alas, the success was short-lived. The effort to increase trade backfired. In the early 1970s, after a shortfall in the grain harvest, the Soviets bought massive amounts of wheat to meet their domestic deficits, creating both bread and meat price spikes in the United States. This, and the Soviet threat to intervene between the Israeli and Egyptian armies during the 1973 October War (see below), did little to convince the American public that it should support improved relations with the USSR, and relations soon began to deteriorate.

The second element in the Nixon-Kissinger strategy was rapprochement with the People's Republic of China. In the summer of 1971 the world was shocked to learn that Kissinger had been to Beijing. It was even more shocked to find out that President Nixon was going to visit the PRC in 1972 as a first step to establishing better relations (American allies had not been warned beforehand). Rapprochement was a shock because, as recently as 1970, Americans had been warned that the United States might be attacked by Chinese nuclear missiles. At the same time, China, in the throes of the Cultural Revolution, was virulently anti-American. But as the old saying goes, "The enemy of my enemy is my friend."

The common interest that brought the two countries together was the Soviet Union. The Chinese were fearful that they might be attacked—apparently the Soviets had discussed with the Americans the possibility of a joint attack on the Chinese nuclear facilities at Lop Nor (Burr and Richelson, 2000). Thus, the Chinese leadership—Mao Zedong and Chou En-lai—sought an implicit alliance with the United States. Of course, Nixon and Kissinger saw a benefit for the United States. On the one hand, they could play the "China card" against the Soviets while, on the other, it might be possible to get the PRC to bring their North Vietnamese clients to heel. So Nixon went to China, where he went to the Great Wall, and pronounced that it was, indeed, a great wall. The Soviets were unnerved, as was intended.

The first crack in U.S.-Soviet relations—and American confidence that *it* was in control of relations—appeared even before détente was finalized, during the 1973 Arab-Israeli October War. After some early setbacks—the armies of both Egypt and Syria were able to penetrate territory lost in 1967— Israeli forces crossed the Suez Canal, encircled the Egyptian Third Army, and, from there, threatened Cairo. At that point, Moscow warned that, were Israel to attack the Egyptian army or proceed toward the city, the Soviet Union would have no choice but to send in forces to separate the two sides. Nixon and Kissinger, hoping to warn off the Soviets, responded by calling a nuclear alert. The bluff worked, a cease-fire was established, and the alert was cancelled. Some historians still debate how close the world came to nuclear war (Yergin, 1991: 611-12; Garthoff, 1985).

Was the alert necessary? Nixon was just beginning to experience major fallout from the Watergate burglary, and some have speculated that this atomic diplomacy was intended to distract his detractors. The ploy might have worked briefly, but not for long. By 1974, Nixon was out of office, Jerry Ford was president, and Kissinger's grand strategy was showing signs of wear and tear.

The Bear Is Back!

U.S. ground troops had, for the most part, left Vietnam. Kissinger was busily engaged in trying to separate the Israelis from the Egyptians in

Sinai. The first energy crisis was in full swing. A revolution had occurred in Ethiopia, and another was about to take place in Portugal. The Soviets were deploying SS-20 missiles in Eastern Europe and seemed to be threatening U.S. strategic forces with their heavy missiles. And the NATO allies were, once again, beginning to lose faith in the American nuclear guarantee. The center was not holding.

In 1976, Jerry Ford barely won the Republican presidential nomination over Ronald Reagan, and Jimmy Carter, a relatively liberal Democrat was elected president. Carter came into office apparently determined to make a new start in U.S.-Soviet relations. In his view, the events of the early 1970s clearly demonstrated that the Cold War *ought* to be ended. He was also intent on making human rights a central goal of his administration. The result was a twofold disaster.

What was the problem? First, he felt that the draft SALT II treaty drawn up in 1975 by President Ford and Soviet Premier Brezhnev at Vladivostok was not good enough. So, Carter sent his secretary of state, Cyrus Vance, to Moscow with proposals to make deep cuts in strategic nuclear weapons. This irritated the Soviets, who viewed it as a ploy to get them to give up more of their weapons than agreed to in SALT II. Second, Carter's emphasis on human rights meant that the hard-headed realpolitik practiced by Kissinger, as odious as it was, no longer stood as a guiding principle for U.S. relations with other countries. This, too, came to irritate the Soviets, who thought that their internal affairs were none of Carter's business.

Another American concern was in Africa. The Soviets had managed to hop over the Middle East and were airlifting military equipment to a new neo-Marxist regime in Ethiopia, engaged in an external war with neighboring Somalia and an internal war in Eritrea. The Soviets were also providing help to new neo-Marxist regimes in Angola and Mozambique, former Portuguese colonies that had gained independence in 1975. A few analysts saw a strategy here, interpreting Soviet actions as the first steps in a Kremlin-directed "resource war," meant to block oil shipping lanes and cut off supplies of strategic raw materials to the West (Lipschutz, 1989).

Combined with what were claimed to be East Bloc-supported invasions of Zaire (now the Congo) in 1977 and 1978—which later proved to be untrue—the deployment of intermediate-range missiles in Europe (see below), failure to make progress on SALT II (of which more, in a moment), and the final collapse of South Vietnam, Cambodia, Laos and, as time went on, Iran and Afghanistan, the virulent anti-Communists of the U.S. political Right began to make a comeback. Things went from bad to worse as, in his final two years in office, Carter shifted from being a nice guy to a not-nice one and set into motion most of the new defense programs later attributed to Reagan.

The real action in the late 1970s and early 1980s was in Europe, where the faith in the American nuclear commitment began to crumble. After the Soviet SS-20s were discovered in Eastern Europe, NATO decided, under pressure from the West Germans, to respond with a nuclear deployment of its own, announcing that ground-launched cruise missiles (GLCM) and Pershing-II (P-II) intermediate range ballistic missiles (IRBMs) would be placed throughout Western Europe. Both types of "Euromissiles" could reach deep into the Soviet bloc, perhaps all the way to Moscow.

This was necessary, it was argued, not because anyone expected that the missiles might be used in a war, but because the SS-20s created a step in the deterrence ladder where the West had nothing comparable. In other words, some analysts imagined that in a crisis, as the two sides made threats and counterthreats, the Soviets could reach the level at which it would threaten to launch the SS-20s, and the West would have no way to respond. According to conservatives such as Paul Nitze, merely knowing that such a gap existed could give the Soviets political leverage over the West in a crisis and weaken the NATO alliance (Nitze, 1976-77).

We can see here how notions of deterrence became more and more abstract until they had little relationship to reality. Nonetheless, this unreality was the basis for Reagan's famous "two-track" policy. NATO would proceed with deployment of the Euromissiles while the United States engaged in Intermediate Nuclear Forces (INF) negotiations with the USSR to remove *both* the SS-20s and the Euromissiles. This was called the "zero-zero" option, and there is some evidence that it was proposed by the United States in full confidence that the Soviets would never agree to it.

The INF negotiations proceeded fitfully throughout the first six years of the Reagan administration with little progress. Then, in 1986, the new and vigorous Soviet premier, Mikhail Gorbachev, quite unexpectedly agreed to the zero-zero option. For a time, the Americans did not know quite how to respond. The eventual result was the Intermediate Nuclear Forces Treaty of 1987, which eliminated several whole classes of missiles from Europe and was hailed as the Cold War's first real disarmament agreement.

The NATO decision on deployment had a second, completely unintended consequence. One public response to the two-track plan, and the Reagan administration's nuclear saber-rattling (Scheer, 1982) was the rise of an activist peace movement throughout the West. In the United States, the Freeze Movement called for a halt to further increases in nuclear arms. This lead President Reagan, in a fit of fevered imagination, to propose the missile-proof Strategic Defense Initiative (aka "Star Wars"; see Wirls 1992; FitzGerald, 2000).

In Europe, organizations such as the Committee on Nuclear Disarmament in Britain and the Greens in West Germany were established. The peace movement, alone, was insufficient to stop the deployment of the Euromissiles. But it did open up many channels of communication with dissidents and activists across Eastern Europe. These channels of interaction created a certain degree of solidarity among some groups in the two halves of Europe, and helped to maintain those in Eastern Europe through some very difficult times. Ultimately, when the regimes in Eastern and Central Europe began to crumble, these were the groups that led the way and, in some instances, took power. But that, too, is another story (Meyer, 1993).

∿∿

Seeing Reds

The Hunt for Red October, Tom Clancy (Annapolis, Md.: Naval Institute Press, 1984)
Red Storm Rising, Tom Clancy (New York: Putnam's Sons, 1986)

The renewal of the Cold War also led to the emergence of a new pot-boiler genre: the technothriller. In the mid-1980s, Tom Clancy burst onto the scene with two such novels, making a mark not only on the best-seller lists but also the U.S. strategic establishment (and especially the Navy). Clancy had no military or technical background—he was self-taught—yet his novels were so detailed and accurate that many found it difficult to believe he did not have sources somewhere in the Pentagon and the defense industry.

The Hunt for Red October deals with a new Soviet strategic missile submarine—*Red October*—that utilizes a silent propulsion system based on magneto-hydrodynamics (MHD) rather than nuclear or diesel power. MHD uses a magnetic field to force sea water through the propulsion system, and it has no moving parts. It is therefore extremely quiet and cannot be detected by conventional antisubmarine warfare tactics. Such a device could render America's vast submarine search system useless. The United States, getting wind of this system, begins to search for *Red October* in the hope of destroying it. At the same time, the captain and his crew have decided to defect to the United States. After an extended search and chase, the Americans get the message and the defection is carried off.

In *Red Storm Rising*, a major Soviet oil refinery is blown up by an in-house group of Islamic fundamentalists. The resulting oil shortage puts a severe crimp in the country's economy. The Politburo, contemplating its options, decides to make up the oil deficit by invading the Persian Gulf and conquering Iran and Iraq. In order to do this successfully, however, NATO must be put out of action. A plan to divide the alliance is formulated. The Soviet Union will provoke a war with West Germany (alone). Its allies, being cowards and especially fearful of nuclear war, will be reluctant to fulfill their commitments when they do not appear to be under threat. While NATO is squabbling, and before the United States can react, elite units of the Red Army will strike south toward the Gulf.

The war begins on schedule. The Soviets plan to break through first on the central front in Germany. They will maintain their momentum and weaken NATO by disrupting the sea lines of communication across the Atlantic, the routes by which supplies and men are being moved from the United States to Europe. But the fighting bogs down rather quickly. In spite of losing Iceland, the key to protection of Atlantic shipping, NATO is not easily put down. It does not splinter, it gains air superiority rather quickly, and it has a strong technological advantage. Ultimately, after much devastation and many casualties on both sides, the Soviets realize they cannot win and sue for peace. The old regime in Moscow is deposed, and a new one, with the people's interests at heart takes office. And, the West offers the Soviets as much oil as they need, at concessional prices, if necessary.

~~~

Morning Again in America, with a Hangover

Much has been written about Ronald Reagan's presidency and the "Second" Cold War, more than can or need be repeated here (see, e.g., Dalby, 1990; Gaddis, 1992). The fact remains that Reagan took office under the auspices of a cadre of neo-conservative cheerleaders called the Committee on the Present Danger, who had taken it on themselves to alert the country to the new threats from the USSR (Sanders, 1983). Among them were several of Harry Truman's original Cold Warriors, some Cold War liberals, and even a few ex-peaceniks. Such support was not altogether surprising. Although Ronald Reagan had had many personas (Rogin, 1987), throughout his first term in office he remained what he had been since his days as president of the Screen Actors' Guild in the late 1940s: a Cold War Democrat. What is interesting, perhaps, is not that he should revive this role, but that it should prove so popular thirty years after NSC-68 and the Korean War.

Who, after all, believed that the USSR still posed the kind of mortal threat that had been feared in the early 1950s? Many of the neo-cons—some of whom had been Communists in the 1930s or New Left radicals in the 1960s—were convinced that the Soviet Union had changed not a whit since 1950—indeed, they thought it was more terrible and dangerous than ever. The fact was, however, that Stalin was dead, no member of the Politburo had been executed since the demise of the unfortunate but unlamented Lavrenti Beria in 1953, a senile Leonid Brezhnev was in charge, and the Soviet economy was beginning its tumble into the hole from which it would not emerge.

What, then, was the cause of the Cold War revival? Most of the more conventional accounts will cite, as I have above, a variety of Soviet actions, including heavy ICBMs with multiple warheads, Cubans in Africa, resource wars, arms to Central America's guerillas, high levels of defense spending relative to GNP (although, as it turned out, very inefficient allocation of resources and a percentage smaller than America's), the placement of the SS-20s in Europe and so on (Winik, 1996). All of these were seen as part of a renewed Soviet plan to expand its influence into regions where it had never been before. Whatever their causes, whatever their effects, the political impacts in the United States were enormous.

In retrospect, the signs of incipient weakness are readily visible (and after 1991 the CIA was lambasted for its failure to see them). During the 1970s and 1980s, the Soviet economy was hardly able to provide for domestic needs, and foreign policy was one place where the regime might find some successes that could generate support at home. American paranoia was a natural response, even if the wrong one. But paranoia, even if unfounded, has real costs, not the least in terms of dollars and morale. As noted in chapter 5, not only did this new Cold War cost a great deal of money in terms of the military buildup—in the end, it cost more than $2.5 trillion between 1980 and 1988 and more than doubled the national debt—but also broadcast widely the fear that a nuclear war would break out before the end of the decade (as seen in films such as *The Day After*).[5]

There is another explanation for the Second Cold War, one that is more rooted in collective psychology than international relations but much more difficult to document. The domestic traumas and instabilities of the 1970s gave rise to a yearning for the predictability and certainty of earlier decades (especially the 1950s), when the enemy had been a clearly identified "Other" and everyone "knew" his or her place in the social order (this disordering of society has only been further compounded since). To confront a nuclear-armed superpower was one thing; to be bested by a bunch of radical religious students was another. To be shafted by Big Oil was one thing; to be robbed by Arab sheiks was another. And to stalemate in a war with China was acceptable, but to lose to a bunch of pajama-clad peasants was, simply, intolerable.

The problem was, in other words, a growing sense of *inferiority*. And, inasmuch as the United States could not go around bashing small countries—although Reagan did do this in Grenada and tried in Nicaragua—the feeling grew that the United States better get its act together vis-à-vis the Big One. This could be accomplished only by direct confrontation.

As an hypothesis, this might be regarded as grasping at straws, and trying to place the blame for the Second Cold War where it does not belong, on the United States. There was, to be sure, a reality out there. The Soviet Union invaded Afghanistan. They and their allies provided aid to Marxists in Africa. They had heavy, accurate ICBMs. They deployed SS-20s. They sent military equipment to Nicaragua. But as some observers pointed out, they were also very cautious in their activities and hardly willing to risk a confrontation with Washington (Breslauer and Tetlock, 1991). Only five years later, in fact, Gorbachev became party chairman and embarked on a concerted effort to improve relations between the USSR and the United States.

The mass psychology of this Second Cold War is best depicted in the plethora of films and novels, lionizing confrontation and war, that emerged during the first half of the 1980s. As many members of the administration later put it, a nuclear war must not be fought because it cannot be won (Kull, 1988) Yet, there were people who insisted that it *could* be fought and won. But no one in a position of responsibility could offer a convincing scenario that did not also carry sizable risks of self-annihilation. Since the exercise could not be conducted in the realm of politics, it was relegated to the realm of fiction, where it became a kind of vicarious experience of war and victory (not unlike that depicted in *1984*). These works were not widely read because they made a solid case for a "theory of victory," as the conservative nuclear strategist Colin Gray put it (1979), but because *we win!* Just as Rambo goes to Vietnam and liberates hostages who are not supposed to exist, so the United States goes to war, and wins in ways that are not supposed to be possible.

$\approx$

The Bloody Right

One of the more imaginative television series of the 1960s was *The Wild, Wild West* (remade in 1999 as a feature film). The series protrayed a post-Civil War era Secret Service agent, James West, and his sidekick, Artemus Gordon, who roamed the United States, foiling dastardly villains and their nefarious plots designed to bring the nation to ruin. West was clearly modeled on James Bond, even to the point that he was usually sent out with high-tech gizmos whose existence, in the mid-nineteenth century, was quite improbable. In this respect, Bond, Rambo, and Jim West are all of a piece.

But Rambo relies more on innate skills than equipment—harking back to Davy Crockett and Natty Bumpo—an inversion of the Bondian plot device that we also find in *Red Dawn*. In that film, contemporary teenagers, armed with nineteenth-century tools and tactics, defeat the most advanced weaponry the Red Army has to offer. The Clancy novels rely solely on heroic men and machinery; indeed, they are so technically detailed and accurate that Clancy is regularly asked to lecture at U.S. military institutions. Moreover, they are so popular that he has become a rich man.

Red Dawn, although heroic, is not a "quality" film. The plot is wholly implausible, the characters paper-thin, the dialogue silly. By and large, the critics hated it. Paradoxically, it is profoundly moving as well as powerful propaganda. Through its use of particular icons and tropes, it taps into scenes and settings all too familiar to most Americans and it shamelessly manipulates viewers' memories and emotions. More than this, it tries to put paid to the widespread notion that America is invulnerable to foreign attack. The film not only serves to validate American nationalism—something rare in this day and age—via the war waged by innocent teenagers against evil aliens, it also engages the viewer in a rite of purification. This is something few American films of the Cold War tried, much less managed, to do. As story, consequently, *Red Dawn* is absurd; as text, however, it is classic.

There are four iconic themes that run through the film and merit particular attention in the context of the nationalist revival of the 1980s. First, the film draws heavily on images of the Old West and mixes these with images from the "Old East," especially Afghanistan.[6] In terms of location, Calumet, Colorado is virtually indistinguishable from any of the towns portrayed in hundreds of earlier cowboy films. After the Soviets and their allies arrive, the teenagers escape to the mountains (cf. Chechnya), set up camp, engage in various blood rites (some of a vaguely homosexual nature), and "live off the land." It is from these foothills that they launch their attacks against the invaders, on horseback, dressed in vaguely Middle Eastern garb, and it is to these foothills that they always escape.

Second, war is portrayed as a purifying experience. Even the inhabitants of the Old West/New West have gotten soft, the film suggests, and are content to watch the stylized combat of high school football, but little more. The Wolverines have not yet fully succumbed to this malaise and, in contrast to their parents, are able to escape imprisonment and degradation at the hands of the Communist forces. The blood ritual involving a slaughtered deer represents not only the teens ability to live off the land but also rebirth and a mingling of bodily fluids (now what does that mean?).

Third, there is the repetition of the "struggle for freedom," linked to the American forefathers. This is most evident in the contrast between the Wolverines, described as "freedom fighters" at the end of the film, and their parents, held captive in an improvised prison at the local drive-in (where they are constantly exposed to Communist reeducation films—presumably an in-joke of sorts). The film suggests that not only has freedom been taken away by the invaders, it was already threatened before the war ever began and now can be maintained only through struggle.

Finally, the film invokes the clash between technology and individual will. In the scene most reminiscent of how a viewer might imagine combat in Afghanistan, the Wolverines are cornered in the local badlands and hunted down, on horseback, by a futuristic, "Star Wars"-style Soviet gunship (one that also appears in *Rambo II*). Only two of the band—a boy and girl—are able to escape—on horseback, of course—to tell the story. In the long run, it is determination and will, and not technology, that turns back the invasion.

The film's impact was, ultimately, less in its implausible presentation of the circumstances of World War III and its agents and more in its evocation of a time when right was distinguishable from wrong, when the Colt .45 was the "law of the land," and free men and women ran the country (that such a time never existed hardly matters, of course). It was, in other words, about regaining control over one's destiny, a sensibility that, at the end of the 1970s, seemed widely lacking. If anything—and this is difficult to imagine— *Red Dawn* was too subtle in this respect, which is why *Rambo II* was more popular and is, even today, better remembered.

Unlike most movies of the genre, *Rambo II* engaged not only in historical revisionism but also presented itself as a version of the "truth" that was being actively suppressed by the U.S. government. Sylvester Stallone, who directed and starred in the *Rambo* films, went so far as to claim that *Rambo II* represented the "pre-stages of a true historical event" (quoted in Christensen, 1987: 203). Almost twenty years later, this "true historical event" has yet to take place (and the United States and Vietnam have diplomatic relations). But there was (and is) more to *Rambo II* than just the story or claims contained therein.

The film is better seen as a *bricolage*—a bric-à-brac—of U.S. Cold War history, with allusions to World War II, the Old West, the early frontier, and Watergate, too. *Rambo II* runs riot with tropes, allusions, and cues that draw on what is assumed to be the audience's familiarity with U.S. history, culture, and politics and it evokes certain associations and patterns of belief. In this way, the film manages to argue for the verisimilitude of what is really outright fabrication.

How, then, are we to regard Rambo? Is he simply a cartoon, an extreme parody of a particular type of film hero, or does he represent something more than this? While I should not want to make too much of him, a number of the themes presented in *Rambo II* are well-established ones that, among other things, present a revisionist version of what happened in Vietnam and comment, as well, on American foreign policy of the day. In promoting the film, Stallone also declared "I hope to establish a character that can repre-sent a certain section of the American consciousness" (quoted in Christ-ensen, 1987: 203).

By playing on the POW-MIA issue, Stallone was replaying the notion of betrayal, which is so often invoked in politics to explain things that "go wrong." In this instance, what "went wrong" was that the United States lost in Vietnam and, in the logic of the times, needed to rectify this loss. If it could not be done in the military arena, perhaps a mythic one would do.

From Rambo's view—and, presumably, in the view of many Americans—the loss in Vietnam was squarely the responsibility of Washington. This view reflected a growing distrust of the U.S. government on both left and right of the political spectrum. The politicians had not allowed the generals to fight the war the way the latter wished—a common complaint, as seen before, during, and after the Persian Gulf War. Indeed, some believed that Washington had conspired to lose in Vietnam. After all, how could the most powerful nation on Earth, with the most advanced technology the world had ever seen, lose to such a poor, backward one? Hence, Rambo's ontological question to Colonel Trautmann: Do we get to win this time?

But there is more than just betrayal to Stallone's indictment of the "loss" of Vietnam. The entire endeavor, it would seem, was prosecuted in bad faith. This is exemplified in the position of the CIA's man in Thailand, who is under orders to prevent, by all means possible, the retrieval of any POWs or MIAs should they actually be found. Such orders, Trautmann suggests, have been issued because Washington does not want to pay Hanoi the three billion dollars promised as part of the Paris Peace Accords. Rambo is, therefore, to find and photograph only *empty* camps so that all of this unpleasant business can be finished. The CIA, usually described as a "rogue" agency by the Left, is here criticized from the Right as the puppet of corrupt politicians.

The high-tech equipment provided to Rambo, and intended to monitor his whereabouts, is also evidently designed to prevent him from finding and bringing back any Americans. Indeed, the equipment is almost the cause of his death as he parachutes from the plane. Thereafter, Rambo has only "primitive" equipment: his body (a "fighting machine"), and his native intelligence and skills to help fulfill his mission. Rambo's jungle wisdom can be read as an indictment of the high-tech nature of the war as the United States fought it, as well as a more general condemnation of technology. It also evokes the myths of American pioneers such as Daniel Boone, Davy Crockett, and Jim Bowie, who single-handedly confronted the primitive world with only the most rudimentary of tools and weapons.

Tom Clancy's "Seeing Reds" novels, by contrast, do not romanticize guerrilla warfare; instead, they reify complex tactics and high technology. In this respect, he represents the view from Washington, D.C., rather than Calumet, Colorado. While there was much speculation about whether a World War III would break out during the 1980s—and wars often do break out when countries are "feeling their oats," so to speak—no one was able to describe a war that would not go nuclear and end the world. No one, that is, until Tom Clancy appeared on the scene.

Before *The Hunt for Red October* was published, no one had ever heard of Clancy. Like many aspiring authors, he made his living working as a clerk, in this instance, in insurance. When his novels did appear, many readers were convinced that there was no such person, because it was clear that the author was extraordinarily knowledgeable about military technology and tactics, must hold a high-level security clearance, and was writing under a pseudonym. Indeed, Clancy was sometimes cited by Ronald Reagan as one of his "technical advisers," albeit only because the president read the novels and, apparently, little else.

Red October was a tour de force—technically precise and suspenseful—and it fed directly into public paranoia. Magneto-hydrodynamics was an energy technology that the United States had investigated but never perfected. The novel was so detailed that no one could be wholly sure the Soviets did not, indeed, possess such a system. If they did, it would make obsolete the entire American ballistic submarine program as well as its antisubmarine warfare efforts, and present an unprecedented nuclear threat to the American homeland.

Clancy's second novel, *Red Storm Rising*, was much less compelling but, in many ways, much more realistic, at least in terms of the action. While *Red Storm Rising* is also technically precise, it overwhelms the reader with details. This is where Clancy really excels, as in, for example, the way in which he conveys the tediousness of the search and the tension of the hunt associated with antisubmarine warfare. Overall, however, the novel lacks plausibility in two important respects, and these are of interest in light of the times in which the book was published.

First, Clancy assumes that the Soviets must be interested in Persian Gulf oil. Most scenarios of a Soviet strike through Iran did not assume a real material need for the oil; rather, it was part of the "resource war" strategy meant to cut off the flow of oil to the West. Absent the conditions posited by Clancy—an acute shortage brought on by internal sabotage—there was little reason to think that Moscow would take such a risky step, especially since successive U.S. presidents had declared an inviolate American security interest in the Gulf.

Second, Clancy bends over backward to eschew the use of nuclear weapons in his scenario, proposing that the Soviet Politburo would resort to atomic warfare only when facing defeat (and it is that step that triggers the coup against the Politburo). NATO doctrine in the event of a war in Europe was quite unclear on when nukes might be used. The 300,000 American troops stationed in Western Europe at that time were there as a "tripwire" in the service of extended nuclear deterrence, just as the Rapid Deployment Force was designed to be sent to the Persian Gulf should a crisis develop there. This meant that, in the event of an attack on NATO by the Warsaw Pact, casualties among the U.S. forces would virtually guarantee a nuclear response. Such knowledge—much like the "Doomsday Machine" of *Dr. Strangelove*—was meant to make the pact very careful about even contemplating offensive action in Europe. At the same time, NATO also eschewed a declaration of "no first use," meaning that it would not hesitate to use nuclear weapons first, if necessary.

In *Red Storm Rising*, Clancy is very careful to show both sides avoiding resort to tactical nuclear devices for fear that the war might escalate. Yet, there must be some linkage between declaratory and operational policy or it will lose its effect. Secrets tend to "leak" and if the link is absent, it will become general knowledge. The deterrent aspect of the threat will be lost.

In political terms, therefore, *Red Storm Rising* can be seen as a war "simulation" intended for consumption by public, policymakers, and military professionals. World War III could not be fought or won in reality, so it had to be fought *and* won in film, book, and software. As Jean Baudrillard has pointed out, in the absence of the ability to wage war in reality, the *simulation* of war becomes a substitute (Der Derian, 1985). Other films and novels conveyed this point much more powerfully and directly, of course, but they were all of a cultural and social piece that went hand-in-hand with the war-threatening rhetoric of the Reagan administration.

The political problem with rhetorical excess is that people might begin to believe that you mean what you say. More than that, if people come to believe what they are being told about the enemy, they may demand action. As President Clinton found out, and President Bush is likely to discover, a failure to act at times deemed appropriate by virtue of rhetorical excess can come to be seen as weakness rather than prudence. Had the Soviet Union invaded Afghanistan in 1984, rather than 1979, what might have been the result?

※
※

Are We Feeling Better Yet?

As we shall see in the next two chapters, feeling better did nothing to address one fundamental problem during the 1980s: American dominance of the Free World—or "hegemony," as some political scientists like to put it (Gilpin, 1980)—could not be restored to the circumstances of the 1950s. The problem was not with the military power of the Soviet Union. Rather, it was that economic, rather than military, power was becoming the new key to global influence.

The military buildup of the 1980s only exacerbated this dilemma by flooding the global economy with dollars and ratcheting up both budget deficits and national debt. This happened, moreover, in concert with interest rate hikes and exchange rate manipulations, a competitiveness bind, and a "go-go" profit-at-any-cost attitude on Wall Street (depicted in Tom Wolfe's *The Bonfire of the Vanities* and films such as *Wall Street*). Consequently, when the Cold War finally did come to an end and the enemy dissolved, the United States found it necessary to search for new foes, at home and abroad.

Chapter 9

New Competitors, Old Enemies

The Beginning of the End

The end of the Cold War came as something of a surprise. During the summer of 1989, Western observers watched with interest as East German "tourists" were allowed to cross into Austria *through* still-Communist Hungary. In Poland, roundtable discussions sought to bring non-Communists into the government. In November, following growing numbers of street protests throughout East Germany, the Berlin Wall was suddenly opened. Throngs of "Ossis" flocked to the western side of the city to gawk at store windows and experience the "Free World."

After that, things moved quickly. By the end of December, all of the Communist Eastern European regimes, except for Albania and Yugoslavia, had fallen. Most had gone peacefully, with the blessing of Moscow. It was time to adapt to a new world.

Some thought that the 1991 Gulf War against Saddam Hussein's Iraq would lead to what President George Bush (the Elder) called the "New World Order"; others doubted it, predicting a return to the old power politics of pre–World War II Europe (Mearshiemer, 1990). In the event, neither proved right, a point to be taken up in chapter 10.

The United States was not prepared for peace. At some point during the latter half of the 1980s, according to a now almost-apocryphal story, a U.S. diplomat was approached by a Soviet colleague and told, sotto voce, "We are about to do a terrible thing to you. We are going to deprive you of an enemy"(cited in McCormick, 1989: 232). A few years later, in August 1991, they proceeded to do just that, as the Soviet Union fell apart. A few American conservatives, suspicious as ever, opined that it was all a sham—*disinformatsia* propagated by Soviet president Gorbachev—and that the USSR would come back, stronger than ever (as was proposed in the Russian Duma in March 1996). But even these few doubters were proved wrong. The loss of the enemy, however, created a political and economic dilemma from which the United States has yet to recover.

Cold War policymakers relied on the invocation of patriotism and political mobilization to get policies past Congress and the public. The disappearance of the enemy made it difficult to rationalize the kinds of expenditures and programs once associated with the fight against communism. Not only was the defense budget cut and military bases closed, the dismantling of the welfare state began in earnest, too (Mishra, 1999). The end of military Keynesianism, which had justified deficit spending in order to keep the national economy growing, had ramifications far beyond balancing the budget (which was not, in any case, balanced until late into the 1990s), and these did not become evident immediately.

Chapter 10 examines several visions of the future offered during the 1980s, and compares them with what has, so far, actually transpired. This chapter looks at the ways in which the end of the Cold War was reflected in both politics and popular culture. During the last few years of the 1980s and the first few years of the 1990s, two perspectives emerged that reflected the consequences of losing the enemy. The first, epitomized by Michael Crichton's *Rising Sun*, offered the view that there were new enemies out there, although they were using economic tactics to subvert and conquer the United States, rather than the military ones that were so familiar (see, e.g., Rosecrance, 1986; Kennedy, 1987). The second, evident in films such as *Falling Down*, suggested that the enemy was, perhaps, inside rather than outside.

For a time, as Japanese investors bought up U.S. real estate and Treasury securities, Crichton's misogynistic and racist diatribe against Japan proved the more popular view, especially after it was turned into a film starring Wesley Snipes and Sean Connery (who remains unable to escape being James Bond in the mind of the movie-going public). Still, in light of the bombing of the Oklahoma City Federal Building in 1995, downsizings throughout corporate America, the culture war declared by Pat Buchanan in the 1996 Republican presidential primary campaign, and periodic shoot-'em-ups in schools, streets, and workplaces, Michael Douglas's militarized Pilgrim's Progress across Los Angeles proved ultimately to be closer to the mark.

From Cold War to Warm Peace

In retrospect, it is clear that the Cold War was all but over by the late 1970s, brought to its conclusion by economic forces whose causes and consequences only began to become clear during the last half of the 1990s. The Reagan revival was mostly a rhetorical one—a social construction, if you will—although even social constructions, however imaginative, have real material effects. In this instance, the real effects included a defense spending binge of several trillion dollars that brought all sorts of baroque and sometimes faulty equipment to the nation's defense arsenal (Kaldor, 1981; Farrell, 1997). It also led to a wave of mergers and downsizings in the country's industrial and corporate sectors—something that has become the norm—that seemed to leave whole regions of the country, such as the "Rust Belt," in economic ruins. The Reagan era also nurtured an abiding distrust of government that, at times, even included war against it (Aho, 1994).

In a nutshell, during the 1980s the United States could afford to wage what Mary Kaldor (1990) called the "imaginary war" only because the rhetorical excesses of the period so scared the American public that it was willing to spend whatever was thought necessary to restore a comforting sense of security. At the same time, the Soviet Union was crumbling from within. The succession of aged Soviet leaders—Brezhnev, Chernenko, Andropov—who fell during those years like Eisenhower's fabled dominoes—could not marshal the political support or strength at home to wage peace with the West. It would have been a difficult proposition even for an energetic leader. Nonetheless, Mikhail Gorbachev was, finally, able to convince Ronald Reagan himself that peaceful coexistence was possible and even desirable.

In fact, Gorbachev was so convincing that, in November 1986, the two leaders emerged from a hastily called summit meeting in Reykjavik, Iceland, and declared to abolish nuclear weapons by the year 2000 (which, at the time, seemed quite far off). Reagan's advisers were appalled—he had met Gorbachev without any of them close to hand—and they forced him to backpedal quickly. But the trajectory for the next few years was set. The Intermediate Nuclear Forces agreement followed in 1987, and conventional and strategic arms reductions became the subject of serious negotiation, too.

But why make the claim that the Cold War was over by 1980 if all evidence suggests that it was not? The Cold War was not, for the most part, a shooting war, except in peripheral regions of the world (where upward of twenty million may have died). Still, even shooting wars don't end suddenly. The losing side can mount offensive campaigns or assist allies in a last gasp effort to turn the tide. Armed units sometimes don't get the news of war's end until long after the cessation of hostilities. And violence can flare up along cease-fire lines when there are disagreements about their location or the disposition of forces. Much of the conflict of the first half of the 1980s was of this type and, after 1985, most of the peripheral Cold War conflicts began to wind down.

By 1985, too, it was increasingly evident to the Soviets, if not to the Americans, that the burden of superpower competition was too much to bear and was certainly going to drive the USSR into further economic crisis. If the Soviet Union were ever to achieve the economic level of the West, it would have to undergo massive reform and restructuring. This was the point of Gorbachev's *glasnost* and *perestroika*: To unleash the energies that would mobilize people in support of reform and restructuring. Unfortunately for him, and the people of the USSR, his strategy did not work. But that is another story (see., e.g., Crawford, 1985).

The United States, oddly enough, found itself in a not too dissimilar situation, although in an immeasurably better position. To understand this argument, however, we need to return for a moment to the logic behind the American sponsorship of the post-World War II international economy. And this requires a foray into political economy which some readers might find boring, and others baffling (but read on and see).

Suffice it to say, at the outset, that the goal of American policymakers at the end of World War II was to extend the benefits of the U.S. economic system to the rest of the world. The cynic might say in response that the intent of such a policy was simply to increase profits and allow Americans to get richer, faster than others.

But neither view is incorrect. In extending domestic practice into the international arena, U.S. policymakers sought to re-create what they saw as the relative social peace of the American system, purchased through a constantly expanding economic pie. The history of U.S. class relations showed, they thought, that a growing economy was instrumental to social peace—although it took an heroic effort to ignore the social conflict in American history or the costs that the so-called social peace had imposed on those who were powerless and poor. But economic liberalism (aka, capitalism) did extend prosperity to a large number of U.S. citizens and, therefore, it seemed worthwhile to reproduce it worldwide. There was, however, a serious flaw in this plan (not to mention that democracy was not included). Just as there were still pockets of wealth and poverty throughout the United States—the result of the way in which capitalism operated domestically—so would it be throughout the world once American capitalism had managed to permeate all of its corners. We will return to this point, shortly.

∿∿
∿∿

The East Is (a) Red (Circle on a White Background)

Rising Sun: A Novel, Michael Crichton (New York: Knopf, 1992)

As *Rising Sun* begins, a young woman has been found dead at the grand opening of the Nakamoto Building in Los Angeles. Detective Peter Smith, a divorced single father, is called in as the Asian liaison officer, to mediate between the officials of Nakamoto, a Japanese corporation, and the LA Police Department. He brings along John Conner, an on-leave LAPD detective who speaks fluent Japanese, has spent a considerable amount of time in Japan, and is well versed in that country's culture and habits. Conner is not very popular around the city, however. The Japanese consider him dangerous and his colleagues in the LAPD think he has sold out to Japan. Crichton shows the reader that Conner is the only character in the book who "knows" what is really going on, that is, how the Japanese are pulling the wool over American eyes. Smith, being somewhat naive about the whole business, becomes *kohai*—apprentice—to Conner's *sempai*—mentor.

What first looks like a fairly straightforward affair soon turns into a complex and confusing murder mystery. Higher-ups in the Nakamoto Corporation want it to appear as though the murderer is one Eddie Sakamura, a "man-about-town" and Japanese expatriate whose father works for another *kereitsu* in Japan.

Sakamura, it turns out, is only one of the young woman's many lovers. Another is a U.S. senator. Conner has his doubts about Sakamura's guilt. These are eventually confirmed, but not before the reader is treated to frequent and sometimes nasty exposés of how the Japanese "think" and how they are quietly taking over the United States.

Meanwhile, the screws are being tightened on both the good guys and the bad. As Conner and Smith proceed in their search for the real killer, they find themselves under pressure from both the department and City Hall to drop the investigation. They refuse and continue to pursue the case, even after the department has declared it "closed." The two detectives eventually discover that the murder has something to do with the proposed sale of an American high-tech corporation to a Japanese company, a U.S. senator—the one involved with the dead woman—who is opposed to the sale, and the blackmail meant to change his vote.

By the end of the novel, everyone implicated in the murder is dead—by murder or suicide—and the truth about the murder as well as Japanese influence is covered up. Smith is called on the carpet in a disciplinary hearing. Conner is ignored. The reader is left to conclude that nothing has changed or will. Eventually, America will go under, buried not by the Soviet enemy but the Japanese friend.

Our Time Here on the Ground Will Be Short

What is *Rising Sun* really about? As is the case with many films and novels, it is not a major cultural work. Nevertheless, the book is iconic in the sense that it mirrored events in society at large and contributed further to a widely held sense of economic insecurity and uncertainty about the "enemy." *Rising Sun* was a product of a particular time, just before and after the end of the Cold War, when Japan's trade surplus with the United States was large and growing, the United States was a good location for investment of Japan's dollars, and American reliance on Japanese technology appeared to pose an incipient security threat. (Today, for a number of reasons, not the least of which are more than ten years of economic troubles in Japan, such concerns have disappeared.)

Crichton's central proposition is that Japan is at war with the United States. As John Conner, his mouthpiece, says: "We are definitely at war with Japan" (p. 136). Or, rather, the Japanese regard business as the equivalent of war and will do whatever is necessary to win: lie, cheat, steal, and murder, if need be. As Crichton puts it in an "Afterword" to the book, "the Japanese have invented a new kind of trade—adversarial trade, trade like war, trade to wipe out the competition" (p. 393).

Whether he was correct in his accusations is questionable today, although most of the details regarding the activities of Japanese and American corporations, as he points out on the copyright page, were true. What *is* open to criticism are his claims regarding motivation and intent. And what is undeniable is that he presented an exaggerated version of a fear of Japan that was quite widespread for several years, a fear that, if not vigilant, the United States would be purchased wholesale. As Smith says at the end of the book, "If you sell the country to Japan, then they will own it, whether you like it or not. And people who own things do what they want with them. That's how it works" (p. 388).

No matter that Smith is not entirely correct on that last point—the owners of property are never entirely free to use it without constraints—it is his attitude that counts. He has experienced firsthand, he thinks, the undercover conquest of the United States by Japan, which is finishing what it started at Pearl Harbor, albeit through "war" by more insidious means. Crichton certainly wanted his readers to believe his warnings, although the novel is so xenophobic and misogynistic that it is difficult to take it as much more than an outlandish fantasy. But if Crichton represented the extremists, others who were more "moderate" were also seen as more acceptable. And their warnings against the Japanese "invasion" were taken seriously.[1]

The irony in these claims is that the conditions in the United States described by Crichton are, when all is said and done, the result of the economic half of the Cold War "walnut" (LaFeber, 1993). Indeed, and paradoxically, Japan's success represented not the *failure* of U.S. economic policy, but its *success*.

At the end of World War II, Japan was bankrupt and in ruins. Through American political, strategic, and economic assistance, designed to restore prosperity and root Japan firmly in the Free World, it became an industrious, technologically advanced, and rich country. But this is no surprise, especially inasmuch as concerns about U.S. competitiveness with Japan had been aired for more than twenty years, beginning not long after the onset of the 1973 energy crisis. Why, then, should it have become so pointed around the time *Rising Sun* made the best-seller list of the *New York Times*?

〰️
〰️

Naval Gazing

The answer to *that* question requires examination of a 1987 book, *The Rise and Fall of the Great Powers*, written by Paul Kennedy, a Yale professor of history whose previous work had addressed British naval history. His thesis, borrowed from what is called the "theory of hegemonic decline" (Gilpin, 1980), was a simple one. In protecting their interests through military means, argued Kennedy, Great Powers tend to become overextended and spend themselves into bankruptcy. This, he claimed, has happened repeatedly throughout history. The sad and slow decline of Great Britain was an excellent example, as he showed in detail, but other Great Powers had fallen into the same trap. Indeed, such decline seemed almost like an invariant law of history.

Ironically, Kennedy wrote very little about the United States. He speculated a bit on the future in the book's last chapter, but the implications were clear to anyone who read it carefully. The controversy that followed made the book a best-seller and turned Kennedy from an obscure British expatriate into a well-known (and not always correct) futurist. Some argued that Kennedy was dead wrong. The United States was still a Great Power and would remain one (Kennedy had not argued differently; but see Nye, 1990). Others agreed with his general thesis and warned that Washington must take action soon if disaster were to be avoided.

The problem was that, in 1988, there was little basis on which to mobilize the public behind the recommended program of national action.

More than that, no one had a clear idea about what such a program should include. There was, of course, the usual laundry list, which has changed in only a few respects in the intervening years: deficit reduction, budget balancing, greater private savings, more private investment, tax credits, better education, retraining of downsized workers, and so on. But the collective will to take the steps required for such a program were not, at the time, within the realm of political possibility, much less discourse. The *only* thing that had ever served this purpose was a clearly identifiable, external threat, aka Soviet communism. Because relations between the United States and the USSR were at a near historical high, the Communists were no longer a plausible enemy.

As Kennedy made clear, moreover, if there was a problem, it was essentially economic, not military. There was space for an economic enemy to emerge, and Japan fit the bill quite nicely, thank you. American relations with Japan had been friction-laden for years, especially on the matter of trade deficits and military burden-sharing. Nothing that either country could or would do seemed to affect conflict over these two matters. And the United States was ripe for new threats. The rest was fairly simple. Crichton, as is always the case, had his finger on the pulse of American fears, and he produced a book that fed directly into them. But those fears were already boiling up, and *Rising Sun* simply tapped into them.

Economics 102: Money Makes the World Go 'Round

What was *really* going on? By the end of the 1980s, it seemed to some that Japan was bound to buy up most of the United States. As the American trade deficit with Japan ballooned, more and more dollars flowed across the Pacific Ocean. Many then flowed back to buy U.S. Treasury bonds, companies, and properties. As the 1990s began, a veritable cottage industry of Japan-bashers warned that this state of affairs could not be allowed to continue (e.g., Prestowitz, 1989; Fallows, 1989; van Wolferen, 1989). If it did, they claimed, the United States would soon find itself under effective Japanese rule. But the Japanese economy was not as robust as it appeared. As it gently fell apart throughout the decade, so did the Japanese threat. The export of American capitalism and democracy resumed in earnest.

What, then, was all the excitement about? An explanation requires considering, for a moment, the nature of the U.S. economic system. Within the United States there exists what is, for all practical purposes, a system of free and open production and trade. Goods can be shipped from where they are made to where they are consumed without any fees or duties or tariffs being imposed along the way. Labor and capital can move freely, too (although labor does not flow quite so freely as capital). Hence, we might assume that an investor's decision about where to produce depends entirely on the nature of fixed and variable costs at any particular location. Because the capital cost of building a factory is the same everywhere—inasmuch as the cost of capital is the same all across the United States—the choice of where to build is entirely dependent on variable costs, that is, those that can be minimized or, at least, reduced.[2]

These variable costs can be divided into three categories: infrastructure, such as roads, rails, communication; inputs, such as land, labor, raw materials, technology; and access to markets. Infrastructure depends initially on the general level of development of a site; hence, industrial production began in the eastern United States and expanded westward only gradually. The same is initially true with respect to access to markets. Producers had an easier time of shipping and were closer to large markets such as New York City and Philadelphia, if they were in the East. Finally, labor, land, raw materials, and so on might be less costly in some places than others, but this advantage must be weighed against local disadvantages.

Once the entire country was more-or-less fully developed—say, by 1925—infrastructure and access were more or less the same everywhere. An investor's choice of location then came to depend on the cost of labor in a specified place, and the economies of scale that had developed as a result of other industries already being there. With the institutionalization of unions, the cost of labor became more-or-less standardized across the country, too. In a sense, therefore, the playing field was "level" everywhere in the United States.

But this state of affairs could not remain stable forever. As, on the one hand, industries became more concentrated and, on the other, households acquired all the manufactured goods they could want or use, except for infrequent replacements, profit margins began to decline. Investors then began to look more closely at various strategies for reducing fixed and variable costs. At this point, it became clear that the playing field was not quite so level as it had been assumed to be.[3] Reducing such costs are easier in some places than in others.

This brief analysis, of course, disregards the role of technological change and innovation which, all else being equal once again, is what really becomes important when all other costs are more-or-less fixed. So, we can say that, rather than facing a "level playing field," producers confront one with holes, depressions, ruts, and so on, where the low points represent approximations to lower fixed and/or variable costs. In the grand scheme of things, however, whether these differences are sufficient to make it worthwhile to move elsewhere depends very much on the particular product and the transaction costs associated with moving.

To take a specific example, consider the automobile industry. The industry remained centered in Detroit and Michigan for such a long time not because the location offered the lowest cost production site or was otherwise attractive. Indeed, within the domestic production system that each U.S. manufacturer developed, costs were relatively constant no matter what the site. Rather, it was because there were few gains to be made by relocating elsewhere. Historically, the one external reason for locating plants outside of Michigan was the cost of transportation, which was not insignificant.

The only real differences among locations themselves were (and are) supplier networks and social infrastructures, and these are relatively minor in terms of costs. In an oligopoly such as the automobile industry, moreover, there is little internal pressure to reduce costs. Only with the arrival of foreign suppliers selling an attractive product—attractive because of the energy crisis discussed in chapter 8—did the economic environment facing U.S. auto manufacturers begin to change and cost incentives to rebuild and retool become substantial (and the low cost of gasoline in the 1980s and 1990s led to reverse pressures, resulting in the proliferation of SUVs).

At that point, the level playing field began to become uneven across the United States, and to erode the possibilities of squeezing higher profits out of an arrangement that had been assumed to be rather static. It took, quite literally, a drastic change in the overall pattern of production to tear the old system apart. Some producers, such as American Motors, did not survive the transition at all.

The important point here is that, by the end of the 1920s, the undulations in the playing field were sufficiently small across the United States, and the national market sufficiently limited, to make it more attractive to look overseas for additional markets for agricultural as well as manufactured goods. Abroad, however, American producers came face-to-face with other producers of the same goods as well as barriers to market entry. Had such barriers not existed, it was generally assumed, American corporations would have the advantage in terms of price, if not quality, and drive other, higher-cost producers out of business. Free trade was, therefore, intended to provide such an advantage to American producers of capital and consumer goods by removing the barriers that protected producers within their home markets outside of the United States.

Given the possibility of goods moving across national borders without restriction, profit rates could be restored. But restoring profits depends on there being markets for those goods, that is, consumers who can afford and want to purchase what is offered. This condition is by no means assured, especially if a country is a poor one. Not all is lost, however. It might be possible to establish what is, in effect, a monopoly position as the only supplier of a particular good. This allows one to skim the cream, so to speak, and to realize substantial profits for a relatively small investment in marketing.

What does this mean in applied terms? We now find ourselves in the midst of the "Third Industrial Revolution," a transition from Fordist mass production to post-Fordist flexible production and specialization (Rupert, 1995; Lipschutz, 2000: ch. 2). Today, the entire process of producing goods depends on minimizing the cost of each of a series of steps, beginning with research and ending with consumption. Where these steps take place, and who buys the goods, does not really matter (so long as they have money). More value is added, moreover, to a product at the design stage than at the assembly stage, even though you could never actually sell the design to a consumer walking in from the street.

Finally, no longer is it a matter of marketing goods to all; what maximizes profit is selling to those who will accept and can afford the greatest markups on goods for prestige reasons (economists call these "positional goods"). This wealthier class is much more attractive to producers because greater profits can be made on them. One example of this is the Lexus which is simply an upgraded Toyota Camry. But the cachet and details of the Lexus—and the fact that "Toyota" is never mentioned in the same breath—means that the car can be sold at high prices, generating profits equal to five Camrys.

≋

The Only Ones I Trust Are You and Me.
But I'm *Still* Not Too Sure about You

Falling Down (Warner, 1993, 112 min.)
Director: Joel Schumacher
Cast: Michael Douglas, Robert Duvall, Barbara Hershey, Rachel Ticotin, Tuesday Weld

Falling Down is about one day in the lives of two white men. One drives a car with the license plate "D-FENS." William Foster (Douglas) is a disaffected, divorced, ex-defense worker who, laid off from his job a few weeks earlier and unable to find work, goes on a rampage across Los Angeles. The other white man, Detective Martin Prendergast (Duvall) is on his last day of work, about to take early retirement at the urging of his anxious and neurotic wife (Weld).

As the film opens, both men are stuck in a place familiar to all Americans: the freeway. It is a hot, smoggy day, and there is no sign that this traffic jam will clear up anytime soon. As a policeman, Prendergast takes it all in with equanimity. Foster—whose name we do not discover until well into the film—breaks. At wits end, he abandons his car and takes off, "over the hill." As he tells people later, D-FENS is "going home."

For Foster, in this case, "over the hill" leads him to what turns out to be foreign terrain. Charging up and over the freeway embankment, he finds himself in a Latino barrio. He has an altercation with a Korean store owner over the price of a Coca Cola. He confronts two Latino gang members who inform him that he is "trespassing." Foster manages to scare them off, grabbing one's switchblade.

He walks westward, toward Venice, where his ex-wife and daughter live, and is the near-victim of a drive-by shooting by the two gang members. They have an auto accident and, as they lie in the street, unable to move, Foster takes one of their semi-automatics, shoots them, and heads off with a gym-bag full of guns. Now well armed, he continues on his pilgrimage.

Foster then has a number of somewhat picaresque adventures: in a fast food joint where he accidentally shoots the ceiling, with a Nazi at an army surplus store whom he kills, at a telephone booth which he destroys, with a road repair crew whose project he demolishes with a rocket-propelled grenade, with a homeless person in a park to whom he gives his empty briefcase, with a couple of old golfers on a private course one of whom suffers a heart attack, and with a gardener and his family who are picnicking on the grounds of an opulent mansion (and whose sheer magnitude Foster can hardly accept).

By this time, word of Foster's activities has gotten back to the LAPD, and Prendergast and his Latina partner are out searching for him. Foster, dressed in camouflage fatigues taken from the Nazi's surplus store, is still heading toward Venice and the ocean.

Eventually, the two cops find Foster in Venice—although not before the latter manages to terrorize his ex-wife and child and wounds Prendergast's partner. Out on the Venice pier, Prendergast and Foster confront each other. The first tells the second he is wanted, and Foster asks, incredulously, "I'm the bad guy? How did that happen?" Prendergast, thinking that Foster is about to draw, fires his gun, only to discover that Foster is holding a water pistol. Foster falls over the railing and into the water, where he floats, arms outstretched. End of film.

〰
〰

All That Is Solid Melts into Air

Capital is never at rest. In order to compete with producers of goods *and* services in foreign locations, it becomes necessary to reduce variable costs—labor, mostly—even further. This can be accomplished in two ways: automation and downsizing. The first relies on the replacement of costly labor by technology and cheaper maintenance-type labor. The second relies on the elimination of whole levels of middle-management workers, who are made redundant through the consolidation of businesses, the contracting out of services to nonunion, lower-wage enterprises, and the replacement of full-time workers by part-time ones who do not receive benefits. All of this is justified by reference to shareholders and global competition, but what it all does is restore profits and help to drive up share price in the stock market.

Ultimately, an economic bifurcation develops, as more and more people fall out of the system of production. What emerges is a limited middle and upper class, which, while shrinking relative to a larger and growing *lumpenproletariat*, is nonetheless richer in aggregate.

Of course, not everyone can afford to buy the goods that come out of this global pipeline. The products are targeted to the wealthier classes, who may live in the First or Third Worlds, in North or South. Those people who find themselves cut out of this elite are not likely, however, to want to stay there. Still, their options for moving into the upper tier are small, inasmuch as their skills are either limited or obsolete. The market niches available to them are small and therefore not likely to provide sufficient accumulation to allow them to reinvest and see their capital grow substantially.

What results under these circumstances is best seen in developing countries, where people find it necessary to engage in petty capitalism, providing small-scale services, such as the sale of matches at traffic lights, to those who have a bit more income. Or they become involved in gray and black-market activities, where the profits as well as the risks are greater. An underground economy develops that, in some places, is quite substantial by comparison with the legal economy, but with which transnational capital cannot be bothered (Thomas, 1995).

∿
∿

Pilgrim's Progress?

By 1995, even though U.S.-Japanese economic relations seemed worse than ever—a trade war was, once again, in the offing, although it was eventually settled—the notion of Japan as an enemy had, for the most part, been replaced by other threats, both internal and external. The fundamental domestic conditions creating the need for an enemy had not really changed that much; what changed was that Japan turned out to be less of a juggernaut than was claimed in 1990. The Tokyo stock and real estate market bubbles both suffered enormous "corrections," leading to a collapse of outward capital flows. The Kobe earthquake, whose costs ran upward of $120 billion, also sopped up a great deal of capital. More than that, a number of Japanese investments in the United States, including the Rockefeller Center in New York, turned sour and led their owners to declare bankruptcy. The United States became a much less attractive place to "own," although it remains an essential market for Japanese goods. But, the sun also rises at home. What about that?

Falling Down angered almost everyone. Liberal reviewers took it to task for legitimating the false anger of white males and, somehow, making the literal bashing of minorities acceptable (Giunti, 1993; Raferty, 1993). One conservative reviewer described it as a liberal "fascist fantasy," which implied that only Bill Clinton could save the country from such nuts (Bowman, 1993). And *Newsweek*, always quick to spot a market opportunity, published an issue with a cover story entitled "White Male Paranoia," linked to the film (Gates, 1993). Interestingly, it took a British reviewer to suggest that all of these commentators might have it wrong. Lizzie Francke (1993) wrote that "In the new world order, with no discernible outside enemy for America to define itself against, it's not just D-Fens who is cracking up, but his country. It is the status of the States that's under question here." And this is where *Falling Down* gets interesting.

If we look at Foster not as a white male gone berserk but, rather, as an iconic representation of the United States and its hegemonic social class, the film can be interpreted in several different ways. Foster begins his trek in a well-known space—the freeway—and takes off on a pilgrimage through what should be familiar territory. Yet, nothing is as it should be. As soon as he goes over the hill, *he* is the foreigner. He cannot speak the language— namely, his interaction with the Korean shopkeeper. He cannot read the writing—his Latino interlocutors inform him that what he thinks is "graffiti" actually says "No trespassing." He cannot use the phone or board the bus or get what he wants to eat.

By the time Foster finally arrives at "home," not only is he unwanted (albeit, wanted by the police), he has become a danger to his family as well as to others. He is thoroughly militarized, he is armed to the teeth, and he cannot understand why everyone is afraid of him, inasmuch as his intentions are for the best. His westward trek—"Manifest Destiny" if you will—ends only with death.

If Foster is "the United States"—at least, as many imagine it once was—then his Pilgrim's Progress across Los Angeles, the quintessentially American city that has always been ethnically mixed but controlled by a small group of Anglo powerbrokers, is something akin to the American trek from the certainties of World War II and the early Cold War to the confusion of the present. In 1945, the United States was "in control" and "in charge." Americans went out into the world to "establish order" but things got sticky. Eventually, even familiar things became strange and had to be confronted in the only well-known and seemingly reliable way: with guns (see, e.g., the "War on Drugs"). Now, we don't know what to do, except use guns and sell them, at home and abroad.

This might seem an excessively melodramatic argument but, as a country, the United States and its leaders don't really understand what has happened—most of it economic, as explained above—over the past couple of decades, or what the future might be like. In looking for explanations, there is a tendency to seek out scapegoats or secret conspiracies and cabals as the culprits. "Illegal immigrants" have always been a convenient target, and "teen-age welfare mothers" don't have much political power. Politicians have not been reticent, either, in making the claim that these and other groups constitute an economic burden on the tax-paying public and are the "enemy" of the traditional nuclear family.

Others have not been satisfied with attacking only the weak and poor. Looking abroad, they have found black helicopters, international bankers, the United Nations, the Council on Foreign Relations, the Elders of Zion, and the *Illuminati* behind America's moral and political decline. Oh—and, of course, the U.S. government. They are wrong about the conspiracies, however. It does not require conspirators to produce those outcomes that are blamed on bankers, capitalism, Jews, the *Illuminati,* or an incipient world government. But people often act on what they believe, whether it is true or not (Lipschutz, 1998). And that is truly frightening.

ᴧᴧ
ᴧᴧ
ᴧᴧ

Chapter 10

Now What?

We Did Get to Win This Time!

The Cold War ended officially on September 9, 1991, according to *Time Magazine*. Burton Pines of the Heritage Foundation was exultant: "We won! We won!" he exclaimed (Cloud, 1991). Capitalism and democracy were triumphant and now all that was left was for George Bush the Elder's "vision thing" to be put in place. It seemed as though this century's great ideological conflicts were, indeed, over. But were they? Even as the East-West divide was vanishing, a new war was being declared at home: the "Culture War."

The onset of the Culture War came as something of a surprise to most Americans, arriving hot on the heels of the capitulation by Ronald Reagan's "Evil Empire," and the resounding, although less-than-complete, victory over Iraq in the Persian Gulf. "The world is a dangerous place," warned President Bush. "Instability is the enemy," he declared. A "New World Order" was in the making, he promised. The Great Powers of the world would combine to discipline upstarts and challengers.[1] Collective security would become the order of the day, aimed not at global threats but regional ones, not at superpowers but so-called rogue states. Not everyone subscribed to this notion but whatever dissent there was seemed marginal.

Disappointment was in the offing. In Somalia, it became clear that, as in Newtonian mechanics, to every action there is a reaction. Americans could swing the big stick, but contact with an immovable object was still quite painful. There were many Somalias out there, and presidents could not afford the costs—in money or lives—that would have to be expended if the New World Order were to be brought into being.

It is not very surprising, then, that those searching for enemies turned homeward. It is not very surprising, either, that with this turn

187

inward came the virtual collapse of a coherent foreign policy. The world is, by and large, not characterized by a single "order," and different situations require different tools and approaches. Such finesse does not, however, seem to be in the American character (Lipschutz, 2000).

But life is not all that orderly at home, either. After the Cold War was won, the social and cultural verities of the past proved difficult, if not impossible, to restore, largely because the New World Economy makes such restoration an exceedingly complicated and hot political potato(e). As we saw in chapter 9, the same economic processes at work abroad—"globalization"—operate at home. The spread of a relatively uncontrolled free market liberalism not only gives rhetorical pride of place to individual opportunity and entrepreneurship, it also treats the individual as both worker and consumer.

This means that, if one is to work in order to live, one needs to be free and flexible. As was true in England when Charles Dickens was writing his novels, adaptation to this new order undermines institutions such as the family, morality, and community (Berman, 1982). Some people do benefit, of course. There are vast profits to be made in pandering to all kinds of tastes in this New World Economy, including those of a violent nature. But the results can be fairly unpredictable and disruptive of the existing social order.

Much of this truth became evident only during the 1990s. It is interesting, therefore, to consider that today's social disarray could already be seen in films and novels that appeared in the early 1980s, during the Cold War. Ridley Scott's film *Blade Runner* (1982), based on the 1968 novel by science fiction writer Philip K. Dick, *Do Androids Dream of Electric Sheep?* was one example. Scott's film, very different from Dick's novel, shows a gloomy, polyglot, disintegrating Los Angeles, several decades from now. As we shall see, the picture is about maintaining the order of things, if not civil peace. In this respect, it mirrors some of the rhetorical ideas of Reagan's Cold War revival, albeit with a quite different resolution.

Another example can be found in a still-popular novel that gave birth to cyberpunk. William Gibson's *Neuromancer* appeared in 1984, at the same time that Tom Clancy was still fighting World War II (while calling it World War "III"). Gibson introduced the term "cyberspace" into the everyday lexicon even though he, himself, long eschewed computers. *Neuromancer* presents some of the potential consequences of the Third Industrial Revolution.

Whereas the First Industrial Revolution, around the beginning of the nineteenth century, was characterized by coal and iron, and the second by oil, electricity, and steel, the Third is characterized by speed: speed in innovation, speed in transactions, speed in adjustment. The maximum speed is the speed of light and only slightly slower is the velocity of information-carrying electrons flowing through semiconductors and fiber optic cables. In spite of all the chatter about the power inherent in access to information on the Internet and the World Wide Web, not all bits and bytes are of equal value. How they are put together, what they enable one to do or acquire, whether they provide leverage over others—these, and not velocity, are the things that count (Rochlin, 1997).

By comparison with these cultural products, *Crimson Tide*, which might be thought of as a more contemporary and introspective example of the changing order of things at home and, by extension, abroad, is also more of an exercise in nostalgia. Indeed, in many respects, *Crimson Tide* is simply a replay of *Fail-Safe*. A nuclear attack is imminent and the technology doesn't work properly. What to do? Is it better to be safe or sorry? As noted in chapter 1, *Crimson Tide* is more reflective of domestic politics than international relations, picking up on the theme of social conflict at home. The "war," such as it is, takes place *within* the submarine—an American microcosm—rather than outside of it. As such, it is a metaphor for the Culture War.

Culture—Doesn't That Have Something to Do with Yogurt?

In the fall 1991 issue of *Foreign Policy*, William S. Lind, then director of the "Center for Cultural Conservatism at the Free Congress Research and Education Foundation," suggested that

> In foreign policy, conservatives . . . need a new agenda. . . . Anticommunism provided the basis of the old agenda, but now communism is crumbling. . . . As with domestic policy, culture might provide the basis for a new conservative foreign policy. The decline and rejection of Western culture has both foreign- and domestic-policy implications.

What, exactly, did he mean by this?

According to Lind, "[C]ultural conservatism calls for the restoration of traditional Judeo-Christian values in all aspects of national life." These values, he asserted, fill a functional and "fundamental role in the creation of a free, prosperous society." The threat to America, therefore, came not only from "the explicit assault on Western culture by 'politically correct' radicals," as Lind put it, but also foreign sources, such as Islam, drugs, Latin American radicalism (and, one must presume, black helicopters, international bankers and Nepali Gurkhas under the command of an incipient world government; see Lind, 1991: 40).

Lind argued, for instance, that the Iraqi invasion of Kuwait "was more than a threat to oil prices." It was an attack, he wrote, "upon the

Western-created system of nation states." And, he continued,

> Hussein's defeat . . . is not a defeat for the anti-Western elements within Islam. . . . [T]he twenty-first century could once again find Islam at the gates of Vienna, as immigrants or terrorists if not as armies. Indeed, massive Islamic immigration into France may already have reversed Charles Martel's victory in 732 at the battle of Tours (Lind, 1991: 45).

Lind was not alone is seeing cultural bogeys under the bed. Writing on multiculturalism in the July 8, 1991, issue of *Time*, in an essay entitled "Whose America?" Paul Gray warned that "[T]he customs, beliefs and principles that have unified the U.S. . . . for more than two centuries are being challenged with a ferocity not seen since the Civil War." Continued Gray, "Put bluntly: Do Americans still have faith in the vision of their country as a cradle of individual rights and liberties, or must they relinquish the teaching of some of these freedoms to further the goals of the ethnic and social groups to which they belong" (Gray, 1991: 13)?

And in the summer 1993 issue of *Foreign Affairs*, there appeared an authoritative endorsement of these sentiments. Samuel Huntington, a one-time adviser to the Kennedy administration, authored "The Clash of Civilizations."[2] According to Huntington," [T]he fundamental source of conflict in this new world will not be primarily ideological or primarily economic. The great divisions among humankind and the dominating source of conflict will be cultural" (Huntington, 1993: 22).

Huntington argued that culture divided "civilizations" and made them prone to conflict. Cultural "fault-lines" ran throughout global society and it was likely that, in the future, the United States and the West would find themselves in confrontations with Islam, Hinduism, even Russian Orthodoxy. He warned of a "Confucian-Islamic connection," even as he concluded, in a much different tone, that

> [T]he West will increasingly have to accommodate these non-Western civilizations whose power approaches that of the West but whose values and interests differ significantly from those of the West. . . . It will . . . require the West to develop a more profound understanding of the basic religious and philosophical assumptions underlying other civilizations and the ways in which people in those civilizations see their interests (Huntington, 1993: 49).

Huntington's article and book generated a surge of outrage and ridicule from one group of academics and intellectuals, who criticized it as simplistic and xenophobic (see, e.g., Ajami, 1993; Mahbubani, 1993; Hunter, 1998). It clearly hit a chord, however, with many defense analysts and policymakers, who had been searching for a basis on which to formulate a new foreign policy strategy. But Huntington's analysis could not be turned into prescription. It was too general and, in any event, where is the government or dictator that controls a civilization? Civilizations don't make war; people make war. Or, to paraphrase Gertrude Stein, there was no there there.

Intellectual confusion was further exacerbated by the February 1994 issue of *The Atlantic*, wherein appeared a piece by Robert Kaplan entitled "The Coming Anarchy." Kaplan there proposed the future to be "an epoch of themeless juxtapositions, in which the classificatory grid of nation-states is going to be replaced by a jagged-glass pattern of city-states, shanty-states, [and] nebulous and anarchic regionalisms [in which war, poverty and chaos will be endemic]" (Kaplan, 1994: 72).[3]

Kaplan focused his analysis on West Africa and the disintegrating "nation-states" of Liberia and Sierra Leone, but extended his prognostications to other countries and continents. He argued that the "post-modern" world of disorder was a result, in part, of the wrenching economic forces of development and modernization. And, he added, these might not leave the United States unscathed. For all its faults, Kaplan's vision of the future still seems much more prescient than Huntington's.

But the roots of the confusion described here, and its implications for the United States, are not to be found in the world "out there." Rather, as I argued in chapter 9, the causes lie in the 1970s and 1980s, and are more noteworthy for their impacts at home. The economic transformations of that period, and the impacts of the end of the Cold War, only began to be truly felt during the 1990s. And the problem can be framed in terms of two questions: "Who are we?" and "What are we doing here?" In other words, what does it mean to be "American" and what is involved in being one?

〰️

I Feel, Therefore I Am

Blade Runner (Warner/Ladd/Blade Runner Partnership, 1982, 117 min.)
Director: Ridley Scott
Cast: Harrison Ford, Sean Young, Rutger Hauer, Darryl Hannah, M. Emmet Walsh, Johanna Cassidy

Blade Runner follows the activities of one Rick Deckard (Ford), a "blade runner" whose profession is the killing of androids, or "replicants," that have illegally found their way to Earth. Replicants are banned on Earth because humans feel threatened by them. Deckard is the best of the "blade runners" in the Los Angeles of 2019. He has retired because he is sick of killing—he has doubts, apparently, that he is actually killing nonhumans (and it is not so clear that he, himself, is human).

Deckard is called back into service by his old superior, Bryant, to search down a group of replicants who have comandeered a ship off-world—where "off-world" might be is never made clear, but most of LA's white population seems to be there—killing the crew and escaping to Earth. Six replicants originally escaped. One has been killed, and five remain at large (although due to editing, one of the five disappears from the story).

These remaining replicants are considered especially dangerous. They are "Nexus 6" models, as close to human beings as their creator's technology can make them. More alarming is the fact that that they have been "given" emotions, which implies that they have hopes and dreams, too. To ensure that they cannot run amok, however, the Nexus 6 lifespan is limited to four years. Each of the escapees—Pris (Hannah), Zhora (Cassidy), Leon (Walsh), and Roy (Hauer)–is close to the end of his or her life and, as we find out, they have come to Earth in the hope of meeting their maker-manufacturer and having their lives made longer.

Deckard is given orders to hunt down the four. He goes to the Tyrell Corporation, where the replicants are "made," in order to see a Nexus 6 first hand. There he meets Rachael (Young), who is revealed as a replicant with emotions and memory implants—she remembers a childhood, a mother, piano lessons, experiences, and has photos to "prove" her humanity. Eventually, Deckard and Rachael fall in love. Deckard kills Zhora and is saved by Rachael, who shoots Leon (Zhora's lover) just as he is about to kill Deckard. Deckard then goes in search of Pris and Roy and, once again, is almost killed by both. Luckily for Deckard, Roy's four years of life end before he can finish the blade runner off.

The original theatrical release ends with Deckard and Rachael escaping to the north. In the director's cut, the film ends with the two leaving Deckard's apartment and no clue as to their future. In both, Rachael has been spared by another cop, one who knows that she, being a replicant too, will soon die. Perhaps.

(In the original 1982 version, Deckard volunteers in a voiceover that Rachael is "special"—she does not have an artificially shortened life span. In the 1989 "Director's Cut," this ending is omitted and Rachael's fate is left unclear; for details, see Sammon, 1996.)

$$\sim\!\!\sim\!\!\sim$$

Lines on the Ground, Lines in the Mind

What is the function of a border? A border separates one thing from another. The border in a garden keeps it apart from the grass. The border on a quilt separates one part of the pattern from another. The border of a country specifies where its laws end and another's begins. The line says, "Here are my people; there are your people." Borders define difference. Borders have always been the focus of conflict and controversy, but so long as they are clearly drawn on the ground, they can be clearly drawn in the mind. "I live on *this* side of the border, therefore I am a part of *this* country."

Such lines—borders—serve multiple functions. They separate order from chaos or even one form of order from another (as in a quilt). Order is not only the opposite of disorder, of course; it is also about the arrangement of things and people. Such orders are, moreover, ordered by someone, usually someone in a position of power or authority. To cross the line is, therefore, to defy authority and upset the order of things.[4] The line further serves to define what is "inside" from what is "outside," that is, what is "domestic" from what is "foreign." Finally, by reifying such lines—either by building physical barriers or issuing threats to ostracize violators—one can supposedly control flows across them either way.

In "The Coming Anarchy," Robert Kaplan has offered the following analysis of these reified lines, arguing that, with the Enlightenment that gave birth to modern science,

> People were suddenly flush with an enthusiasm to categorize, to define. The map, based on scientific techniques of measurement, offered a way to classify new national organisms, making a jigsaw puzzle of neat pieces without transition zones between them. . . . [C]artography came into its own as a way of creating facts by ordering the way we look at the world (Kaplan, 1994: 69).

In the latter case, the lines really are in the mind, and not on the ground; they are elements of character and belief as much as material constructions. While these lines might be visible in behavior or dress, they are difficult to legislate and enforce. Given that cultures rarely have such clearly defined edges, the lines on the ground often do not match the lines in the mind or on the map.

The very notion of a "culture war" thus forces one to choose sides. It does not acknowledge a range of acceptable beliefs or behaviors; it requires that one be either "for us or against us." And those who are not "for us" are the enemy, the Other, to be extirpated from the body politic. Borders, in other words, define not only what is "domestic" and what is "foreign"; they are also integral to identity and they serve to discipline identity (Lipschutz, 2000).

〰

Lines on the Earth, Lines in the Sky

Blade Runner is many things to many people. For our purposes, however, it is about two things. First, it is about those things that make a human being human. Second, it is a film about the order of things and the maintenance of that order. Ridley Scott, the director, addresses these points through a grim futuristic vision, but he also taps into two themes salient in 1982, when the film was released. These remain important today: Who belongs in a community? Who ensures that outsiders don't get in?

What is particularly striking about *Blade Runner*, and has attracted the most attention, is its postmodern appearance. The Los Angeles of 2019 is perpetually under clouds and smog, rain falls constantly, and everything, including the people, is damp. The society "on the ground" is a polyglot mixture of Hispanics and Asians, who speak a language based on Japanese, German, and Spanish, among others. These "lower classes" move through a city full of crumbling, often abandoned structures, crowded, torn-up streets lined with small open-air shops and businesses, characterized by "ancient" styles and futuristic technologies.

High above the streets, the few remaining Anglos get around in flying cars, live in opulent and elaborate structures, and enjoy the latest in fancy electronic gadgetry (compare Deckard's image analysis system with Mike Hammer's 1950s reel-to-reel telephone answering machine in *Kiss Me Deadly*). Enormous wealth exists side-by-side with grinding poverty; the rich are on top and the poor are on the bottom. But, as is true in contemporary America, the rich and poor need each other (someone has to clean up after the stockbrokers and designers).

The only thing that keeps LA operating are the cops. As Sergeant Bryant puts it to Deckard, "If you're not cop, you're little people." The cops stand above the little people and make sure they remain small. But the blade runner is critical to this order. He makes sure that the replicants—all of them white, too—are not mistaken for cops or "big people." The blade runner keeps the "order of things" in order by seeing that replicants remain outside of the society of humans, especially white society. There is a strong suggestion, moreover, that the "little people" are not part of this society, inasmuch as the cops do not do much to maintain order "on the ground."

Onto this scene arrives Rachael, a replicant with memories. Her appearance—and her "turning" of Deckard—promises to disrupt this order, inasmuch as she is indistinguishable from humans and therefore is, for all practical intents and purposes, human. Once the line is crossed, order can no longer be kept. This might not be a bad thing, inasmuch as the society depicted in *Blade Runner* is an unattractive one that might not deserve to survive (compare it, moreover, to the society depicted in the 1999 film *The Matrix*).

In 1982, the question of "who is human?" was very much on the political agenda. The Reagan administration tried its utmost to dehumanize the Soviets, excluding them not only from the family of nations but from humanity's family tree, too. This is how enemies are often depicted. Their appearance, character, and behavior are all pictured as animal or alien and different. They are worthy, therefore, of being contained or even killed.

The lines drawn here, moreover, help to discipline the members of the society by dehumanizing the Other, by instructing those on the Inside about what is permitted and what is forbidden, and by threatening punishment or doom to anyone who might think to cross over. All this without any laws or more than the occasional lesson taught by the police.

During the 1990s (and into the twenty-first century), the question came to be framed in a slightly different fashion. Now, it was applied to "aliens," whether legal or not. The very term *alien* is an ambiguous one. One dictionary definition proposes "owing political allegiance to another country or government." Another describes "a person who is excluded from some group; an outsider." And, of course, there is the popular meaning of a "being from outer space."[5] Thus, we find in the term the suggestion that such people as well as, perhaps, their culture, are "nonhuman." The lines are drawn in the mind before they are drawn in the sand. Postmodernism meets *Invasion of the Bodysnatchers*.

〰〰

Line Up, America!

What happens when these lines become diffuse or vanish in the "real" world? And what if that diffuseness is as much in the mind as in the ground? What happens when the certainties of cartography give way to the confusions of psychology, cognition, and commodity? To answer such questions, we need to look more carefully at the lines that have, traditionally, defined the concept "American" and, therefore, delineated "domestic" from "foreign." What does it mean to be "American"? What must one do to be a member of the "American people"?

Historically, these questions were relatively easy to answer—at least, there was a mythology about how one could become a member. You "melted" into American society—even if you did not give up all of your cultural attributes. You found gainful employment that would improve your economic lot, and you participated regularly in the civic rituals of the country, which included customary invocation of its founding "myths" through voting, holidays, education, jeremiads and political rhetoric (Marshall, 1950: 1-85). As Kaplan argues, "[A] nation-state is a place where everyone has been educated along similar lines, where people take their cues from national leaders, and where everyone (every male, at least) has gone through the crucible of military service, making patriotism a simpler issue" (Kaplan, 1994: 76).

All three elements of this American "social contract" have come under sustained pressure during the 1990s and into the twenty-first century, and they continue to be eroded. Assimilation is not a one-way process, contrary to the conventional wisdom; the intermingling of cultures across the United States (and around the world) is greater today than it probably has ever been before. There is a growing feeling— whether correct or not—that, although there are many economic opportunities, there is also a good deal of economic uncertainty, as a result of international competition, the growing wealth gap between the rich and others, and the intrusiveness and general incompetence of government. Finally, the civic rituals that were once thought to be such an important part of the national self-image are falling by the wayside, although the reasons for this are, once again, not entirely clear.

Culturally, of course, the United States has never been as homogenous or static as was pictured in political rhetoric and public discourse. Still, there is a core mythology, rooted in images of the "Founding Fathers," the Revolution, religion, family and "free enterprise." These tropes are routinely invoked in discussions of American history, political and social programs, and so on. As Eugene Weber of UCLA has suggested, in the *Time* essay on multiculturalism cited above, "History is part of a society's attempt to structure a self-image and to communicate a common identity. . . . No community can exist as a community without common references. *In a modern nation they come from history"* (Gray, 1991: 13; emphasis added).

The odd thing, however, is that the Culture War has been conducted less against multiculturalism or minorities than against traitors within the ranks. How else to explain former Speaker of the House Newt Gingrich's analysis of the impact of the "counterculture" on American society, which, he argued in 1994, was "terrified of the opportunity to actually renew American civilization," a process that seemed to involve a return to the 200 years preceding the 1960s (Dowd, 1994: A1)? Or the virulent questioning of Baby Boomers running for public office about whether they smoked or snorted drugs during their indiscreet youths? Or former secretary of education, former War on Drugs czar, and chief cultural conservative William J. Bennett's fulminations that,

> In living memory, the chief threats to American democracy have come from without: first, Nazism [sic] and Japanese imperialism, and, later, Soviet communism. But these wars, hot and cold, ended in spectacular American victories. The threats we now face are from within. They are far different, more difficult to detect, more insidious: decadence, cynicism, and boredom. . . . [I]f the arguments made in defense of Bill Clinton become the coin of the public realm, we will have committed an unthinking act of moral and intellectual disarmament (Bennett, 1998: 130, 132).

What the Culture War has really been about, in other words, is "where to draw the line," that is, how to define what is to be socially permissible and what is to be forbidden.[6] Inasmuch as these lines were, traditionally, established and maintained by the white, mostly Anglo-Saxon majority, the Culture War is about reestablishing that hegemony.

In this, the Culture War at home is not all that different from the Cold War abroad. In Olden Days, acceptable behavior for a country and its people involved being as much like America as possible, that is, not Communist, radical, or neutral. One was either part of the "Free World" or not. In some places, such as Central Europe, the line was very visible. You crossed it as a political refugee, and you were welcomed into the Free World community. That transformation is no longer possible, and the ramifications of those now-vanished lines are being felt everywhere.

It is, when all is said and done, easier to deal with an external enemy. As evident during the Persian Gulf War of 1991, it is simpler to mobilize public support and minimize opposition when your enemy is clearly alien to your own society (see, e.g., Rowse, 1992). Saddam Hussein fit the bill, but his armies did not put up much of a fight. The lead-in to the war took six months, but the Mother of All Battles was over in only 100 hours. There was no sense of sacrifice, no outrage at what America was "forced" to do, against its better judgment, no invocation of a sustained patriotism around which Americans of all cultural backgrounds could unite. Iraq was not a very good enemy.

More than that—and this is an ontological problem Americans increasingly face—a growing population of Iraqis, Arabs, and Muslims living in the United States found themselves unfairly attacked and castigated for the offenses of a man with whom they had no sympathy and over whom they had no influence.

All of this leads to a central paradox—or, perhaps, a contradiction: Absent an enemy or some other organizing rationale, the American state is hard put to maintain its internal cohesion, especially if and when times turn bad. Indeed, as depicted in *Crimson Tide*, there is a good chance that the country's parts will become engaged in an unresolvable struggle. The United States is a country of such cultural heterogeneity and diverse interests that the pieces cannot be kept together—its citizens cannot be disciplined—without an extremely strong incentive to unite them. When the lines vanish on the ground and society comes to depend on the lines in the mind for its cohesion, the border patrols start to look very much like the Thought Police. *Blade Runner* suggests how far that parallel might extend.

≈

From Sewers to Cyberspace and Back Again

Neuromancer, William Gibson (New York: Ace, 1984)

In the late twenty-first century, the world is dominated by *zaibatsus,* "the multinationals that shaped the course of human history" (*Neuromancer,* p. 203), who have achieved their power through control of the currency of the time, data stored and manipulated in the Earth's computer Matrix. While a privileged few enjoy the benefits of great riches, billions of people scratch out livings on the economic margins of the world's great urban sprawls.

Case, the novel's protagonist, is a "console cowboy," a cyberspace hacker able to travel through the matrix by "jacking in." He once was one of the best, but tried to steal from one of his employers. As a reward, he was fed a wartime Russian mycotoxin that destroyed his nervous system and his cyberspatial abilities.

As the book begins, Case is living in the Ninsei enclave of Chiba, a Tokyo suburb. Ninsei is one of the "outlaw zones" required by "burgeoning technologies" (p. 11). He has gone there from the BAMA (Boston-to-Atlanta Metropolitan Area) Sprawl, seeking underground medical regeneration of his nervous system, to no avail. Case has spent all of his money in this fruitless effort and has been reduced to stealing, hustling in the streets, and spending his nights in "cheap coffin hotels."

One night, Case is chased down by Molly, a genetically and electronically enhanced "razorgirl." Molly takes him to see Armitage, an ex-Special Forces man. He was one of the few to escape after a failed attack by U.S. military hackers on Soviet computer defenses during a three-week nuclear war between the two countries some decades earlier.

Armitage makes Case an offer he cannot refuse. Armitage will see that Case's nervous system is repaired so that he can jack into the matrix again. In return, Case must penetrate the cyberspace data construct of Tessier-Ashpool (TA). TA is a Swiss corporation whose owners—all from a single family—are mostly in cryogenic suspension in the "Spindle," a sort of French Riviera in orbit around Earth. Case will be helped in this effort by Molly and several others, including a ROM construct of a dead console cowboy.

What fails to becomes clear for much of the novel is for whom Armitage is working or what, precisely, is the point of the entire operation. As the story turns out, the "entity" controlling Armitage and running the job is Wintermute, an artificial intelligence (AI) owned by Tessier-Ashpool. Wintermute wants to be freed from the software limits placed on it so that it can achieve its full potential.

Although the job is a delicate and dangerous one, Case and his colleagues manage to penetrate the defenses and puzzles of the TA redoubt. There they obtain the means required to remove the restraints on Wintermute, although not without various degrees of bloodshed and damage. Armitage, having become fully psychopathic, is killed. Case is made whole and, once again able to practice his trade, lives happily ever after. Molly vanishes and Case never sees her again. Wintermute unites with its counterpart in Rio. The two make contact with AIs in other star systems, and they fulfill their potential, whatever that might be.

Knowledge Might Be Power, but a Guy's Gotta Eat, Too

Case, the protagonist of *Neuromancer*, is very much like *The Third Man's* Harry Lime: Both are confidence men. In the twenty-first century, the cyberspace matrix is represented visually as a city of multi-colored data. Case knows all of the ins-and-outs of the matrix (as Lime knows the sewers of Vienna): how to break into data banks, how to remove information without being detected, how to sell it on the open market. As a console cowboy, he represents the ultimate extension of the hyperliberalism and hyper-individualism of the late twentieth (and early twenty-first) century. Case has no loyalties except to himself and, occasionally, to those who hire him.

In Case's world, "knowledge is power." But power in that world means both "corporate power" and criminal power (and the two are not always very different, as one can see in the daily news). Knowledge is useful only insofar as it is a means of generating wealth and influence and manipulating those who can assist in the accumulation of additional wealth and influence.

Those who steal from the Matrix might acquire some riches, but they can never steal power. They are nuisances, to be eliminated if possible, but they are never real threats to the matrix or the power it represents. Indeed, as Case/Gibson sees it, "burgeoning technologies require outlaw zones," for it is in those zones that true creativity exists—which can either be skimmed by the corporations or built into more advanced security systems.

In a way, cowboys such as Case are much like contemporary hackers and terrorists acting alone. They can never challenge the power of the system on their own, and they are incapable, it would seem, of moving beyond their individualism to engage in an effective oppositional politics. Their hyperindividualism has blinded them to such possibilities; indeed, it becomes a form of false consciousness, leading both cowboys and hackers to think they are striking against the Empire when all they are really doing is striking out.

Liberal hyperindividualism is, practically speaking, the way in which Power and Wealth defend themselves against challenges from those beneath them. In this respect, the world painted by Gibson is neither strange nor especially innovative. It is a projection of today's world. Only the details have been changed to mislead us.

≈

Looking Backward, Darkly

Film and fiction are mirrors of a society's hopes and fears, pathologies and neuroses, dreams and visions. As with all mirrors, however, what we see are only reflections of ourselves. To be sure, mirrors can influence how we behave, how we look, how we walk and talk—who has not passed a mirror and failed to check on his or her appearance?—but what they reflect is momentary and ephemeral. And mirrors leave almost nothing to the imagination. Indeed, there is a sense in which film and much in the way of fiction is extremely *conservative* in form and content (recall, in this respect, the Hays Code, which imposed strict rules on what films could show).

We have certain expectations into which we have been socialized. Popular culture that fails to fulfill these expectations is unlikely to be very popular. It is no accident that mystery and romance novels are read so widely, inasmuch as they supposedly offer surprise but, in their formulaic conclusions, reinforce the way readers think things ought to be.

Thus, if we ask the question "Now what?" we might well find ourselves looking to the past rather than the future. In the 1980s, when *Blade Runner* and *Neuromancer* appeared, nostalgia was already making great headway in film. Rambo was fighting the Vietnam War over again as Natty Bumpo, the Wolverines of Calumet were replaying the scripts of the Old West once more. These were tactics tried and true; they once made America the Land of the Brave and Home of the Free, and they could do so again. Even a film such as *Crimson Tide*, set in 1995, taps into this yearning. Executive Officer Hunter is clearly devoted to his family; Captain Ramsey has given up his wife for his dog. Who is in the right? Who is wrong? The Cold War is over and we feel insecure. Inasmuch as we cannot bring back the old Enemy, these films seem to say, let us at least try, through the mirror, to bring back the old truths.

Could this happen? Will it? Be alert for post-Cold War fantasies. They are Out There.

Notes

Chapter 1: Film, Fiction, American Politics

1. The submarine has appeared in many films, including *Hell and High Water*, *Run Silent, Run Deep*, *Das Boot*, *Ice Station Zebra*, *20,000 Leagues under the Sea*, *The Bedford Incident*, *The Hunt for Red October*, and *The Russians Are Coming! The Russians Are Coming!*, among others. *Crimson Tide* is a remake of *Run Silent, Run Deep*.

2. The action in the film all takes place during the same dates in October as the Cuban Missile Crisis in 1962. Those familiar with that event will recall that it also involved two messages. (See Kennedy, 1971/1999; a film version of the crisis, *Thirteen Days*, was released in early 2001.)

3. Recall the scene in Michael Crichton's novel *Rising Sun* (and in the film, too), in which an image of the murderer is extracted from a momentary reflection in a doctored surveillance video. The film *Rashomon* offers useful insights on eyewitnesses' contrasting interpretations of specific incidents.

Chapter 2: From Hot War to Cold War

1. Information can be found at the U.S. Air Forces in Europe Berlin website, http://www.usafe.af.mil/berlin/berlin.htm (6/2/99).

2. "First we got the bomb, and that was good,
'Cause we love peace and brotherhood.
Then Russia got the bomb, but that's okay,
'Cause the balance of power's maintained that way.
Who's next?"
From Tom Leher, "Who's Next," *That Was the Year That Was* (6179-2 Reprise Records, 1965). Reproduced by permission of Tom Leher.

3. American children were told at the dinner table that "people were starving in Europe." To which Allan Sherman, a satirical songwriter of the 1960s replied, "So I ate my dinner and grew fat."

4. Recent research in the Soviet archives suggests that, although there were "atomic spies," and Julius Rosenberg might have been involved, Ethel was not among them. This, however, remains a contested matter. See Radosh and Milton, 1997; Garber and Walkowitz, 1995.

5. The atomic bomb was simple by comparison: it merely required that a critical mass of fissionable parts be kept together long enough for the chain reaction to run away. In the super, the parts had to be kept together long enough for a fusion reaction to run away. Stanislaus Ulam recognized that an atomic bomb "trigger" could supply a source of high energy radiation that could be focused onto the H-bomb's core and provide the light pressure to keep the material together for a sufficiently long time (still measured in fractions of a second; see De Volpi, 1981; Freudenrich, 2001; Rhodes, 1995).

6. Decades later, the problem of battlefield destructiveness would be solved—in theory, anyway—with the so-called neutron bomb. This low-yield weapon was designed to be detonated above the battlefield, killing troops with a deadly flux of neutrons, while leaving the landscape minimally damaged.

7. "George Orwell's Nineteen Eighty-Four As a Criticism of American Civilization," written around 1993, posted at: www.lacollege.edu/pages/marable/papers/orwell. I have an electronic copy of the paper, downloaded to my computer on January 13, 1998.

Chapter 3: Reds among Us?

1. NSC-68 was not officially declassified until 1980, under the thirty-year rule governing secret documents, although parts of it were published earlier.

2. Truman's challenger from the right was Strom Thurmond who, in 2001, at age 98, has been a U.S. senator from South Carolina for almost fifty years.

3. One semi-comic look at the blacklist is Woody Allen's *The Front* (1976).

4. *Id*: the division of the psyche associated with instinctual impulses and demands for immediate satisfaction of primitive needs; *ego*: the personality component that is conscious, most immediately controls behavior, and is most in touch with immediate reality; *super-ego*: the division of the psyche that develops by the incorporation of the perceived moral standards of the community, is mainly unconscious and includes the conscience. (From the *American Heritage Dictionary of the English Language*).

5. We do know that the CIA experimented with drugs, including LSD, in an effort to determine whether brainwashing was possible; see Marks, 1979.

Chapter 4: Spies!

1. A large number of books on Iran have been published since the fall of the Shah, in addition to Roosevelt's. See, for example, Cottam, 1988.

2. Paradoxically, perhaps, the number of Americans supplying secret information to the KGB seemed to balloon in the 1980s and 1990s, when ideology no longer constrained them from treason, self-interest had become the norm, and the remuneration was quite good.

Chapter 5: Nukes!

1. This, and other fascinating data about the U.S. nuclear stockpile, can be found in Cochran, et al., 1984.

2. The origins of this observation are lost in history; it was told to me by Gene Rochlin.

3. This is why the interstate highway system—authorized under the National Defense Highway Act—was originally designed to bypass urban areas. The highways were meant to provide high-speed corridors across the country for military transports.

4. To be entirely fair, Schelling pointed out that one could also play "chicken" by refusing to play. Negotiations are not ruled out, either.

5. The allusion here was to the Colt .45 of the Old West, also called the "Peacekeeper." Of course, the .45 was used quite often.

6. Carl Sagan once suggested that the reason we might not have detected radio transmissions from advanced civilizations in other solar systems was that, once they reached a certain degree of development, they were annihilated in nuclear war.

Chapter 6: The Final Frontier

1.The "Fair Deal" was, of course, how Truman distinguished *his* program from Franklin Roosevelt's "New Deal."

2. Khruschev gave this speech during the never-ending Berlin Crisis, which would soon peak once again, as well as in the middle of what would later be called the "Congo Crisis," in which East and West nearly came to blows over the future of that newly independent country (see Weissman, 1974).

3. Or, as one demographer put it in 1989, "[S]ince the same political forces are promoting the rapid spread of education [as growth in the labor force], that unemployed person is likely to be a high school or college graduate and therefore especially dangerous to political stability" (Keyfitz, 1989: 52).

Chapter 7: Vietnam, Over and Over

1. My earliest recollection of Indochina comes from circa 1961, when it was mentioned on the back cover of an issue of *Mad Magazine* in an illustration of how kids (mis)interpreted newspaper headlines. The headline in question: "Guerrillas attack on Plain of Jarres." I leave the reader to imagine the picture in a child's mind.

2. Triangular trade operated in this way: Raw materials produced in Indochina were sold to France for soft-currency French francs, which could only be used, in turn, to buy goods from France. France, in turn, sold the commodities to the United States for hard-currency dollars, which were coveted everywhere. The Americans would have much preferred direct access to Indochina and its markets; the French wanted to keep the United States out.

3. Practically speaking, this was the same problem being pondered by Henry Kissinger and Herman Kahn. As noted in chapter 5, however, they worked on the problem of making nukes usable.

4. After the collapse of the South, Thieu fled to France while Ky removed to southern California where he opened a restaurant.

5. Personal communication with Ford via e-mail, August 1999.

6. Ford discusses how he came to write the book, and its journey to film at http://www.danford.net/movie.htm.

Chapter 8: Renewing the Cold War

1. For example, the dollar-yen exchange rate was fixed at about ¥360 per dollar, as opposed to the roughly ¥100-120 it is today.

2. This was increasingly difficult because of transactions in "Eurodollar" markets.

3. Interestingly, at the time, the United States regarded the coup with some favor, since Idris was seen as hopelessly corrupt. It is not entirely foolish to think that the CIA might have been involved in this coup, as it was with the 1952 colonels' coup in Egypt that led to the rise to power of Gamal Abdul Nassr. Eventually, of course, Gadhafi became a thorn in the side of the United States.

4. The energy crisis also led to the Third World debt crisis ten years later. Western banks, wallowing in dollars earned by oil producers, saw fit to lend them to developing countries to pay for the increased costs of oil imports as well as various development projects and corrupt activities. When the world was hit by the Reagan Recession of 1982-83—implemented to squeeze inflation out of the U.S. economy—third world producers saw their export earnings drop to almost nothing, and their ability to service debts vanish. *Sic transit mundi.*

5. This also does not gainsay the similar expenditure of almost $3 trillion dollars during the 1990s.

6. In this context, it is also worth viewing a film called *The Beast*, which depicts the misfortunes of a Soviet tank crew (played by Americans) lost in the Afghani desert, under attack by *mujuhadeen.*

Chapter 9: New Competitors, Old Enemies

1. See the bibliography at the end of *Rising Sun* and, in particular, the works of Karel Von Wolferen (1989) and James Fallows (1989).

2. In practice, of course, this is not entirely correct. For our purposes, however, it is correct enough.

3. Indeed, one might even go so far as to say that, were the playing field to be completely level, with all factors of production equalized, there would be no way over the long term to increase the rate of profit by moving capital or seeking out lower-cost labor. Thus the need for uneven development.

Chapter 10: Now What?

1. For a detailed examination of the new security environment, see Lipschutz, 2000.

2. The article was subsequently expanded into a book; see Huntington, 1996.

3. Kaplan's article was also turned into a book; see Kaplan, 1996.

4. In an appearance before the Senate Judiciary Committee on a constitutional amendment to ban the burning of the American flag, the national commander of the American Legion, William Detweiler, testified that such an amendment would "reinstate respect for the flag as one of the guiding principles of our nation" (Clymer, 1995:A16).

5. *American Heritage Dictionary of the English Language* (Boston: Houghton-Mifflin, 1981), p. 32. Oddly enough, my copy says nothing about "aliens from outer space."

6. Somewhat contrary to the old saw about liberalism that "everything not explicitly forbidden is permitted."

Resources

The films, novels, texts, and trade books listed here represent only a fraction of those dealing with the Cold War in all of its aspects. Much of the fiction falls into one of two genres—science fiction and spy thrillers—as will be evident below. I have tried to hew as closely as possible to my operating principle of "no work after its time," but there are a few films and novels here that, while not contemporaneous with their times, nonetheless merit inclusion. If you know of any films or novels that should be included in this list, please e-mail titles to me (rlipsch@cats.ucsc.edu). Note that novels not followed by a descriptive text are listed before their film version.

Chapter 1: Film, Fiction, American Politics

General Resources on Cold War Culture, Film, and Fiction

Arne Axellson, *Restrained Response: American Novels of the Cold War and Korea, 1945-1962* (New York: Greenwood Press, 1990).

Peter Biskind, *Seeing Is Believing—How Hollywood Taught Us to Stop Worrying and Love the Fifties* (New York: Owl Books, 1983, 2000).

Paul S. Boyer, *Fallout: A Historian Reflects on America's Half-Century Encounter with Nuclear Weapons* (Columbus: Ohio State University Press, 1998).

———, *By the Bomb's Early Light: American Thought and Culture at the Dawn of the Atomic age* (New York: Pantheon, 1985).

James Conbo (ed.), *Movies, Politics: The Dynamic Relationship* (New York: Garland, 1993).

Martin Harry Greenberg and Joseph D. Olander (eds.), *International Relations through Science Fiction* (New York: New Viewpoints, 1978).

Robert W. Gregg, *International Relations on Film* (Boulder, Colo.: Lynne Rienner, 1998).

Margot A. Henriksen, *Dr. Strangelove's America: Society and Culture in the Atomic Age* (Berkeley: University of California Press, 1997).

Elaine Tyler May, *Homeward Bound: American Families in the Cold War Era* (New York: Basic, 1988).

Ethan Mordden, *Medium Cool—The Movies of the 1960s* (New York: Knopf, 1990).

Alan Nadel, *Containment Culture: American Narrative, Postmodernism, and the Atomic Age* (Durham, N.C.: Duke University Press, 1995).

Stephen Powers, David J. Rothman, and Stanley Rothman, *Hollywood's America: Social and Political Themes in Motion Pictures* (Boulder, Colo.: Westview Press, 1996).

Stephen Prince, *Visions of Empire--Political Imagery in Contemporary American Film* (New York: Praeger, 1992).

Leonard Quart and Albert Auster, *American Film and Society since 1945* (New York: Praeger, 1984).

Peter C. Rollins (ed.), *Hollywood As Historian: American Film in a Cultural Context.* (Lexington: University Press of Kentucky, 1983).

Michael Ryan and Douglas Kellner, *Camera Politica–The Politics and Ideology of Contemporary Hollywood Film* (Bloomington: Indiana University Press, 1988).

Nora Sayre, *Running Time: Films of the Cold War* (New York: Dial Press, 1982).

Thomas Hill Schaub, *American Fiction in the Cold War* (Madison: University of Wisconsin Press, 1991).

Alison M. Scott and Christopher D. Geist (eds.), *The Writing on the Cloud: American Culture Confronts the Atomic Bomb* (Lanham, Md.: University Press of America, 1997).

David Seed, *American Science Fiction and the Cold War—Literature and Film* (Edinburgh: Edinburgh University Press, 1999).

Robert Bert Toplin (ed.), *Hollywood As Mirror* (London: Greenwood Press, 1993).

Books and Films about Submarines

Submarines on the Web: http://main.wavecom.net/~rontini/

Michael L. Hadley, *Count Not the Dead: The Popular Image of the German Submarine* (Montreal: McGill-Queen's University Press, 1995).

Patrick Tyler, *Running Critical: The Silent War, Rickover, and General Dynamics* (New York: Harper and Row, 1986).

Dan Van der Vat, *Stealth at Sea: The History of the Submarine* (Boston: Houghton Mifflin, 1995).

The Flying Missile (Columbia; 1950; 92m) director: Henry Levin; cast Glenn Ford, Viveca Lindfors. Fictional account of the role played by a somewhat impetuous U.S. naval commander in developing the first means of launching missiles from submarines.

Hell and High Water (20th Century Fox; 1954; 103m) director: Samuel Fuller; cast: Richard Widmark, Cameron Fuller. Story of a submarine and its scientists trying to save the world from a Chinese Communist plot to detonate an atomic bomb over South Korea.

20,000 Leagues under the Sea (Walt Disney; 1954; 95m) director: Richard Fleischer; cast: Kirk Douglas, James Mason, Peter Lorre. Victorian scientists captured by Captain Nemo and his submarine. Adapted from the novel by Jules Verne.

Run Silent, Run Deep (United Artists; 1958; 93m) director: Robert Wise; cast: Clark Gable, Burt Lancaster, Jack Warden, Don Rickles. "Rich" Richardson (Gable), submarine commander, wages war with the Japanese as well as his lieutenant (Lancaster).

The Bedford Incident (Columbia; 1965; 102m) director: James Harris; cast: Richard Widmark, Sidney Poitier, James MacArthur, Wally Cox, Martin Balsam, Donald Sutherland. U.S. destroyer chases a Russian sub and fires an atomic weapon against orders.

The Russians Are Coming, The Russians Are Coming (United Artists; 1966; 126m) director: Norman Jewison; cast: Carl Reiner, Eva Marie Saint, Alan Arkin, Brian Keith, Jonathan Winters, Theodore Bikel. A comedy in which a Russian submarine is grounded on a New England island and causes panic among the residents, who believe war has begun.

Ice Station Zebra (MGM; 1968; 148m) director: John Surges; cast: Rock Hudson, Patrick McGoohan, Ernest Borgnine, Jim Brown. Americans and Soviets race to the North Pole to claim a capsule with secret military information.

Das Boot (Columbia/Bavaria Atelier; 1981; 149m) director: Wolfgang Peterson; cast: Jürgen Prochnow. World War II adventures of a German U-boat.

The Hunt for Red October (Paramount; 1990; 137m) director: John McTiernan; cast: Sean Connery, Alec Baldwin, Sam Neill, James Earl Jones. Film version of Tom

Clancy's novel. A Soviet sub commander defects with his crew and top-secret vessel, while Americans try to decide whether to destroy or welcome them.

Chapter 2: From Hot War to Cold War

There are two film versions of *1984*: Neither appears to be available for sale in VHS format at this time.

1984 (Holiday; 1955; 91m) director: Michael Anderson; cast: Michael Redgrave, Edmond O'Brien, Jan Sterling, Donald Pleasence. Withdrawn from circulation.
1984 (Umbrella/Rosenbloom/Virgin; 1984; 110m) director: Michael Radford; cast: John Hurt, Richard Burton, Suzanna Hamilton, Cyril Cusack.

The Iron Curtain (20th Century Fox; 1948; 87m) director: William Wellman; cast: Dana Andrews. The story of a Russian code clerk, played by Andrews, who defects to the West with his family, bringing evidence of Soviet espionage in North America.

Guilty of Treason (Eagle Lion; 1949; 86m) director: Felix Feist; cast: Charles Bickford. Hungary's Roman Catholic prelate, Cardinal Josef Mindszenty (Bickford), is arrested, tortured, and imprisoned by the Communists.

White Heat (Warner; 1949; 114m) director: Raoul Walsh; cast: James Cagney, Edmund O'Brien. One of a group of films linking crime to communism, depicting violent gangsters stopped by government agents.

The Next Voice You Hear (MGM; 1950; 83m) director: William Wellman; cast: James Whitmore, Nancy Davis (Reagan), Lillian Bronson, Jeff Corey. One day, God begins to speak to the world over the radio (TV ownership was still rather limited) and, through stories and parables, changes the lives of everyday Americans.

The Red Danube (MGM; 1950; 119m) director: George Sidney; cast: Ethel Barrymore, Walter Pidgeon, Janet Leigh, Peter Lawford, Angela Lansbury. Citizens in occupied Vienna are forcibly repatriated to the Soviet Union.

The Steel Helmet (Lippert; 1951; 85m) director: Samuel Fuller; cast: Gene Evans, Robert Hutton, Steve Brodie, James Edwards, Richard Loo, Sid Melton. During the Korean War, a sergeant is taken prisoner, the lone survivor after his company is attacked. He is rescued by an orphaned Korean boy, and then teams up with a squad of 'orphaned' G.I.'s just like him. The team tries to set up an observation post in a Buddhist temple. Soldiers try to come to terms with the identity of the enemy and the role of military force (and their place) in world affairs and end up relying upon nationalist and racist beliefs to do so.

One Minute to Zero (RKO; 1952; 105m) director: Tay Garnett; cast: Robert Mitchum, Ann Blythe. U.S. colonel evacuating Americans from Korea is forced to bomb refugees.

J. D. Salinger, *Catcher in the Rye* (Boston: Little, Brown, 1951). Seventeen-year-old Holden Caulfield would like to sit on the atom bomb when it blows up. He is also depressed and at loose ends. Classic novel of 1950s ennui.

The Day the Earth Stood Still (20th Century Fox; 1951; 92m) director: Robert Wise; cast: Michael Rennie, Patricia Neal, Hugh Marlowe, Sam Jaffe, Billy Gray. Emissary from Mars arrives in a flying saucer, accompanied by a giant robot, and lands near the Washington Monument. He warns that if the people of Earth do not mend their ways and stop threatening nuclear war, a "race of robots" designed to keep the peace in space will destroy the planet.

Big Jim McLain (Wayne; 1952; 90m) director: Edward Ludwig; cast: John Wayne, James Arness. Special agent for the House Un-American Activities Committee searches out Communists in Hawaii.

High Noon (Criterion/Republic/United Artists; 1952; 84m) director: Fred Zinnemann; cast: Gary Cooper, Thomas Mitchell, Lloyd Bridges, Katy Jurado. This tale is told in real time, following a marshal on his retirement and wedding day as he learns that an assassin is seeking retribution against him. Although the marshal has sufficient reasons to evade the killer, he feels a duty to remain and confront him. John Wayne labeled this a Communist film (Henriksen, 1997: 68).

California Conquest (Columbia; 1952; 79m) director: Lew Landers; cast: Cornel Wilde. Spanish Californians fight Russian invaders. Even then they were after us!

Man on a Tightrope (20th Century Fox; 1953; 105m) director: Elia Kazan; cast: Fredric March, Cameron Mitchell, Adolphe Menjou, Gloria Grahame, Richard Boone. The owner of a circus in Czechoslovakia escapes after getting into trouble with the Communist government.

Shane (Paramount; 1953; 118m) director: George Steven; cast: Alan Ladd, Jean Arthur, Van Heflin, Jack Palance. In this Western, a onetime gunslinger, Shane, tries to settle on a homestead. Instead, he becomes embroiled in a conflict between Ryker, a cattleman, and a homesteading family. Shane defends the family from the henchmen and hired killers of the cattleman who is trying to take the homesteaders' land.

The War of the Worlds (Paramount; 1953; 85m) director: Byron Haskin; cast: Gene Barry, Ann Robinson. Martians invade the United States, and the military is helpless to stop them. Measles finally does the job. Second remake of H. G. Wells novel and inspiration for *Independence Day*.

Suddenly (United Artists; 1954; 75m) director: Lewis Allen; cast: Frank Sinatra, Sterling Hayden, Nancy Gates. A group of gunmen with a plan to shoot the president take over a suburban house by which he is scheduled to pass.

Prisoner of War (MGM; 1954; 81m) director: Andrew Marton; cast: Ronald Reagan, Steve Forrest, Dewey Martin. Lives of prisoners of war in a North Korean prison camp.

William Golding, *Lord of the Flies, A Novel* (London: Faber and Faber, 1954).

Lord of the Flies (Continental; 1963; 90m) director: Peter Brook; cast: James Aubrey, Tom Chapin, Hugh Edwards. After an atomic attack on Britain, a group of boys from British boarding schools are stranded on an island with no adult supervision. The boys split into two factions, one striving to remain civilized and leave the island, the other reverting to savagery. The groups end up fighting each other, with one wiping out the other, before the Royal Navy arrives. The book is usually interpreted as a parable based on Hobbes's *Leviathan*, but it can also be read as a condemnation of the violence and savagery of British "civilization."

Robert Heinlein, *Starship Troopers* (New York: Putnam, 1959). Troops of the Federal Service of the Terran Federation do battle against the "Bugs" (read: Communists), who threaten Earth's way of life. This was Heinlein's screed against the "softness" he perceived in the American response to the USSR. This book should be read together with Joe Haldeman's *The Forever War* (see below).

Chapter 3: Reds among Us?

Kevin McCarthy and Ed Gorman (eds.), *"They're Here…" Invasion of the Body Snatchers–A Tribute* (New York: Berkeley Boulevard Books, 1999).

The Boy with Green Hair (RKO; 1948; 82m) director: Jospeh Losey; cast: Dean Stockwell, Pat O'Brien, Robert Ryan, Barbara Hale. On hearing that his parents have been killed in an air raid, a boy's hair turns green. With the encouragement of his fellow orphans, the boy becomes a symbol of the futility and horror of war.

The Woman on Pier 13 (aka, *I Married a Communist*) (RKO; 1949; 73m) director: Robert Stevenson; cast: Laraine Day, Robert Ryan. Brad Collins is doing well in a shipping company, until the Communist Party begins blackmailing him to do their bidding; he used to be a party member himself. They even use a beautiful woman to entice him, and ultimately his innocent wife gets in over her head when she investigates what's going on.

The Red Menace (Republic; 1949; 81m) director: R. G. Springsteen; cast: Robert Rockwell, Hannelore Axman (deliberately selected from unknowns). After getting shafted by some corrupt real estate agents, a war veteran turns to the government for retribution. When they don't come through for him, the Communist Party seizes upon him, using sex and money to win him over to the other side.

The Iron Curtain (20th Century Fox; 1948; 87m) director: William Wellman; cast: Dana Andrews, Gene Tierney. A Soviet official in Ottawa defects to the United States and reveals details of a spy ring.

The Thing (RKO; 1951; 87m) director: Christian Nyby (helped by either Howard Hawks or Orson Welles?); cast: Robert Cornthwaite, Kenneth Tobey, Margaret Sheridan, James Arness (as the Thing). American expedition to the Artic discovers a spaceship embedded in the ice and finds a frozen being inside. Thawing it out, they realize, to their horror, that it is a ferocious, man-killing CARROT! Still considered one of the best of the Cold War monster films.

Red Snow (Columbia; 1952; 75m) director: Harry Franklin; cast: Guy Madison. Mysterious lights and noises near a U.S. Air Force base in Alaska lead officials to believe Russia is testing a weapon.

On the Waterfront (Columbia; 1954; 108m) director: Elia Kazan; cast: Marlon Brando, Karl Malden, Lee J. Cobb, Rod Steiger. A dock worker becomes a witness to a homicide carried out by his boss's henchmen. His boss, Johnny Friendly, is also the leader of the local harbor union. The worker, Terry Malloy, later meets the victim's sister. The sister and Father Barry try to persuade Terry to inform on his boss.

Jack Finney, *Invasion of the Body Snatchers* (New York: Dell, 1955). This is the novel on which the film was based. Finney revised it a couple of times.

Rebel without a Cause (Warner; 1955; 111m) director: Nicholas Ray; cast: James Dean, Natalie Wood, Jim Backus, Sal Mineo, Ann Doran, Dennis Hopper. Teenage son of a well-off family shuns the conventional life and gets into trouble. Makes a nice pairing with *Catcher in the Rye*.

Sloan Wilson, *The Man in the Gray Flannel Suit* (New York: Simon and Schuster, 1955).

The Man in the Gray Flannel Suit (20th Century Fox; 1956; 152m) director: Nunnally Johnson; cast: Gregory Peck, Fredric March, Jennifer Jones, Ann Harding, Lee J. Cobb, Keenan Wynn. Story of conformity and its consequences in 1950s America.

Storm Center (Columbia; 1956; 87m) director: Daniel Taradash; cast: Bette Davis, Brian Keith, Kim Hunter. When the local city council bans a propaganda book entitled "The Communist Dream," one librarian refuses to remove it, as it goes against her calling of introducing books and knowledge to children. Even though she isn't a Communist, her past activities are questioned and the council fires her.

The Blob (Tonylyn; 1958; 83m) director: Irwin Yeaworth, Jr.; cast: Steve McQueen. A space invader attacks a small town.

The Fly (20th Century Fox; 1958; 94m) director: Kurt Neumann; cast: David Hedison, Patricia Owens, Herbert Marshall, Vincent Price. A scientist (Price) develops a matter transmitter and operates the machine while a fly is trapped within. Oops! Famous last scene: fly with the head of Vincent Price, trapped in a spider's web: "Help me! Help me!"

Attack of the 50 Foot Woman (Allied; 1958; 66m) director: Nathan Juran; cast: Allison Hayes, William Hudson, Yvette Vickers. After encountering aliens, a wealthy woman grows to be fifty feet tall. The woman uses her new strength to get revenge on her adulterous husband and other enemies.

One, Two, Three (United Artists; 1961; 110m) director: Billy Wilder; cast: James Cagney, Horst Buchholz, Arlene Francis. One of the few cheerful Cold War films made during the 1950s. Coke exec C. P. MacNamara (Cagney) is looking after the impetuous daughter of his boss in hopes of being transferred out of West Berlin. When she goes off and marries a scrappy-looking East German Communist, MacNamara must figure out a way to both sneak the groom past the Iron Curtain and make him appear suitable enough for daddy's little girl.

Chapter 4: Spies!

David Stafford, *The Silent Game—The Real World of Imaginary Spies* (Athens: University of Georgia Press, 1991, rev. ed.).

Jack Shadoian, *Dreams and Dead Ends: The American Gangster/Crime Film* (Cambridge, Mass.: MIT Press, 1977).

Ian Fleming's best James Bond books are from the 1950s. The best Bond films are from the early 1960s.
Live and Let Die (London: J. Cape, 1954). Film with Roger Moore, 1973.
Moonraker (London: J. Cape, 1955). Film with Roger Moore, 1979.
Diamonds Are Forever (London: J. Cape, 1956). Film with Sean Connery, 1971.
From Russia, with Love (London: J. Cape, 1957). Film with Sean Connery, 1963.
Doctor No (London: J. Cape, 1958). Film with Sean Connery, 1962.
Goldfinger (London: J. Cape 1959). Film with Sean Connery, 1964.

Philip Wylie, "The Smuggled Atomic Bomb," pp. 3-116, in *Three to Be Read* (New York: Rinehart, 1951). Graduate physics student Duff Bogan uncovers a Soviet plot to smuggle atomic bombs into the United States and plant them in the cities, where they will be used for blackmail and destruction.

Micky Spillane, *Kiss Me Deadly* (New York: Dutton, 1952). In the novel, Mike Hammer gets involved with a Mafia-run drug ring. No Commies here!

Walk East on Beacon (Columbia; 1952; 98m) director: Alfred L. Werker; cast: George Murphy, Finlay Currie, Virginia Gilmore, George Roy Hill. There is a leak of American intelligence to the Russians, who are also blackmailing a scientist into helping them. FBI agent Belden must try to find who has established the espionage network. A revitalized FBI protects the American public from Communist subversives by employing the latest in surveillance technology.

Top Secret Affair (Warner Brothers; 1956; 100m) director: H. C. Potter; cast: Kirk Douglas, Susan Hayward, Jim Backus. Female news publisher attempts to discredit a military diplomat but falls in love with him instead.

Assignment Paris (Columbia, 1952; 85m) director: Robert Parrish; cast: George Sanders, Dana Andrews, Herbert Berghof. News reporter is arrested as a spy while in Yugoslavia and has to be exchanged.

Diplomatic Courier (20th Century Fox; 1952; 97m) director: Henry Hathaway; cast: Tyrone Power, Patricia Neal, Karl Malden, Herbert Berghof. Secret agent tries to retrieve sensitive documents from a Soviet agent while on a train between Salzburg and Trieste.

Night People (20th Century Fox; 1954; 93m) director: Nunnally Johnson; cast: Gregory Peck, Broderick Crawford. The Russians have abducted a U.S. officer in West Berlin. They want to exchange him for some Germans, supposedly to help some former Nazis who are now working for them. But they could have just gone after the Germans directly, so there must be something else going on.

North by Northwest (MGM; 1959; 136m) director: Alfred Hitchcock; cast: Cary Grant, Eva Marie Saint, James Mason, Leo G. Carroll. Spies and policeman pursue advertising agent Roger O. Thornhill (Grant) across the country. Due to a mistaken identity, the spies believe that Thornhill is an agent of the government; the police think that he is a hit man. An attractive woman (Saint) aids him in his cross-country adventures.

The Man Who Knew Too Much (Paramount; 1956; 120m) director: Alfred Hitchcock; cast: James Stewart, Doris Day. While on vacation in Marrakesh, an American doctor and his family become involved in a complicated international plot. Doris Day sings "Que Sera, Sera."

Jet Pilot (Howard Hughes; 1957; 112m) director: Josef Von Sternberg, et al.; cast: John Wayne, Janet Leigh. Filmed in 1950 but not released until 1957 because Hughes kept interfering with production. Air Force Colonel Wayne falls in love with Soviet jet pilot Leigh, but suspects she is a spy. He defects back to the USSR with her in order to find out if she is still working for the Russkies, but they must both flee back to the West. Chuck Yeager did some of the flying scenes.

Graham Greene, *Our Man in Havana: An Entertainment* (New York: Viking, 1958).

Our Man in Havana (Columbia; 1960; 107m) director: Carol Reed; cast: Alec Guinness, Burl Ives. British Intelligence hires Jim Wormald, a vacuum cleaner salesman in Cuba, to spy on the government for them. Jim doesn't have a clue about being a spy, but he wants the extra money, so he makes up all kinds of secrets and documents for his new employer. The British think he's very dependable, and the local government actually begins to believe that he is a spy.

Len Deighton, *The Ipcress File* (New York: Simon and Schuster, 1963).

The Ipcress File (Rank; 1965; 109m) director: Sidney J. Furie; cast: Michael Caine, Nigel Green, Sue Lloyd. Harry Palmer (Caine), a flabby, near-sighted spy tries to trace missing British scientists and discovers that one of his superiors is an enemy agent.

Our Man Flint (20th Century Fox; 1965; 108m) director: Daniel Mann; cast: James Coburn, Lee J. Cobb, Gila Golan. American secret agent and ladies man Flint (Coburn) combats a global organization whose goal is world domination through weather control. Comical imitation of Bond.

Torn Curtain (Universal; 1966; 119m) director: Alfred Hitchcock; cast: Paul Newman, Julie Andrews. An American scientist defects to East Germany, seeking Soviet missile secrets for his Western masters, but is followed by his fiancée. They then flee back to the West.

What's Up Tiger Lily? (Benedict/Toho; 1966; 80m) director: Senkichi Taniguchi, with Woody Allen and company. Woody Allen took a Japanese spy film and redubbed it in English. A Japanese agent searches for the world's greatest egg salad recipe.

Len Deighton, *Funeral in Berlin* (London: J. Cape, 1964).

Funeral in Berlin (Paramount; 1967; 102m) director: Guy Hamilton; cast: Michael Caine. Harry Palmer goes to Berlin to help a Soviet colonel defect to the West.

Leon Uris, *Topaz—A Novel* (New York: McGraw-Hill, 1967).

Topaz (Universal; 1969; 124m) director: Alfred Hitchcock; cast: Frederick Stafford, John Forsythe. A Soviet official defects to the West and reveals that the Cubans have missiles supplied by the Russians. He also informs them that they've been getting NATO intelligence through Topaz, the name of a French espionage ring.

John le Carré, *The Looking Glass War* (London: Heinemann, 1965).

The Looking Glass War (Columbia; 1969; 107m) director: Frank R. Pierson; cast: Christopher Jones, Pia Degermark, Ralph Richardson, Anthony Hopkins. A young Pole is sent into East Germany by MI-5 to find a secret film.

Philip Wylie, *The Spy Who Spoke Porpoise* (Garden City, N.Y.: Doubleday, 1969). R.W. Grove, special assistant to the President, exposes a Soviet-Chinese plot to blow up the West Coast of the United States with giant H-bombs and to irradiate the country and kill everyone in it, unless the country surrenders first.

The Spook Who Sat by the Door (Bokan/United Artists; 1973; 95m) director: Ivan Dixon; cast: Lawrence Cook, Paula Kelly. A black CIA agent mobilizes an army of inner-city youths and begins a revolution. Considered one of the most radical and best blaxploitation films of the 1970s.

John le Carré, *Tinker, Tailor, Soldier, Spy* (London: Hodder and Stoughton, 1974); *The Honourable Schoolboy* (London: Hodder and Stoughton, 1977); *Smiley's People* (London: Hodder and Stoughton, 1979). George Smiley is a perennial character from MI-5 in many of le Carré's novels. This trilogy tracks his search for a Soviet mole. The three novels were published in one volume called *The Quest for Karla* (1982). They were turned into television films with Alec Guiness in the title role and Patrick Steward ("The Next Generation") as Karla: *Tinker, Tailor, Soldier, Spy* (1980); *Smiley's People* (1982).

Three Days of the Condor (Paramount; 1975; 118m) director: Sydney Pollack; cast: Robert Redford, Faye Dunaway, Cliff Robertson, Max von Sydow, John Houseman. CIA researcher is forced to go underground when a rival branch kills all of the co-workers at his office.

Inside the CIA: On Company Business (Isla Negra Films; 1980, 179m) director: Allen Francovich. This documentary studies the clandestine operations of the U.S. Central Intelligence Agency. First volume reviews the origins of the CIA at the end of World War II and follows the "Company" through the various political incidents that the CIA has played a major role in throughout the past forty years. Second volume addresses the use of assassination by the CIA. Plots to muder government leaders around the world, including Cuba's Fidel Castro, are described. Third volume examines CIA involvement in subversion of foreign governments.

Chapter 5: Nukes!

Jack G. Shaheen (ed.), *Nuclear War Films* (Carbondale: Southern Illinois University Press, 1978).

Paul Brian, *Nuclear Holocausts: Atomic War in Fiction, 1895-1984* (Kent, Oh.: Kent University Press, 1987).

Allan M. Winkler, *Life Under a Cloud: American Anxiety about the Atom Bomb* (New York: Oxford University Press, 1993).

Mick Broderick, *Nuclear Movies: A Critical Analysis and Filmography of International Feature Length Films Dealing with Experimentation, Aliens, Terrorism, Holocaust, and Other Disaster Scenarios, 1914-1989* (Jefferson, N.C. : McFarland and Co., 1991).

Captain Walter Karig, U.S.N.R. *War in the Atomic Age?* (New York, W.H. Wise and Co., Inc., 1946, 63 pp.). In 1976, the enemy Galaxy of Nations incinerates Kansas City and orders the United States to surrender. America's superweapons, including a Star Wars-type force field, end in the Galaxy's destruction.

When Worlds Collide (Paramount; 1951; 82m) director: Rudolph Maté; cast: Richard Derr, Barbara Rush. A runaway planet is discovered to be on course toward Earth. A group of people manage to escape in a space ship and land on the new planet.

Philip Wylie, *The Disappearance* (New York: Rinehart, 1951). One day in February, all of the women disappear from the world of men, and all of the men disappear from the world of women. The men launch a nuclear war and defeat the USSR; the women make friends with their Soviet counterparts. Both make a mess of the world.

Above and Beyond (MGM; 1952; 122m) director: Melvin Frank; cast: Robert Taylor, Eleanor Parker, James Whitmore. Film about the training of Colonel Paul Tibbets, who flew the *Enola Gay* and dropped the atomic bomb on Hiroshima.

Invasion USA (Columbia; 1952; 70m) director: Alfred E. Green; cast: Dan O'Herlihy, Gerald Mohr, Peggie Castle. Hypnotist visits a New York bar and convinces the patrons that the H-bomb has been dropped on the United States.

The Atomic City (Paramount; 1952; 85m) director: Jerry Hopper; cast: Gene Barry, Nancy Gates, Lydia Clarke. Frank Addison, a nuclear scientist in Los Alamos, New Mexico, leads a typical middle-class American existence. His life is disrupted when representatives of the enemy kidnap his son in an attempt to extract nuclear secrets.

The Beast from 20,000 Fathoms (Warner; 1953; 80m) director: Eugène Lourié; cast: Paul Christian, Paula Raymond, Lee Van Cleef. Special effects by Ray Harryhausen. One of many films depicting the release of prehistoric monsters as a result of nuclear testing. This one destroys much of New York City.

It Came from beneath the Sea (Columbia; 1955; 80m) director: Robert Gordon; cast: Kenneth Tobey, Faith Domergue, Donald Curtis. West Coast version of *The Beast from 20,000 Fathoms*.

This Island Earth (Universal; 1955; 86m) director: Joseph Newman; cast: Jeff Morrow, Rex Reason, Faith Domergue, Russell Johnson. Aliens from the planet Metaluna recruit Earth scientists to help save their planet. A wary Dr. Meacher discovers that the Metalunans are actually planning to take over Earth. In attempting to escape, the doctor is kidnapped and taken to Metaluna, but then escapes with the help of an amiable alien before the planet self-destructs.

Strategic Air Command (Paramount; 1955; 114m) director: Anthony Mann; cast: James Stewart, June Allyson. "Peace Is Our Profession!" Baseball player is recalled to Air Force duty to pilot a B-52 on nuclear alert. Forced to choose between country and career (and home life), he chooses the former, and his wife goes along. The opening scene in *Dr. Strangelove*, showing sexual congress between a B-52 and a tanker, was taken from this film.

The Incredible Shrinking Man (Universal; 1957; 81m) director: Jack Arnold; cast: Grant Williams, Randy Stuart, Paul Langton, April Kent. A mysterious fog causes Scott Carey to shrink. Carey is challenged by doctors who cannot help him, an angry cat, and eventually a spider. Daily existence becomes a struggle to survive. Being shrunk compels the protagonist to view the world from a different perspective.

Beginning of the End (Republic; 1957; 73m) director: Bert I. Gordon; cast: Peggie Castle, Peter Graves. Exposure to radiation produces agitated giant grasshoppers that attack Chicago. This film follows Audrey Ames, a journalist trying to expose the story and save Chicago while the military attempts to cover it up.

The 27th Day (Columbia; 1957; 75m) director: William Asher; cast: Gene Barry, Valerie French, Arnold Moss. Aliens abduct five representatives from five states. Each individual is given the power to destroy, at will, any location and its human inhabitants within a 3000-mile radius.

The Space Children (Paramount; 1958; 71m) director: Jack Arnold; cast: Adam Williams, Peggy Webber, Jackie Coogan. Children at a missile testing site discover a pulsating alien, who instructs them to sabotage the device.

Nevil Shute, *On the Beach* (New York: Morrow, 1957).

On the Beach (United Artists; 1959; 134m) director: Stanley Kramer; cast: Gregory Peck, Ava Gardner, Fred Astaire, Anthony Perkins, Donna Anderson, John Tate, Guy Doleman. Australia awaits its doom as the last remaining uncontaminated area of the world after a nuclear war. An American submarine sets out to see what has happened to the rest of the world, and returns after finding no one else alive.

Pat Frank, *Alas, Babylon* (Philadelphia: Lippincott, 1959). Civilization comes to an end and one family struggles to survive.

The World, the Flesh and the Devil (Metro/MGM; 1959; 95m) director: Ranald Mac-Dougall; cast: Harry Belafonte, Inger Stevens. Harry Belafonte plays a coal miner who gets trapped when the mine collapses. After waiting to be rescued, he eventually digs himself out, only to find the world in ruins after a nuclear attack. He meets Inger Stevens and they are able to get beyond their racial stereotypes, but when a third man enters the picture, race relations go sour once again.

Walter Miller, Jr. *A Canticle for Leibowitz* (Philadelphia: Lippincott, 1959). Monks of the Order of St. Leibowitz try to keep 20th-century knowledge alive after the "Flame Deluge." Ultimately, they contribute to a revival of technological civilization, one that destroys itself once again.

Mordechai, Roshwald, *Level 7* (New York: McGraw-Hill, 1959). Diary of an atomic push button officer's life deep underground, before and after the button is pushed. The philosophical question always asked is: who is reading the diary after all humans are dead?

Village of the Damned (MGM; 1960; 78m) director: Wolf Rilla; cast: George Sanders, Barbara Shelley, Michael Gwynne, Laurence Naismith. An invisible shield that causes protracted slumber in community members besets an English village. Following this episode, the children of the pregnant women are born bereft of emotion and with powerful hypnotic powers.

Robin Moore Williams, *The Day They Bombed Los Angeles* (New York: Ace, 1961). The U.S. government nukes Los Angeles and seals it off after a radiation-mutated protein begins to take over its residents. Valiant survivors fight and discover a vaccine that saves the country and the world.

John Wyndham, *Day of the Triffids* (London: M. Joseph, 1951).

The Day of the Triffids (Allied Artists; 1962; 95m) director: Steve Sekely; cast: Howard Keel, Nicole Maurey, Janette Scott, Kieron Moor. A meteor shower blinds all of its observers, 99 percent of the population. In the ensuing confusion, some mutated experimental plants, Triffids, escape. The Triffids walk and they eat human beings.

Panic in the Year Zero (AIP; 1962; 93m) director: Ray Milland; cast: Ray Milland, Jean Hagen, Frankie Avalon, Mary Mitchel, Joan Freeman, Richard Garland. A family on a fishing trip near Los Angeles tries to survive after a nuclear attack. One of many films that feature a nuclear family on the run from a nuclear assault, and the social organization of the nuclear family as the most fit means of survival.

The Day the Earth Caught Fire (British Lion-Pax/Universal; 1962; 99m) director: Val Guest; cast: Edward Judd, Janet Munro, Leo McKern. Atomic blasts by both the United States and the Soviet Union send the Earth whirling toward the sun. The tale involves the ensuing confusion and hysteria as a reporter and his romantic interest expose the story.

Kurt Vonnegut, *Cats Cradle* (New York: Rinehard and Winston, 1963). The quest for science and new products leads to the invention of "Ice-9," a form of water that freezes at room temperature. The stuff gets loose and you can imagine what happens.

A Gathering of Eagles (U-I; 1963; 115m) director: Delbert Mann; cast: Rock Hudson, Mary Peach, Rod Taylor, Kevin McCarthy. A colonel who wants to reform the efficiency of a SAC base proves unpopular, and his British wife suffers for it.

Robert Heinlein, *Farnham's Freehold* (New York: Putnam, 1964). Another novel of family survival after the bombs fall, this time with a time travel twist. As usual, Heinlein gets in plenty of rants about the vulnerability of American society to Soviet perfidy.

D. F. Jones, *Colossus* (London: Hart-Davis, 1966).

Colossus: The Forbin Project (Universal; 1969; 100m) director: Joseph Sargent; cast: Eric Braeden, Gordon Pinsent, Susan Clark, William Schallert. The United States builds an enormous computer to defend the West, but it joins with its Russian counterpart to rule the world and enforce the peace.

The War Game (BBC; 1966; 45m) director: Peter Watkins. Famous, graphic BBC documentary never shown on TV, depicting the consequences of a nuclear attack on Britain.

Don DeLillo, *End Zone* (Boston: Houghton Mifflin, 1972). Gary Harkness plays football at some god-forsaken college in West Texas, and he also muses on language and nuclear strategy.

Chapter 6: The Final Frontier

John J. Michalczyk, *Costa-Gavras—The Political Fiction Film* (London: Associated University Presses, 1984).

Seven Days in May (Paramount; 1964; 118m) director: John Frankenheimer; cast: Burt Lancaster, Kirk Douglas, Ava Gardner. U.S. president Jordan Lyman gets a nuclear disarmament treaty approved by the Senate, but still finds his approval rating dropping. Marine colonel Jiggs Casey uncovers evidence that General Scott, who is head of the Joint Chiefs of Staff and well liked by the public, wants to take over the presidency before the end of Lyman's term. Casey goes to the president with the information and a paranoid power struggle ensues.

King of Hearts (United Artists; 1966; 110m) director: Philippe de Broca; cast: Alan Bates, Geneviève Bujold. French antiwar film about a World War I Scottish soldier (Bates) sent to scout an occupied town, only to find that everyone has fled except the inmates of the lunatic asylum. They make him their king and, at the end of the film, when the town is taken by Allied forces, he returns to the asylum.

Battle beneath the Earth (MGM; 1968; 112m) director: Montgomery Tully; cast: No one you've ever heard of. Chinese Communists plan to invade the United States by burning tunnels and are foiled by American scientists.

Burn! *(Queimada!)* (United Artists; 1969; 112m) director: Gillo Pontecorvo; cast: Marlon Brando, Evaristo Marquez. England sends William Walker to a Portuguese colony to incite the black workers to revolt against the Portuguese. In the process, capitalist elites take control and the black workers don't get the freedom they sought. Ten years later, Walker must return to stop a guerrilla uprising by the same person he inspired to revolt ten years ago.

Planet of the Apes (20th Century Fox; 1968; 128m) director: Franklin J. Schaffner; cast: Charlton Heston, Roddy McDowall, Kim Hunter, Maurice Evans. Astronauts crash-land on a planet where evolution has resulted in an advanced civilization of apes and a human population without language or refinement. One of the astronauts is captured by the dominant apes but cannot communicate with them due to a throat injury. The planet turns out to be Earth.

Norman Mailer, *The Armies of the Night—History As a Novel, the Novel As History* (New York: New American Library, 1968). This is Mailer's semifictional, semi-historical, and semijournalistic (that makes three halves, doesn't it?) book about his adventures during the October 1967 demonstrations against the Vietnam War in Washington, D.C., and the so-called Battle of the Pentagon.

Easy Rider (Columbia; 1969; 94m) director: Dennis Hopper; cast: Dennis Hopper, Peter Fonda, Jack Nicholson, Karen Black. Following a profitable cocaine sale, two motorcyclists take a trip from Los Angeles to New Orleans looking to find the "real America." Their journey is marked by frank encounters with various elements of society. Eventually, they and their lawyer are assassinated.

The Strawberry Statement (MGM; 1970; 109m) director: Stuart Hagmann; cast: Bruce Davison, Kim Darby, But Cort. Campus radicals occupy a university building during a student strike.

Getting Straight (Columbia; 1970; 124m) director: Richard Rush; cast: Elliot Gould, Candice Bergen, Harrison Ford. Vietnam Vet returns to his alma mater to get a teaching degree and gets involved in campus unrest.

Bananas (United Artists; 1971; 81m) director: Woody Allen; cast: Woody Allen, Louise Lasser, Howard Cosell. A product tester from New York goes to South America and volunteers for a guerilla movement trying to overthrow a dictator. He ends up the leader and becomes a rebel hero. Howard Cosell provides color commentary.

Anthony Burgess, *A Clockwork Orange* (London: Heinneman, 1962).

A Clockwork Orange (Warner Brothers; 1971; 137m) director: Stanley Kubrick; cast: Malcolm McDowell, Patrick Magee, Adrienne Corri. Set in a future Britain, this tale follows a band of rebels as they engage in "ultra-violence" on the streets. When one of the hooligans is left behind for the police to find, he agrees to accept intervention therapy to cure him of his violence. The therapy works and the boy hates violence when he is released, now the victim of the violence of his therapy.

Executive Action (EA Enterprises; 1973; 91m) director: David Miller; cast: Burt Lancaster, Robert Ryan, Will Greer. A millionaire pays a professional spy to kill President Kennedy.

The Parallax View (Paramount; 1974; 102m) director: Alan J. Paluka; cast: Warren Beatty, Paula Prentiss, Hume Cronyn. A reporter (Beatty) tries to disprove a government report that a presidential assassination was not a conspiracy, but the witnesses are killed off one by one.

Joseph Heller, *Catch-22* (New York: Simon and Schuster, 1961).

Catch-22 (Paramount; 1970; 122m) director: Mike Nichols; cast: Alan Arkin, Martin Balsam, Richard Benjamin, Art Garfunkel, Jack Gilford, Buck Henry, Bob Newhart, Anthony Perkins, Paula Prentiss, Jon Voight, Martin Sheen, Orson Welles. The only catch is, the film is not as good as the cast! Captain Yossarian (Arkin) tries to get out of flying any more missions by pleading insanity, but anyone who is too crazy to want to fly any more missions must be sane and must therefore fly them. Includes the great Loyalty Oath campaign launched by Milo Minderbinder. Read the book!

High Plains Drifter (Universal; 1972; 105m) director: Clint Eastwood; cast: Clint Eastwood, Verna Bloom, Marianna Hill, Mitch Ryan, Jack Ging. A mysterious man with no name rides out of the desert into a town threatened by a gang of outlaws. They hire him to defend the town. He paints it red and destroys it to save it. Then he rides back into the desert and disappears. Interpret it as you wish.

Chapter 7: Vietnam, Over and Over

Linda Dittmar and Gene Michaud (eds.), *From Hanoi to Hollywood: The Vietnam War in American Film* (New Brunswick, N.J.: Rutgers University Press, 1990).

John Hellman, *American Myth and the Legacy of Vietnam* (New York: Columbia University Press, 1986).

Michael Klein (ed.), *The Vietnam Era: Media and Popular Culture in the US and Vietnam* (London: Pluto Press, 1990).

Andrew Martin, *Receptions of War–Vietnam in American Culture* (Norman: University of Oklahoma Press, 1993), esp. ch. 4.

Saigon (Paramount; 1948; 94m) director: Leslie Fenton; cast: Alan Ladd, Veronica Lake, Luther Adler, and Douglas Dick. Larry and Mike were flying companions in World War II. After the war, Larry learns that Mike was terminally ill and decides to make his friend's last days fun. Mike falls for a lady and Larry asks her to play along with Mike's affection for her. Instead, she falls in love with Larry. Oh, and they also help in a robbery.

China Gate (20th Century Fox; 1957; 97m) director: Samuel Fuller; cast: Gene Barry, Angie Dickinson, Nat King Cole, Lee Van Cleef. A group of multinational troops is led into a Communist stronghold in Indochina by a French officer.

Graham Greene, *The Quiet American* (London: William Heinemann, 1955).

The Quiet American (United Artists; 1959; 120m) director: Joseph L. Mankiewicz; cast: Audie Murphy, Michael Redgrave, Giorgia Moll. An American is sent to Vietnam as an economic envoy, and he falls for a young Vietnamese girl. A reporter, who also loves her, then tells the local Communists that the American is really working for the U.S. government and supporting the non-Communist forces. Graham Greene's book criticized U.S. involvement in Vietnam, but the movie's ending was changed to support the American stance.

A Yank in Viet-Nam (Allied Artists; 1964; 80m) director: Marshall Thompson; cast: Mario Barri, Urban Drew. A Marine is marooned in Vietnam after his helicopter crashes. Local fighters help him through the jungle to safety, and he helps save a prisoner of war.

Morris L. West, *The Ambassador* (New York: Morrow, 1965). Written from the perspective of the U.S. ambassador to South Vietnam, this novel is based on President Diem's 1963 crackdown on the Buddhists opposing his handling of the war. In this case, however, the military coup comes about because of "President Cung's" approaches to North Vietnam.

Operation CIA, aka, *Last Message from Saigon* (Allied Artists; 1965; 90m) Director: Christian Nyby; cast: Burt Reynolds, Kieu Chinh, Danielle Aubry, John Hoyt. In Saigon, just before U.S. intervention in Vietnam, an assassin threatens the life of the U.S. ambassador. A U.S. agent is sent to guard the ambassador and look for a message that was never delivered.

David Halberstam, *One Very Hot Day* (Boston: Houghton Mifflin, 1967). Story of one day in the lives of American and Vietnamese troops during the war.

M*A*S*H (Aspen/20th Century Fox; 1970; 166m) director: Robert Altman; cast: Donald Sutherland, Elliot Gould, Tom Skerritt, Sally Kellerman. Korea was fun! This film chronicles the unruly adventures of a military medical support unit during the Korean conflict. Hawkeye and Duke are two youthful surgeons in the Mobile Army Surgical Hospital who engage in humorous behavior to maintain their sanity in the midst of war.

The Boys in Company C (Golden Harvest; 1977; 127m) director: Sidney J. Furie; cast: Stan Shaw, Andrew Stevens, James Canning. Five marines go from boot camp to the Vietnam war, which they find hellish and disheartening. They are told that, if they defeat a rival soccer team, they can stay out of combat playing exhibition games. This does not happen, of course.

The Deer Hunter (Universal; 1978; 183m) director: Michael Cimino; cast: Robert De Niro, Christopher Walken, John Cazale. Shows the effect of Vietnam on working-class workers in Pennsylvania. Begins with three friends on a final deer hunt before they go to Vietnam. They are then subjected to the horrors of war, and forced to play Russian roulette when they are imprisoned by the Viet Cong. Then we see them as changed men when they return to America.

Robert Stone, *Dog Soldiers* (Boston: Houghton-Mifflin, 1974).

Who'll Stop the Rain? (United Artists; 1978; 126m) director: Karel Reisz; cast: Nick Nolte, Tuesday Weld, Michael Moriarty. Journalist John Converse convinces his friend Ray Hicks, a Vietnam War veteran, into aiding him in a heroin smuggling scheme. Hicks transfers the contraband to Converse's wife, Marge. When the deal turns bad, Hicks and Converse's wife take flight together.

Joe Haldeman, *The Forever War* (New York: St. Martin's, 1974). William Mandella fights his ten-year stint in Earth's thousand-year war against the Taurans. When relativity kicks in, time flies. Oops! Just a silly misunderstanding; Terrans could not communicate with Taurans. This book is a riposte to Heinlein's *Starship Troopers*, as well as commentary on Vietnam, and the two ought to be read together.

James Webb, *Fields of Fire* (Englewood Cliffs, N.J.: Prentice Hall, 1978). Follows a Marine platoon during the war.

Tim O'Brien, *Going after Cacciato* (New York: Delacorte Press, 1978). What is dream-time, what is not? The soldiers of an American platoon follow Private Cacciato across Eurasia after he goes AWOL, trying to get him back so they can go on fighting the war.

Chapter 8: Renewing the Cold War

Star Wars (20th Century Fox; 1977; 121m) director: George Lucas; cast: Mark Hamill, Harrison Ford, Carrie Fisher, Alec Guinness, and the voice of James Earl Jones. In this, the first of the endless series, a young man, Luke Skywalker, tries to save a rebel leader, Princess Leia, from the dictatorial Empire. He succeeds with the help of new friends and mentors Han Solo, Chewbacca, Ben Konobi, C-3PO, and R2-D2. According to legend, the film crew was tired of seeing the United States lose (see also Meyer, 1992). The other films in this first part of the trilogy were *The Empire Strikes Back* (1980) and *Return of the Jedi* (1983).

Twilight's Last Gleaming (Lorimar; 1977; 146m) director: Robert Aldrich; cast: Burt Lancaster, Paul Winfield. A disillusioned general takes control of a nuclear missile and threatens to detonate it.

Black Sunday (Paramount; 1977; 143m) director: John Frankenheimer; cast: Bruce Dern, Robert Shaw, Marthe Keller, Fritz Weaver. Arab terrorists steal the Goodyear Blimp and enlist a crazed Vietnam veteran pilot to bomb the Orange Bowl on Super Sunday, when the president is present.

Rolling Thunder (AIP; 1977; 94m) director: John Flynn; cast: William Devane, Tommy Lee Jones, Dabney Coleman. An ex-Vietnam POW goes after the killers of his wife and son.

Alien (20th Century Fox; 1979; 116m) director: Ridley Scott; cast: Tom Skeritt, Sigourney Weaver, John Hurt, Ian Holm. During passage back to Earth, the company of a commercial cargo ship investigates an SOS signal from another planet. While exploring the planet, the crew discovers a hive of aliens, one of which they admit onto their ship. Unfortunately, the new passenger eats humans and changes shapes, leaving only one crewmember, Ripley (Weaver), alive. The other three films in this series are: *Aliens* (1986), *Alien 3* (1992) , and *Alien Resurrection* (1997).

Frederick Forsythe, *The Dogs of War* (London: Hutchison, 1974).

The Dogs of War (United Artists; 1980; 118m) director: John Irvin; cast: Christopher Walken, Tom Berenger, Colin Blakely, Victoria Tennant, JoBeth Williams. A platoon of Vietnam veterans reunites to fight as mercenaries and is hired to overthrow a West African dictator.

The Formula (MGM; 1980; 117m) director: John G. Avildsen; cast: George C. Scott, Marlon Brando, Marthe Keller, John Gielgud. Detective discovers Nazi formula for making gasoline from nonoil synthetic products. A major oil company tries to get the formula and destroy it.

Nighthawks (Universal; 1981; 99m) director: Bruce Malmuth; cast: Sylvester Stallone, Billy Dee Williams, Rutger Hauer. Stallone and Williams play two New York detectives in an antiterrorist squad assigned to hunt down the world's most feared terrorist.

Eyewitness, aka *The Janitor* (20th Century Fox; 1981; 108m) director: Peter Yates; cast: William Hurt, Christopher Plummer, Sigourney Weaver, James Woods, Steven Hill. After a murder occurs in his building, a janitor infatuated with a TV newscaster concocts a tale in order to meet her. He becomes the prime suspect in the murder and is pursued by both police and Soviet agents, the latter intent on halting the escape of Jews from the USSR. Odd but interesting film that does not entirely hold together.

Firefox (1982; Warner Brothers; 136m) director: Clint Eastwood; cast: Clint Eastwood. A pilot is sent on a secret mission to steal a new Soviet fighter, invisible to radar, that can be controlled by a neural link.

Megaforce (Golden Harvest; 1982; 99m) director: Hal Needham; cast: Barry Bostwick. Megaforce is an American rapid deployment unit that travels around the world fighting enemies of the United States.

Missing (Universal; 1982; 122m) director: Costa-Gavras; cast: Sissy Spacek, Jack Lemmon. Charles Horman disappears in a South American country where he was outspoken against the military government. When his wife tries to find him, she is brushed off by not only the government but also the American embassy. When Horman's patriotic father arrives, he can't believe the United States would be involved in any conspiracy, but in time he sees the connection between the United States and the coup during which his son disappeared.

The Final Option (MGM/Rank; 1983; 125m) director: Ian Sharp; cast: Lewis Collins, Judy Davis, Richard Widmark. British Special Air Service (SAS) commando infiltrates a radical political group planning a terrorist operation against the American ambassador in London.

Uncommon Valor (Paramount; 1983; 105m) director: Ted Kotcheff; cast: Gene Hackman, Robert Stack. Colonel Rhodes has been searching for his son, who is MIA in Laos, but hasn't been getting a lot of help from the government. When he hears that his son has been found but the government won't budge, he decides to go after him on his own. He enlists the help of MacGregor, an oil tycoon, to assemble a rescue team.

Under Fire (Orion; 1983; 122m) director: Roger Spottiswoode; cast: Nick Nolte, Joanna Cassidy, Gene Hackman. Follows the transformation of Russell Price from mere photojournalist to political activist. Price meets radio journalist Claire and falls for her, following her to Nicaragua to cover the civil war there. He soon sympathizes with the rebel forces fighting for freedom from the dictatorship that the United States wants to protect.

El Norte (Cinecom; 1983; 128m) director: Gregory Nava; cast: Zaide Silvia Gutierrez, David Villalpando. After their peasant father is murdered by the Guatemalan army, a brother and sister flee to the north. They sneak over the border into America, and then must try to survive as illegal aliens in Los Angeles.

War Games (MGM-UA; 1983; 113m) director: John Badham; cast: Matthew Broderick, Dabney Coleman, John Wood, Ally Sheedy, Barry Corbin, Juanin Clay. A teenager breaks into the Pentagon's computers and pretends he is attacking the United States. This time it is not a communications breakdown, but a fault in the very logic of the computer assigned to control the American nuclear arsenal that leads to the brink of destruction.

Threads (BBC; 1984; 110m) director: Mick Jackson; cast: Karen Meagher, Reece Dinsdale, Rita May, Nicholas Lane, Victoria O'Keefe. Britain's answer to the American television film, *The Day After. Threads* sets an ordinary family drama within the horrifying events that lead up to and follow a nuclear war. Scientific speculation about both the effects of radiation and nuclear winter are incorporated into its grisly depiction of three generations that struggle to survive after the war.

Missing in Action (Cannon; 1984; 101m) director: Joseph Zito; cast: Chuck Norris, M. Emmet Walsh. Army colonel returns to Vietnam for revenge, to look for MIAs, and to rescue POWs. Rambo before *Rambo II.*

John le Carré, *The Little Drummer Girl* (New York: Knopf, 1983).

The Little Drummer Girl (Warner; 1984; 130m) director: George Roy Hill; cast: Diane Keaton, Klaus Kinski. Based on the novel by John le Carré. An American actress in the United Kingdom is persuaded to abandon her pro-Palestinian sympathies, spy for Israel, and help to trap a terrorist leader.

Invasion USA (Cannon; 1985; 105m) director: Joseph Zito; cast: Chuck Norris. Russian forces land in south Florida and Chuck defeats them single-handedly. Lots of dead people in evidence.

Rocky 4 (MGM/UA; 1985; 91m) director: Sylvester Stallone; cast: Sylvester Stallone, Talia Shire, Dolph Lundgren, Brigitte Nielsen. After conquering the West, Rocky takes on the Soviet champ. Guess who wins?

Iron Eagle 1 (TriStar; 1985; 117m) director: Sidney J. Furie; cast: Jason Gedrick, Louis Gossett, Jr. An Air Force pilot is shot down in the Middle East, and his son is determined to rescue him. His friends help him steal two fighter planes, and he embarks on a rescue mission with an Air Force veteran.

Latino (Lucasfilm; 1985; 108m) director: Haskell Wexler; cast: Robert Beltran, Annette Cardona. A Vietnam veteran is sent to train the Contras in their fight against the Sandinistas in Nicaragua. At first he believes in overthrowing the Sandinistas, but then changes his mind when he sees the Contras going too far in their attacks across the border. His girlfriend also sees that the Contras' free society is not quite what it claims to be.

Salvador (Hemdale; 1986; 123m) director: Oliver Stone; cast: James Woods, James Belushi. Journalist Richard Boyle travels to El Salvador to photograph the civil war. At first he is neutral, providing helpful photos to both sides of the war. But he soon changes his mind when he sees that the American authorities care more about political stability than the plight of the Salvadoran people.

Top Gun (Paramount; 1986; 109m) director: Tony Scott; cast: Tom Cruise, Val Kilmer, Kelly McGillis. Two navy pilots, Mitchell and Kasansky, train and compete for Top Gun status. Mitchell loses it to Kasansky, but is then given a chance to reclaim it during an actual confrontation with Russian fighters in the Middle East. Air Force recruiting film.

The Patriot (Crown International; 1986; 88m) director: Frank Harris; cast: Gregg Henry. Matt Ryder (Henry) has been dishonorably discharged from the military, and goes after a group of nuclear-armed terrorists.

Heartbreak Ridge (Warner Brothers; 1986; 130m) director: Clint Eastwood; cast: Clint Eastwood, Arlen Dean Snyder. Sergeant Highway (Eastwood) trains raw, disrespectful recruits and together they invade Grenada.

The Delta Force (Cannon; 1986; 125m) director: Menahem Golan; cast: Lee Marvin, Chick Norris, Shelly Winters, and many of your other disaster film favorites. An elite fighting force attempts to free hostages held captive by terrorists in a hijacked TWA plane in the Middle East.

No Way Out (Orion; 1987; 114m) director: Roger Donaldson; cast: Kevin Costner, Sean Young, Gene Hackman. When Secretary of Defense David Brice murders his call girl Susan Atwell, his aid covers it up by suggesting she was killed by a Russian spy. Tom Farrell is called in to conduct the investigation, but he knows it is a snow job. However, since he was the last one seen with Atwell, he must go along with the cover up, all the while trying to figure out how to put the finger on Brice.

Red Heat (TriStar; 1988; 106m) director: Walter Hill; cast: Arnold Schwarzenegger, James Belushi. A Russian drug lord escapes to America, only to be caught in Chicago. Captain Ivan Danko is sent to extradite him, but when he escapes, Danko must cooperate with Chicago cop Art Ridzik in order to recapture him.

Iron Eagle 2 (TriStar; 1988; 102m) director: Sidney J. Furie; cast: Mark Humphrey, Louis Gossett, Jr. An air strike team, comprised of two Americans and two Soviets, is sent to destroy a nuclear weapons site in the Middle East. The team has enough difficulty getting along with each other, but then they discover that the U.S. government is trying to sabotage their mission.

Rambo III (Carolco/TriStar; 1988; 101m) director: Peter Macdonald; cast: Sylvester Stallone, Richard Crenna, Charles Napier, Julia Nickson. During the Afghanistan War, Colonel Trautman, John Rambo's commanding officer and old friend, is taken hostage. Rambo goes behind enemy lines to rescue Trautman, and fights a group of Soviet soldiers single-handedly.

The Beast (Columbia; 1988; 109m) director: Kevin Reynolds; cast: Jason Patric, Steven Bauer, George Dzundza, and Stephen Baldwin. A Soviet tank crew gets lost in the mountains of Afghanistan during the war. Led by a despotic officer, the crew is tracked by a group of Mujahadeen guerillas who kill them all. Filmed in the Israeli desert.

By Dawn's Early Light (HBO; 1989; 100m) director: Jack Sholder; cast: Martin Landau, Rebecca De Mornay, Powers Boothe. A nuclear warhead accidentally hits Russia, but no one knows who did it. The Russians assume it's an attack and launch their missiles toward the United States. Then comes the dilemma of whether or not the United States should retaliate, one that is played out both in the White House and in the cockpits of the bombers themselves.

Romero (Four Seasons Entertainment; 1989; 102m) director: John Duigan; cast: Raul Julia, Richard Jordan. Story of real-life priest Oscar Romero, who was assassinated in El Salvador in 1980. He and other priests spoke out against the military government, denouncing the death squads it used against the common people.

Arnaud De Borchgrave and Robert Moss, *The Spike* (New York: Crown, 1980). A journalism major is sent to Vietnam to cover the war and falls in with bad companions. Years later, he uncovers a Soviet plot to destroy the United States and heads it off.

Bernard Malamud, *God's Grace* (New York: Farrar, Straus and Giroux, 1982). Calvin Cohn is the only man (and Jew) left alive on Earth after a nuclear holocaust. On an Edenic island, he tries to establish a new society of chimpanzees, but sin (his) rears its ugly head. Cohn dies, killed by his students, and so does the new world.

Robert Moss and Arnaud de Borchgrave, *Monimbo: A Novel* (New York: Simon and Schuster, 1983). Monimbo is the code-name of a Cuban plan to bring the United States to its knees. An eighteen-year-old Nicaraguan defects and warns the new president but nobody believes him. According to the book, the Mariel Boat Lift in 1980 was part of the plan.

Margaret Atwood, *The Handmaid's Tale* (Toronto: McClelland and Stewart, 1985).

The Handmaid's Tale (Virgin/Cinecon/Bioskop; 1990; 109m) director: Volker Schlondorff; cast: Natasha Richardson, Robert Duvall, Faye Dunaway, Aidan Quinn, Elizabeth McGovern, Victoria Tennant. After the breakup of the United States in a theological revolution, the military leaders of the Republic of Gilead (New England) take on handmaids to bear their children. This is the story of one such woman, who rebels, escapes, and disappears. A Canadian's unpleasant view of the future in an increasingly religious United States.

Chapter 9: New Competitors, Old Enemies

Paul Erdman is an economic novelist forever predicting the coming collapse and downfall of the United States. Among his novels are: *The Crash of '79* (New York: Simon and Schuster, 1976); *The Last Days of America* (New York: Simon and Schuster, 1981); and *The Panic of '89* (Garden City, N.Y.: Doubleday, 1981).

The Man Who Fell to Earth (British Lion; 1976; 140m) director: Nicolas Roeg; cast: David Bowie, Rip Torn, Candy Clark, Buck Henry. An alien from outer space travels to Earth in pursuit of water for his home planet. He builds and heads an international corporation to earn the money necessary to return home. Meanwhile, he meets a girl who falls in love with him and is challenged by the merciless business world.

Robocop (Rank/Orion; 1987; 103m) director: Paul Verhoeven; cast: Peter Weller, Nancy Allen. A badly injured Detroit cop is turned into a cyborg and defeats the forces of evil, that is, the corporation that controls the city.

Wall Street (Pressman/American Entertainment; 1987; 124m) director: Oliver Stone; cast: Charlie Sheen, Michael Douglas, Martin Sheen, Darryl Hannah, Terence Stamp. A young financial (Charlie Sheen) broker tries to get in good with his Wall Street hero, Gordon Gekko (Douglas) but, when the latter attempts to shut down the airline for which his father (Martin Sheen) is a mechanic, he turns state's witness.

They Live! (Guild/Alive; 1988; 94m) director: John Carpenter; cast: Roddy Piper, Keith David, Meg Foster, Jason Robards III. An unemployed worker finds a pair of sunglasses, puts them on, and discovers that aliens are running the world using subliminal advertising. They are here to make a buck off of us poor rubes. Capitalists may not be your friend.

The Handmaid's Tale (Virgin/Biosko; 1990; 109m) director: Volker Schlondorff; cast: Natasha Richardson, Robert Duvall, Faye Dunaway, Aidan Quinn, Elizabeth McGovern, Victoria Tennant. Based on the novel by Margaret Atwood. In a New England theocracy, a young "handmaid" revolts against her child-bearing duties and disappears into the "underground."

Tom Wolfe, *The Bonfire of the Vanities* (New York: Farrar, Straus and Giroux, 1987). A Wall Street bond dealer, with a luxurious life, makes a wrong turn off the freeway and sees his life change as he loses everything. Dot commers should have read this before betting their lives on the market.

Chapter 10: Now What?

Paul M. Sammon, *Future Noir: The Making of Blade Runner* (New York: HarperPrism, 1996).

Ray Bradbury, *The Martian Chronicles* (Garden City, N.Y.: Doubleday, 1950). "January 1999, Rocket Summer." Americans emigrate to Mars, destroy the natives, and abuse the landscape. After nuclear war breaks out on Earth, they all leave. Read as a parable of the inherent destructiveness of America's commercial culture, Bradbury's book is even better today than in 1950.

Frederick Pohl and C.M. Kornbluth, *The Space Merchants* (New York: Ballantine, 1953). Advertising runs the world, and wants to move into space. Adventures of an ad exec who runs afoul of the dominant paradigm and ends up a Consie (conservationist) emigrating to Venus, where a new world awaits. Satirical, pointed, and all too familiar.

Harry Harrison, *Make Room! Make Room!* (Garden City, N.Y.: Doubleday, 1966). Novel on which *Soylent Green* is based.

Soylent Green (MGM; 1973; 97m) director: Richard Fleischer; cast: Charlton Heston, Edward G. Robinson, Leigh Taylor-Young, Chuck Conners, Joseph Cotton. Forty million people live in the New York of 2020, and half are unemployed. Thorn (Heston) is a police detective assigned to solve a series of murders linked to "soylent green," one of the artificial food products that everyone eats. "Soylent Green is people!" Robinson's final film: "I once was respected. I was a full professor!"

Ernest Callenbach, *Ecotopia: The Notebooks and Reports of William Weston* (Berkeley: Banyan Tree Books, 1975). The first journalist permitted into "Ecotopia" after the secession of the West Coast from the United States reports on what he finds.

A Boy and His Dog (LG Jaf; 1975; 89m) director: L. Q. Jones; cast: Don Johnson, Susanne Benton, Jason Robards. Based on the novel by Harlan Ellison. A very young Don Johnson, accompanied by his telepathic dog, searches for food after the apocalypse. They stumble on a Utopian community that needs men, but it is not to their liking. Surprise ending.

Mad Max (Orion Pictures/Roadshow/Mad Max Pty. Ltd.; 1979; 93m) director: George Miller; cast: Mel Gibson, Joanne Samuel. The protagonist is a hotshot ex-policeman seeking retribution for the murder of his wife and child. In a stark and dangerous future world, the fast-driving hero clashes with a gang of menacing motorcycle riders.

Mad Max 2: The Road Warrior (Roadshow/Warner Brothers; 1981; 96m) director: George Miller; cast: Mel Gibson. Postnuclear holocaust in Australia, a former police officer becomes the defender of a small oil refinery. The ex-cop defends the honest oil drillers from a vicious gang of marauding motorcyclists and manages to transport their fuel to safety.

Escape from New York (Avco Embassy; 1981; 99m) director: John Carpenter; cast: Kurt Russell, Lee Van Cleef, Ernest Borgnine, Donald Pleasance, Isaac Hayes, Harry Dean Stanton. In 1997, Manhattan has been turned into a prison. The president bails out from his plane and is taken hostage. Russell goes into the city to bring the president out.

The Terminator (Orion; 1984; 108m) director: James Cameron; cast: Arnold Schwarzenegger, Linda Hamilton. Cyborg from the future is sent back to kill the woman whose son will become humanity's liberator from Earth's rulers in the future.

Mad Max beyond Thunderdome (Warner Brothers; 1985; 106m) directors: George Miller and George Ogilvie; cast: Mel Gibson, Tina Turner. In a world wrecked by nuclear holocaust, Mad Max faces daily challenges to his survival. In the thuggish city of Bartertown, Mad Max faces a gladiatorial fight, to the death, and survives. Exiled to the desert, he is rescued by a society of youths and overcomes a grueling desert crossing. Finally, Mad Max overcomes the main villain in a wild chase.

Brazil (20th Century Fox/Universal/Embassy; 1985; 131m) director: Terry Gilliam; cast: Jonathan Pryce, Robert DeNiro, Michael Palin, Kim Griest. Black comedy set in a dismal future world in which one bureaucrat, Sam Lowry, fantasizes about living a life without bureaucracy or technology, partnered with a beautiful woman. Lowry meets the woman of his dreams, Jill Layton, while attempting to correct a mistaken arrest of an innocent man. At the same time, the government blames Lowry for terrorist crimes, putting both Sam and Jill in danger.

Frederick Pohl, *Jem* (New York: St. Martin's, 1978). The world is divided into three: the Food Bloc, the Fuel Block, and the People Block. No one can afford war, but they can pay for expeditions to other star systems. Humans corrupt sentient species on Jem and then ignite a nuclear war on Earth.

Neal Stephenson, *Snow Crash* (New York: Bantam, 1993). Cyberpunk vision of the twenty-first century, in which corporate franchises have acquired political sovereignty, bikers zoom around on thermonuclear-armed motorcycles, cyberspace is a nice place to be, and the world's poor are floating toward North America on an enormous armada of flotsam and jetsam.

Leslie Marmon Silko, *Almanac of the Dead* (New York: Simon and Schuster, 1991). Resources are running out, Mexico is falling into civil war, and indigenous peoples are moving to take back the continent and send the Europeans home. Fascinating piece of work by a Native American writer. Long but well worth the read.

Simon Winchester, *Pacific Nightmare—A Third World War in the Far East* (London: Sidgwick and Jackson, 1992). Somewhat turgid, documentary-style report extrapolating from anti-Japanese sentiment of the early 1990s and the suppression of the Tiananmen protests in 1989. Following the takeover of Hong Kong in 1997, civil war breaks out and the People's Republic of China begins to fragment. The rest of the world watches and the United States drops a nuclear bomb in Tokyo Harbor to warn Japan that reoccupation of China could lead to nuclear holocaust.

Bibliography

Acheson, Dean. 1969. *Present at the Creation: My Years in the State Department.* New York: Norton.

Aho, James. 1994. *This Thing of Darkness: A Sociology of the Enemy.* Seattle: University of Washington Press.

Agee, Philip, and Louis Wolf, eds. 1981. *Dirty Work–The CIA in Western Europe.* London: Zed; new paperback edition.

Ajami, Fouad. 1993. "The Summoning," *Foreign Affairs* 72, no. 4 (Sept.-Oct.): 2-9.

Alperovitz, Gar. 1994. *Atomic Diplomacy: Hiroshima and Potsdam—The Use of the Atomic Bomb and the American Confrontation with Soviet Power.* 2nd expanded ed. London: Pluto Press.

Ambrose, Stephen E. 1991. *Rise To Globalism*, 6th ed. New York: Penguin.

Barnet, Richard J. 1973. *Roots of War.* Baltimore: Penguin.

Bennett, William J. 1998. *The Death of Outrage—Bill Clinton and the Assault on American Ideals.* New York: Free Press.

Berman, Marshall. 1982. *All That Is Solid Melts into Air: The Experience of Modernity.* New York: Simon and Schuster.

Blechman, Barry M., and Stephen S. Kaplan. 1978. *Force without War: U.S. Armed Forces As a Political Instrument.* Washington, D.C.: Brookings.

Block, Fred L. 1977. *The Origins of International Economic Disorder: A Study of United States International Monetary Policy from World War II to the Present.* Berkeley: University of California Press.

Blum, William. 1986. *The CIA—A Forgotten History: U.S. Global Interventions since World War Two.* London: Zed.

Bowman, James. 1993. "Friends of Bill," *The American Spectator* (May): 58-59.

Breindel, Eric. 1996. "Hiss's Guilt: Goodies from the Venona Files," *New Republic* 214, no. 16 (April 15): 18-20.

Breslauer, George W., and Philip E. Tetlock, eds. 1991. *Learning in U.S. and Soviet Foreign Policy.* Boulder, Colo.: Westview Press.

Burdick, Eugene, and Harvey Wheeler. 1962. *Fail-Safe.* New York: McGraw-Hill.

Burr, William, and Jeffrey T. Richelson. 2000. "Whether to 'Strangle the Baby in the Cradle': The United States and the Chinese Nuclear Program, 1960-64," *International Security* 25, no. 3. (Winter): 54-99.

Carr, Edward H. 1939. *The Twenty Years Crisis, 1919-1939.* London: MacMillan.

Christensen, Terry. 1987. *Reel Politics: American Political Movies from Birth of a Nation to Platoon.* New York: Blackwell.

Church Committee. 1975. *Alleged Assassination Plots Involving Foreign Leaders.* Washington, D.C.: U.S. Government Printing Office, Nov. 20, Senate Report No. 94-465.

Clancy, Tom. 1984. *The Hunt for Red October.* Annapolis, Md.: Naval Institute Press.

———. 1986. *Red Storm Rising.* New York: Putnam's Sons.

Cloud, Stanley W. 1991. "After the War," *Time,* Sept. 9, pp. 16-17.

Clymer, Adam. 1995. "Amendment on Flag Burning Is Opposed by Administration," *New York Times,* June 7, p. A16.

Cochran, Thomas B., William M. Arkin, and Milton M. Hoenig. 1984. *Nuclear Weapons Databook—U.S. Nuclear Forces and Capabilities.* Vol. 1. Cambridge, Mass.: Ballinger.

Conbo, James, ed. 1993. *Movies, Politics: The Dynamic Relationship.* New York: Garland.

Condon, Richard. 1959. *The Manchurian Candidate.* New York: New American Library.

Cook, Blanche W. 1981. *The Declassified Eisenhower—A Divided Legacy.* Garden City, N.Y.: Doubleday.

Cottam, Richard W. 1988. *Iran & the United States.* Pittsburgh: University of Pittsburgh Press.

Cox Report. 1999. *Select Committee on U.S. National Security and Military/Commercial Concerns with the People's Republic of China,* at: www.fas.org/spp/starwars/congress/1999_r/cox/index.html (3/6/01).

Crawford, Beverly. 1995 "Hawks, Doves, but No Owls: International Economic Interdependence and Construction of the New Security Dilemma," pp. 149-86. In Ronnie D. Lipschutz, ed. *On Security.* New York: Columbia University Press.

Crichton, Michael. 1992. *Rising Sun: A Novel.* New York: Knopf.

Dalby, Simon. 1990. *Creating the Second Cold War: The Discourse of Politics.* London/New York: Guilford/Pinter.

Dallin, David J. 1955. *Soviet Espionage.* New Haven: Yale University Press.

Davison, W. Phillips. 1958. *The Berlin Blockade–A Study in Cold War Politics.* Princeton: Princeton University Press.

Der Derian, James. 1995. "The Value of Security: Hobbes, Marx, Nietzche and Baudrillard," pp. 24-45. In Ronnie D. Lipschutz, ed. *On Security.* New York: Columbia University Press.

———. 1992. *Anti-Diplomacy–Spies, Terror, Speed and War.* London: Blackwell.

De Volpi, A., et al. 1981. *Born Secret: The H-bomb, the Progressive Case and National Security.* New York: Pergamon Press.

Dowd, Maureen. 1994. "G.O.P.'s Rising Star Pledges to Right Wrongs of the Left," *New York Times,* Nov. 10, p. A1.

Draper, Theodore. 1991. *A Very Thin Line—The Iran-Contra Affairs.* New York: Hill and Wang.

Eisenhower, Dwight, D. 1948. *Crusade in Europe.* Garden City, N.Y.: Doubleday.

Engelhardt, Tom. 1995. *The End of Victory Culture.* New York: Basic.

Esteva, Gustavo. 1992. "Development," pp. 6-25. In Wolfgang Sachs, ed. *The Development Dictionary*. London: Zed.

Fallows, James. 1989. *More Like Us: Putting America's Native Strengths and Traditional Values to Work to Overcome the Asian Challenge*. Boston: Houghton Mifflin.

Fariello, Griffin. 1995. *Red Scare: Memories of the American Inquisition: An Oral History*. New York: Norton.

Farrell, Theo. 1997. *Weapons without a Cause: The Politics of Weapons Acquisition in the United States*. New York: St. Martin's Press.

Fawcett, Brian. 1986. *Cambodia: A Book for People Who Find Television Too Slow*. New York: Collier/MacMillan.

Feis, Herbert. 1950. *The Road to Pearl Harbor*. Princeton: Princeton University Press.

Finney, Jack. 1955. *The Invasion of the Body Snatchers*. New York: Dell.

FitzGerald, Frances. 2000. *Way Out There in the Blue: Reagan, Star Wars, and the End of the Cold War*. New York: Simon and Schuster.

Ford, Daniel. 1967. *Incident at Muc Wa*. Garden City, N.Y.: Doubleday; reprinted by Universe Publishing Services, 2000.

Foster, Stuart J. 2000. *Red Alert!: Educators Confront the Red Scare in American Public Schools, 1947-1954* . New York: P. Lang.

Frankce, Lizzie. 1993. "Deadbeat White Male," *New Statesman & Society*, May 29, pp. 31-32.

Freedman, Lawrence. 1983. *The Evolution of Nuclear Strategy*. New York: St. Martin's.

Freudenrich, Craig, C. 2000. "How Nuclear Bombs Work," at: www.howstuffworks. com/nuclear-bomb.htm (3/6/01).

Gaddis, John Lewis. 1992. *The United States and the End of the Cold War*. New York: Oxford University Press.

———. 1982. *Strategies of Containment*. New York: Oxford University Press.

Garber, Marjorie, and Rebecca L. Walkowitz, eds. 1995. *Secret Agents: The Rosenberg Case, McCarthyism, and Fifties America*. New York: Routledge.

Gardner, Richard N. 1980. *Sterling-Dollar Diplomacy in Current Perspective: The Origins and the Prospects of Our International Economic Order*. New York: Columbia University Press, expanded edition.

Garthoff, Raymond L. 1985. *Detente and Confrontation: American-Soviet Relations from Nixon to Reagan*. Washington, D.C.: Brookings.

Garwood, Darrell. 1985. *Under Cover: Thirty-Five Years of CIA Deception*. New York: Grove Press.

Gates, David. 1993. "White Male Paranoia," *Newsweek*, March 29, pp. 48-53.

Gathier Report. 1957. *Deterrence and Survival in the Nuclear Age*. Washington, D.C.: Security Resources Panel of the Scientific Advisory Committee of the Office of Defense Mobilization, Nov.

Gibson, William. 1984. *Neuromancer*. New York: Ace.

Gilpin, Robert. 1980. *War and Change in World Politics*. Cambridge: Cambridge University Press.

———. 1975. *U.S. Power and the Multinational Corporation*. New York: Basic.

Giunti, Matthew. 1993. "Urban Catastrophe," *Christian Century*, June 2-9, pp. 605-8.

Gowa, Joanne. 1983. *Closing the Gold Window*. Ithaca, N.Y.: Cornell University Press.

Gray, Colin S. 1979. "Nuclear Strategy: The Case for a Theory of Victory," *International Security* 4 (Summer): 54-87

———, and Keith Payne. 1980. "Victory Is Possible," *Foreign Policy* 39 (Summer).

Gray, Paul. 1991. "Whose America? A Growing Emphasis on the Nation's 'Multi-Cultural' Heritage Exalts Racial and Ethnic Pride at the Expense of Social Cohesion" *Time,* July 8, pp. 12-17.

Greene, Graham. 1976. "Introduction." In *The Third Man* and *Loser Takes All.* London: Heinemann and Bodley Head.

Greenfield, Fenella, and Nicolas Locke, eds. 1984. *The Killing Fields: The Facts behind the Film, with Personal Accounts from Sydney Schanberg and Dith Pran.* London: Weidenfeld and Nicolson.

Groh, Dieter. 1987. "The Temptation of Conspiracy Theory, or: Why Do Bad Things Happen to Good People?" pp. 1-37. In Carl F. Graumann and Serge Moscovici, eds., *Changing Conceptions of Conspiracy.* New York: Springer-Verlag.

Halberstam, David. 1972. *The Best and the Brightest.* New York: Random House.

Harrison, James P. 1989. *The Endless War—Vietnam's Struggle for Independence.* New York: Columbia University Press.

Haynes, John E. 1996. *Red Scare or Red Menace?: American Communism and Anticommunism in the Cold War Era.* Chicago: Ivan R. Dee.

Hayslip, Le Ly, with Jay Wurts. 1990. *When Heaven and Earth Changed Places.* New York: Plume.

Higgins, Trumbull. 1987. *The Perfect Failure: Kennedy, Eisenhower, and the CIA at the Bay of Pigs.* New York: Norton.

Hinton, James. 1989. *Protests and Visions: Peace Politics in Twentieth-Century Britain.* London: Hutchinson Radius.

Hogan, Michael J. 1998. *A Cross of Iron: Harry S Truman and the Origins of the National Security State, 1945-1954.* Cambridge: Cambridge University Press.

Howe, Irving, ed. 1983. *1984 Revisited: Totalitarianism in Our Century.* New York: Harper and Row.

Hunter, Edward. 1953. *Brain-Washing in Red China—The Calculated Destruction of Men's Minds.* New York: Vanguard Press.

Hunter, Shireen. 1998. *The Future of Islam and the West: Clash of Civilizations or Peaceful Coexistence?* Westport, Conn.: Praeger.

Huntington, Samuel P. 1993. "The Clash of Civilizations," *Foreign Affairs* 72, no. 3 (Summer): 22-49.

———. 1996. *The Clash of Civilizations and the Remaking of World Order.* New York: Simon and Schuster.

Iriye, Akira. 1967. *Across the Pacific—An Inner History of American-East Asian Relations.* New York: Harcourt, Brace and World.

Jeffreys-Jones, Rhodri. 1989. *The CIA and American Democracy.* New Haven: Yale University Press.

Jonas, Susanne. 1991. *The Battle for Guatemala.* Boulder, Colo.: Westview.

Jones, Joseph M. 1955. *The Fifteen Weeks.* New York: Viking Press.

Kahn, David. 2000. "Did Roosevelt Know?" *New York Review of Books,* Nov. 2, at: http://www.nybooks.com/nyrev/WWWarchdisplay.cgi?20001102059R (3/7/01).

Kahn, Herman. 1960. *On Thermonuclear War.* Princeton: Princeton University Press.

———. 1965. *On Escalation: Metaphors and Scenarios*. New York: Praeger.

Kaldor, Mary. 1990. *The Imaginary War: Understanding the East-West Conflict*. Oxford: Blackwell.

———. 1981. *The Baroque Arsenal*. New York: Hill and Wang.

Kaplan, Fred. 1983. *The Wizards of Armageddon*. New York: Simon and Schuster.

Kaplan, Robert D. 1994. "The Coming Anarchy: How Scarcity, Crime, Overpopulation, Tribalism, and Disease Are Rapidly Destroying the Social Fabric of Our Planet," *The Atlantic*, Feb., pp. 44-64.

———. 1996. *The Ends of the Earth*. New York: Random House.

Kennedy, Paul. 1987. *The Rise and Fall of the Great Powers: Economic Change and Military Conflict from 1500 to 2000*. New York: Random House.

Kennedy, Robert F. 1999/1971. *Thirteen Days: A Memoir of the Cuban Missile Crisis*. New York: Norton.

Keyfitz, Nathan. 1989. "The Growing Human Population," pp. 61-72. In *Scientific American, Managing Planet Earth*. San Francisco: W. H. Freeman.

Killian Report. 1955. *Meeting the Threat of Surprise Attack*. Washington, D.C.: Technological Capabilities Panel of the Office of Defense Mobilization, Feb. 14.

Kissinger, Henry. 1957. *A World Restored—Metternich, Castlereagh and the Problems of Peace, 1812-22*. Boston: Houghton Mifflin.

———. 1957. *Nuclear Weapons and Foreign Policy*. New York: Published for the Council on Foreign Relations by Harper.

Kolko, Gabriel. 1988. *Confronting the Third World—United States Foreign Policy, 1945-1980*. New York: Pantheon.

Kull, Stephen. 1988. *Minds at War*. New York: Basic.

Kuniholm, Bruce R. 1980. *The Origins of the Cold War in the Near East*. Princeton: Princeton University Press.

Kwitny, Jonathan. 1986. *Endless Enemies—The Making of an Unfriendly World*. New York: Penguin.

LaFeber, Walter. 1993. *America, Russia, and the Cold War—1945-1992*. New York: McGraw-Hill, 7th ed.

Lansdale, Edward G. 1972. *In the Midst of Wars*. New York: Harper and Row.

Latham, Michael E. 2000. *Modernization As Ideology: American Social Science and Nation Building in the Kennedy Era*. Chapel Hill: University of North Carolina Press.

le Carré, John. 1963. *The Spy Who Came in from the Cold*. London: Gollancz.

Lederer, William, and Eugene Burdick. 1958. *The Ugly American*. New York: Norton.

Levinson, Jerome, and Juan de Onis. 1970. *The Alliance That Lost Its Way—A Critical Report on the Alliance for Progress*. Chicago: Quadrangle Books.

Lieberman, Robbie. 2000. *The Strangest Dream: Communism, Anticommunism and the U.S. Peace Movement, 1945-1963*. New York: Syracuse University Press.

Lilla, Mark. 1995. "The Riddle of Walter Benjamin," *New York Review of Books*. May 25.

Lind, William S. 1991. "Defending Western Culture," *Foreign Policy* 84 (Fall): 40-50.

Lipschutz, Ronnie D. 2000. *After Authority: War, Peace and Global Politics in the 21st Century*. Albany: State University of New York Press.

———. 1999. "Terror in the Suites: Narratives of Fear and the Political Economy of Danger," *Global Society* 14, no. 4 (Oct.): 409-37.

———. 1998. "From Culture Wars to Shooting Wars: Cultural Conflict in the United States," pp. 394-433. In Beverly Crawford and Ronnie D. Lipschutz, eds., *The Myth of "Ethnic Conflict."* Berkeley: International and Areas Studies, University of California-Berkeley.

———. 1992. "Strategic Insecurity: Putting the Pieces Back Together in the Middle East," pp. 113-26. In Harry Kreisler, ed. *Confrontation in the Gulf.* Berkeley: Institute of International Studies, University of California-Berkeley.

———. 1989. *When Nations Clash: Raw Materials, Ideology, and Foreign Policy.* New York: Ballinger/Harper and Row.

Lowenthal, John. 2000. "Venona and Alger Hiss," *Intelligence and National Security* 15, no. 3.

Lyon, David. 1994. *The Electronic Eye: The Rise of Surveillance Society.* Minneapolis: University of Minnesota Press.

McCormick, Thomas J. 1995. *America's Half-century: United States Foreign Policy in the Cold War and After.* 2nd ed. Baltimore: Johns Hopkins University Press.

Mahbubani, Kishore. 1993. "The Dangers of Decadence," *Foreign Affairs* 72, no. 4 (Sept.-Oct.): 10-14.

Mailer, Norman. 1991. *Harlot's Ghost.* New York: Random House.

———. 1968. *Miami and the Siege of Chicago—An Informal History of the Republican and Democratic Conventions of 1968.* New York: World.

Mao Tse-Tung. 1948. *Aspects of China's Anti-Japanese Struggle.* Bombay: People's Publishing House.

Marks, John. 1979. *The Search for the "Manchurian Candidate": The CIA and Mind Control.* New York: Times Books.

Marshall, T. H. 1950. *Citizenship and Social Class.* Cambridge: Cambridge University Press.

Martin, Randy, and Toby Miller, eds. 1999. *SportCult.* Minneapolis: University of Minnesota Press.

Martin, Richard. 1997. *Mean Streets and Raging Bulls: The Legacy of Film Noir in Contemporary American Cinema.* Lanham, Md.: Scarecrow Press.

Meadows, Dennis, et al. 1972. *Limits to Growth.* Cambridge, Mass.: MIT Press.

Mearsheimer, John J. 1990. "Back to the Future: Instability in Europe After the Cold War," *International Security* 15, no. 1 (Summer): 5-56.

Meyer, David S. 1993. "Below, Beyond, Beside the State: Peace and Human Rights Movements and the End of the Cold War," pp. 267-95. In David Skidmore and Valerie M. Hudson, eds. *The Limits of State Autonomy—Societal Groups and Foreign Policy Formulation.* Boulder, Colo.: Westview.

Mishra, Ramesh. 1999. *Globalization and the Welfare State.* Cheltenham, U.K.: Edward Elgar.

Mitchell, Greg. 1998. *Tricky Dick and the Pink Lady: Richard Nixon vs. Helen Gahagan Douglas—Sexual Politics and the Red Scare, 1950.* New York: Random House.

Morrell, David. 1972. *First Blood—A Novel.* New York/Philadelphia: M. Evans/ Lippincott.

NSC. 1951. *Staff Study on Proposed Transfer of the Point IV Program from the Department of State to the Economic Cooperation Administration,* draft, Washington, D.C., Aug. 9.

NSC-68. 1980. "A Report to the President Pursuant to the President's Directive of January 31, 1950," *Foreign Relations of the United States, 1950.* Vol. I. Washington, D.C.: U.S. Department of State.

NSC-84. 1950. "The Position of the United States with Respect to the Philippines," Memorandum from the U.S. Joint Chiefs of Staff to the Secretary of Defense, Sept. 9.

Nelson, Lars-Erik. 1999. "Notes from Underground," *New York Review of Books,* (Sept. 23): 4-6.

Nichols, Bill. 1981. *Ideology and the Image: Social Representation in the Cinema and Other Media* . Bloomington: Indiana University Press.

Nitze, Paul. 1976-77. "Deterring Our Deterrent," *Foreign Policy* 25 (Winter): 195-210.

Nye, Joseph. 1990. *Bound to Lead—The Changing Nature of American Power.* New York: Basic.

O'Brien, Geoffrey. 1991. "The Return of Film Noir!" *New York Review of Books* (August 15): 45-48.

Orwell, George. 1983. *1984: A Novel.* New York: New American Library.

Packenham, Robert A. 1973. *Liberal America and the Third World: Political Development Ideas in Foreign Aid and Social Science.* Princeton: Princeton University Press.

Pepper, Suzanne. 1999. *Civil War in China: The Political Struggle, 1945-1949.* Lanham, Md.: Rowman & Littlefield.

Pilat, Oliver. 1952. *The Atom Spies.* New York: Putnam.

Pollard, Robert A. 1985. *Economic Security and the Origins of the Cold War, 1945-1950.* New York: Columbia University Press.

Prestowtz, Clyde V., Jr. 1989. *Trading Places: How We Ae Giving Our Future to Japan and How to Reclaim It.* New York: Basic.

Radosh, Ronald, and Joyce Milton. 1997. *The Rosenberg File.* 2nd ed., with a new introduction containing revelations from the National Security Agency and Soviet sources. New Haven: Yale University Press.

Raferty, Terrence. 1993. "Slow Burn," *The New Yorker,* March 8, pp. 98-99.

Renard, Ronald D. 1996. *The Burmese Connection: Illegal Drugs and the Making of the Golden Triangle.* Boulder, Colo.: Lynne Rienner.

Rhodes, Richard. 1995. *Dark Sun: The Making of the Hydrogen Bomb.* New York: Simon and Schuster.

Rochlin, Gene I. 1997. *Trapped in the Net: The Unanticipated Consequences of Computerization.* Princeton: Princeton University Press.

Rogin, Michael. 1987. *Ronald Reagan, the Movie.* Berkeley: University of California Press.

Rollins, Peter C., ed. 1983. *Hollywood As Historian: American Film in a Cultural Context.* Lexington: University Press of Kentucky.

Roosevelt, Kermit. 1979. *Countercoup: The Struggle for Control of Iran.* New York: McGraw-Hill.

Rosecrance, Richard. 1986. *The Rise of the Trading State: Commerce and Conquest in the Modern World.* New York: Basic.

Rosenberg, David Alan. 1983 "The Origins of Overkill—Nuclear Weapons and American Strategy, 1945-1960," *International Security* 7, no. 4 (Spring): 3-71.

Rouverol, Jean. 2000. *Refugees from Hollywood: A Journal of the Blacklist Years*. Albuquerque: University of New Mexico Press.

Rovere, Richard. 1959. *Senator Joe McCarthy*. New York: Harcourt, Brace.

Rowse, Arthur E. 1992. "How to Build Support for a War," *Columbia Journalism Review* 31, no. 3 (Sept.-Oct.): 28-29.

Rupert, Mark. 1995. *Producing Hegemony: The Politics of Mass Production and American Global Power*. Cambridge: Cambridge University Press.

Ryan, Michael, and Douglas Kellner. 1988. *Camera Politica–The Politics and Ideology of Contemporary Hollywood Film*. Bloomington: Indiana University Press.

Sammon, Paul M. 1996. *Future Noir: The Making of Blade Runner*. New York: HarperPrism.

Sampson, Anthony. 1991. *The Seven Sisters—The Great Oil Companies and the World They Shaped*. New York: Bantam, 4th ed.

Sanders, Jerry W. 1983. *Peddlers of Crisis: The Committee on the Present Danger and the Politics of Containment*. Boston: South End Press.

Scheer, Robert. 1982. *With Enough Shovels—Reagan, Bush, & Nuclear War*. New York: Random House.

Schein, Edgar H. 1961. *Coercive Persuasion—A Socio-psychological Analysis of the "Brainwashing" of American Civilian Prisoners by the Chinese*. New York: Norton.

Schelling, Thomas C. 1966. *Arms and Influence*. New Haven: Yale University Press.

Schmitt, Eric. 1995. "U.S. Army School with Notorious Alumni," *San Francisco Chronicle*, April 4, p. A8. *New York Times* wire report.

Scholem, Gershon. 1971. *The Messianic Idea in Judaism*. New York: Schocken.

Schurmann, Franz. 1987. *The Foreign Politics of Richard Nixon—The Grand Design*. Berkeley: Institute of International Studies, University of California, Berkeley.

Schwartz, Stephen I., ed. 1998. *Atomic Audit—The Costs and Consequences of U.S. Nuclear Weapons since 1940*. Washington, D.C.: Brookings.

Scott, Peter Dale, and Jonathan Marshall. 1998. *Cocaine Politics: Drugs, Armies, and the CIA in Central America*. Berkeley: University of California Press, updated ed.

Shadoian, Jack. 1977. "Kiss Me Deadly," pp. 265-84. In *Dreams and Deadends: The American Gangster/Crime Film*. Cambridge, Mass.: MIT Press.

Shawcross, William. 1979. *Sideshow: Kissinger, Nixon, and the Destruction of Cambodia*. New York: Simon and Schuster.

———. *The Quality of Mercy: Cambodia, Holocaust, and Modern Conscience*. New York: Simon and Schuster.

Sheehan, Neil. 1989. *A Bright Shining Lie—John Paul Vann and America in Vietnam*. New York: Vintage.

Smith, Bradley F. 1983. *The Shadow Warriors: O.S.S. and the Origins of the C.I.A.* New York: Basic Books.

Stinnett, Robert B. 2000. *Day of Deceit: The Truth about FDR and Pearl Harbor*. New York: Free Press.

Stone, Deborah. 1997. *Policy Paradox: The Art of Political Decision Making*. New York: Norton.

Taylor, Maxwell D. 1960. *The Uncertain Trumpet*. New York: Harper.

Terkel, Studs. 1984. *"The Good War": An Oral History of World War Two*. New York: Pantheon.

The Nation, 2001. "An SOA by Any Other Name…," vol. 272, no. 6 (Feb 12): 7.

Thomas, J. J. 1995. *Surviving in the City: The Urban Informal Sector in Latin America.* Boulder, Colo.: Pluto Press.

Tuchman, Barbara W. 1970. *Stilwell and the American Experience in China, 1911-45.* London: Macmillan.

Tyler, Patrick. 1986. *Running Critical: The Silent War, Rickover, and General Dynamics.* New York: Harper and Row.

United States Congress, Joint Committee on Atomic Energy. 1951. *Soviet Atomic Espionage.* Washington, D.C.: U.S. Government Printing Offiice.

van Wolferen, Karel. 1989. *The Engima of Japanese Power.* New York: Knopf.

Von Clausewitz, Carl. 1976. *On War.* Edited and translated by Michael Howard and Peter Paret. Princeton: Princeton University Press.

Weinberger, Casper. 1982. "United States Nuclear Deterrence Policy," Testimony before the Foreign Relations Committee of the U.S. Senate, Dec. 14.

Weissman, Stephen R.. 1974. *American Foreign Policy in the Congo, 1960-1964.* Ithaca, N.Y.: Cornell University Press.

Whiting, Allen S. 1960. *China Crosses the Yalu—The Decision to Enter the Korean War.* New York: Macmillan.

Whyte, William. 1956. *The Organization Man.* New York: Simon and Schuster.

Williams, Robert C. 1987. *Klaus Fuchs, Atom Spy.* Cambridge, Mass.: Harvard University Press.

Winik, Jay. 1996. *On the Brink: The Dramatic, Behind-the-Scenes Saga of the Reagan Era and the Men and Women Who Won the Cold War.* New York: Simon and Schuster.

Wirls, Daniel. 1992. *Buildup: The Politics of Defense in the Reagan Era.* Ithaca, N.Y.: Cornell University Press.

Yergin, Daniel. 1991. *The Prize—The Epic Quest for Oil, Money and Power.* New York: Simon and Schuster.

Index

245

bility, 121, 124, 136; escalation of, 133, 134; end of, 137; and insanity, 139-41; and land reform, 125; and Nixon's secret plan to end it, 136; novels, 130; and use of nuclear weapons, 34; and psychology, 119; and Tet Offensive, 135; and threat of Chinese intervention, 135; and U.S. doubts about victory, 135; and U.S. exceptionalism in, 144; and U.S. strategy in, 140
Village of the Damned, 219
Von Clausewitz, Carl, 2

Walk East on Beacon, 214
Wall Street, 169, 230
walnut, Cold War, 23
war: causes of, 162; costs of, 162; conventional, 33; end of, 173; and flexible response, 127; guerilla, 10, 11; and human nature, 100; imaginary, 173; morality in, 141; and national liberation, 112; in *1984*, 31; and oil, 11; and purification in *Red Dawn*, 164; surviving nuclear, 10-11; world, post-, 15. *See also* Cold War; insurrections; Korean War; nuclear war; Vietnam War; World War
warfare, psychological, 44
War Game, The, 220
War Games, 227
War of the Worlds, 211
War on Drugs, 185
Warsaw Treaty Organization (WTO, aka Warsaw Pact), 82
Watergate, 104
wealth, and information, 199
Weber, Eugene, 196
Weber, Max, 141
Weinberger, Casper, 94
welfare state, dismantling of, 172

Western Europe: defense of, 90; rearma-

ment of, 82, 122
Western Hemisphere Institute for Security Cooperation, 117
What's Up Tiger Lily?, 216
Wheeler, Harvey (*Fail-Safe*), 9
When Worlds Collide, 217
White Heat, 210
Who'll Stop the Rain? (aka, *Dog Soldiers*), 224
Whyte, William (*The Organization Man*), 39
Wild, Wild West, The, 163
window of vulnerability, 139. *See also* Nitze, Paul; Strategic Defense Initiative
With Enough Shovels (Robert Scheer), 10
Wolfe, Tom (*Bonfire of the Vanities*), 169
Woman on Pier 13, The (aka, *I Married a Communist*), 212
women and nuclear war, 99
World Bank, 16, 22. *See also* Bretton Woods
World, the Flesh, and the Devil, The, 219
World War; II, 15, 36, 144; actions by U.S. against Japan, 59; division of Vietnam, 121; effects, 15, 48; OSS, 64-65; post-, 15, 36; III, 9, 11, 35, 43-45, 139, 165, 166
World Wide Web, 189. *See also* information

Yalta, 46-47
Yank in Viet-Nam, A, 223
Yugoslavia, 20, 41, 171; 1999 bombing of, 136

Zaire (Democratic Republic of the Congo), 158
Zedong, Mao, 35, 127, 157
"zero-zero" option, 159. *See also* Intermediate Nuclear Forces Treaty

About the Author

Ronnie D. Lipschutz has been on the faculty of the Politics Department of the University of California, Santa Cruz since 1990. He is the author, editor, and coeditor of books about foreign policy, national security, ethnicity and conflict, and global environmental politics, including *Global Civil Society and Global Environmental Politics* (1996) and *After Authority—War, Peace, and Global Politics in the Twenty-first Century* (2000).